Blossoming Beyond the Desert

A Feminine Reimagining
of the Passover Seder's Healing Legacy

SHELLE GOLDSTEIN

Tikkun Publishing

PRAISE FROM READERS OF

Blossoming Beyond the Desert

"In reading *Blossoming Beyond the Desert*, I felt like an honored guest at Shelle Goldstein's lavish table, where the ancient ritual of the Passover Seder has been transformed into the delicacies that nourish and delight the hungry soul. This book is a treasured resource of blessings, poetry, questions, stories and wisdom that has the power to guide us towards awareness, healing, connection, and wholeness. *Shechina* shines through every word."

—Rabbi Shefa Gold, author, *Are We There Yet? Travel as a Spiritual Practice*

"This beautifully written personal reflection on the deeper meaning of Passover opens up new ways to understand the rituals and practices of this important Jewish holiday. Shelle Goldstein masterfully weaves her own story of spiritual transformation with the stories of the women of the Exodus, while illuminating the role of the 'divine feminine' in Jewish spiritual life. Readers are invited to do their own God-wrestling while venturing into the mysteries of ancient tradition."

—Estelle Frankel, MS MFT (practicing psychotherapist), spiritual companion, teacher of Jewish mysticism, and author of *Sacred Therapy* and *The Wisdom of Not Knowing*

"Why is this book about Passover different from all the other books out there? With this book, Shelle Goldstein uncovers the beauty of traditions, both ancient and modern, explores and shares the spiritual essence behind the holiday, and finds, magnifies, and poetically expresses a feminine voice in and through the story long silenced by history. It is a beautiful and meaningful read that will give you a new take on the holiday you thought you knew."

—Cantor Sally Neff, The Reform Temple of Rockland

Blossoming Beyond the Desert is a beautiful and inspiring story of Shelle Goldstein's process of awakening, finding her voice, and ultimately becoming a spiritual presence in her Jewish community.

"Having awakened tearfully from a dream about her children losing the connection to their Jewish heritage and ancestry, she was inspired to find and cultivate a meaningful living connection to her Jewish roots, as well as something larger and more encompassing that she could pass on to her beloved children and grandchildren.

"*Blossoming Beyond the Desert* interweaves Shelle Goldstein's individual journey of liberation and healing with the courage, compassion, and wisdom of the feminist perspective on the Exodus story. *Blossoming in the Desert* is an invitation to the reader's own self-exploration, and a rare gem that reaches beyond the personal to the universal.

—Michele Weissman, Diamond Approach teacher

Blossoming Beyond the Desert: A Feminine Reimagining of the Passover Seder's Healing Legacy, by Shelle Goldstein. Copyright © 2023. All rights reserved.

No part of this publication may be reproduced, distributed, or transmitted in any form or by any means, including photocopying, recording, or other electronic or mechanical methods, without the prior written permission of the publisher, except in the case of brief quotations embodied in critical reviews and certain other noncommercial uses permitted by copyright law. For permission requests, write to the publisher, addressed "Attention: Permissions Coordinator," at the address below:

Shelle Goldstein
Tikkun Publishing
shellego@optonline.net

Cover Design / Book Layout / Typesetting:
Isabel Robalo / isadesign.net

Editing:
Naomi Rose / naomirose.net
Elizabeth Kracht/elizabethkracht.com

Printed in the United States of America
First printing 2023

ISBN# 979-8-9873703-0-8

For my Grandchildren

Jeremy, Emily, Ben, Becca, Hannah, Ava

who are my teachers.

The best of our tradition, its Light, Love,

Compassion, and Wisdom,

is embodied in each of you.

Contents

Introduction

THE DREAM

Years ago, before my grandchildren were even a twinkle in their parents' eyes, one night I had a dream:

> I felt my family's Jewish ties fraying and fading away,
>
> that my grown children had lost their connection to our heritage,
>
> that there would be no Jewish connection for my grandchildren-to-be,
>
> and that I had betrayed all the generations that had come before me, as well as those that would follow.
>
> I awakened from the dream with my pillow dampened by tears.

The Jewish people's beginnings and history have always been the backdrop of my family's Jewish identity, warmly acknowledged and celebrated at our holiday gatherings, including Passover. While not a foreground presence of our everyday lives, they were such stable features in the background that I never gave much thought to them *not* serving as a guiding principle for my family—until I learned that my husband and I were going to become grandparents. At that point, my dream felt prescient, an impending reality.

I could feel the heritage that my ancestors fought to preserve becoming increasingly insignificant, the freedom to practice (or not practice) our religion taken for granted. The ability to live according to our values and ideals was something that so many generations of my people had given their lives for. How could I not honor their struggle? For thousands of years, they had prevailed over powerful enemies. I couldn't allow our heritage to be lost to the next generation—my children and theirs—by the enemy of indifference.

But what could I do to stop this downward spiral?

I knew that I had to learn more about my religion, but I had a nagging feeling that I needed something more than that. My cultural and ethnic identification with Judaism wasn't going to be enough to create a bond between my family and our religious tradition. It wasn't going to be enough for me, either.

THE SEDER AS A PATH TO BRING JUDAISM TO LIFE

There is a saying in both Jewish and Buddhist circles: "When the student is ready, the teacher will appear." My teachers appeared in the form of my future grandchildren. As my first grandchild, Jeremy, neared birth, I realized that if he was going have the honor of carrying my father's Hebrew name, *Avram Moshe* (Abraham Moses), I wanted him to have a sense of the warmth and pride in the heritage that had meant so much to my father. I wanted him to feel that he was part of an unbroken chain of Judaism worthy of preserving for future generations, and to appreciate the ways its ancient wisdom still serves as a guide for living today.

And I realized that what I wanted for him was also what I wanted for myself. Just as I needed to learn more about my tradition, I also needed to cultivate an emotional and spiritual connection to it. Because he lived on the West Coast and would miss many of our East Coast holiday celebrations, it became even more important to me.

So I began to wander the spiritual in search of a path that would offer relevance, wisdom, and meaning—something that I could relate to, and be inspired and sustained by; something that would connect me, and hopefully my family, to a whole greater than ourselves. Although I sensed the richness of our history and the deep wisdom it held, I had no real knowledge of it. I couldn't feel it. The books I read and classes I took left me feeling dry and empty. I wanted to drink from a well of spiritually healing waters, but there

was no oasis in this desert. If only I had felt this when my father was alive…
but now he was gone.

It never occurred to me that what I was seeking was already a part of my
life, that the path would be revealed through the most celebrated and cherished festival on the Jewish calendar: the Passover Seder. The Passover Seder
tells the story of the Exodus, the liberation of the ancient Hebrews from bondage in Egypt. And yet, it is much more than a story of an ancient event that
happened to some other people at some other time. It's a story about what's
happening to us, now. In fact, the *Haggadah* (the Seder text) instructs each
of us in every generation to feel that we ourselves have been liberated from
slavery in whatever form it takes—be it physical, psychological, or spiritual.

When I took this mandate seriously and began to look at my own life, the
instructions of the Passover Seder went from being an abstract exercise to a
path that could lead me to real psychological freedom.

And I asked myself: "Why wasn't I able to recognize the depth of the
Exodus's poignant and powerful narrative until now? Why didn't I appreciate the spiritual and universal truths embedded in the messages of the Seder
until now?"

The more attention I gave to these questions, and to the answers that
slowly came forth, the more I found much about the Seder that could be experienced as a journey of healing. What I hadn't realized until now was that the
Seder was not just some old, tired Jewish ritual: it was a contemporary journey
of healing. The text's ancient wisdom could be revealed and carried into *our*
lives today—we who are living and seeking to blossom beyond the desert.

THE MISSING FEMININE PRESENCE

It's been said that 90 percent of the Jewish community attend Seders each year.
Many find deep meaning in this timeless ritual. Yet for others who are more
secular, less observant, this ancient event has become a dry ceremony devoid
of spirit—merely an "appetizer" before the festive meal. While most people
don't want to miss participating in a Seder, there's been a growing sense that
many Seders have been missing something: the ability to connect our hearts to
our sacred texts. Perhaps this is because the treasures in these texts have been
hidden in plain sight.

This has especially been true for today's "women of a certain age," who have often been denied access to religious education. Women like me, who have been hungry for something more meaningful than what many of our mothers and grandmothers experienced, and for the Jewish spiritual connection they were denied.

Why have men and women played such different parts in our celebrations—men in the lead roles, and women's contributions confined to the kitchen—thereby depriving our families and communities of a richer, more feminine-infused consciousness? If women are half of the *Uni-verse* (the One-song), why, for most of our history, have women been singing the minor parts?

I didn't fully realize this inequity until I became immersed in my "Seder project"—which, in the course of time, grew into this book. I was struck by the gross imbalance (as well as the lack of recognition and appreciation) of this "half" of the Whole of Creation not being fully included in the Jewish observance of the Passover journey. And I realized that it was time for both voices—the masculine and the feminine—to come together in harmony; for both our energies to complement each other. This is the reason why *Blossoming Beyond the Desert* carries the subtitle: *A Feminine Reimagining of the Healing Legacy of the Passover Seder.*

Yet in focusing on the experiences of women, this book is not meant to negate or minimize the vast contributions of men, nor to emphasize the competition or differences between men and women. Rather, it is about *feminine and masculine energies*, about correcting the historic overvaluation of the masculine at the expense of the feminine. It's about bringing both into balance.

THE NEED TO BALANCE THE MASCULINE AND FEMININE ENERGIES

Both the masculine and the feminine are needed and of value. The masculine energies of assertiveness, courage, intellect, power, and strength are what's behind the desired effects of men going out into the world on their Hero's journey to overcome obstacles, slay their dragons, hone their skills, and find their true selves.

But even these prized attributes can become liabilities when not moderated by the feminine energies of wisdom, grace, love, and compassion. We have witnessed repeatedly, both in Judaism's patriarchal tradition and in the world beyond it, how easily assertiveness turns into aggression, how unchecked power and strength become discrimination and domination.

The time is right to balance the masculine energies with our feminine energies, including our inherent sense of receptivity, creativity, and profound connection that we women feel by virtue of our ability to bear children, regardless of whether we do. It's not only the bearing of children: it's also the ongoing nurturance. Those women who nurture and carry the seeds of new life inside their wombs for nine months are then immersed in their children's optimal development for decades until the children can fly on their own. And even after they're grown and live separate lives, the deep connection between the generations endures.

Women bring a different consciousness to the world: one that is imbued with the experience of connection, relationship, and interdependence. But we can also be fiercely protective of those we care for, embodying the spirit of the peaceful warrior. These attributes emerge from a different journey than men's Hero's journey. It's not about going *out* into the world to find our true selves, but rather going *in* to the mind-body that opens us to different levels of consciousness.

And yet for too long, there has been a lack of appreciation for these capacities by the world's religions and cultures—even by women themselves. Too many of us have internalized the minor, "less-than" key that many believed was the only song we could sing. It's time to heal this fracture. Let us own the clear, confident voices with which we have been endowed, and take our rightful place in the Wholeness of Creation, so that we, too, are part of the One-Voice: singing its praises, softening its suffering, embodying its beauty and goodness.

THE INTENTIONS OF THIS BOOK

To Illuminate the Timeless Teachings of the Seder

In writing and sharing *Blossoming Beyond the Desert*, my intention is to illuminate the timeless teachings of the Passover Seder, with its themes of change, growth, and moving beyond our limitations toward freedom. In its earlier version, the book did not focus on the Feminine.

To Focus on the Feminine Journey in the Seder

But when I learned the Hebrew word for intention, *kavannah* ("the direction of the heart"), I knew that the book would have to focus more on women, whose voices in relation to the Passover journey have been given scant attention.

To Help Both Women and Men Heal from Constrictions on Freedom and Authenticity

My heart was also directed to a focus on *healing* from the psychological constriction that keeps women from living with a sense of freedom and authenticity (a struggle for men, as well). While the book is written from a feminine perspective, my hope is that it will enable the Passover ritual to be experienced in fresh, new ways—ways that will elevate its holiness and touch *all* our hearts so that in, the words of revered Rabbi Abraham Isaac Kook, "The old shall become new and the new shall become holy."

To Have Universal Resonance, Regardless of Spiritual Path

While this book's offerings are grounded in Judaism, the religious tradition into which I was born and with which I am strongly identified, another *kavannah* is for it to have *universal* resonance, to transcend our different spiritual paths and to articulate a vision of a world in which freedom—in the broadest sense of the word—belongs to all.

WHAT'S INCLUDED IN THIS BOOK

The musings and messages in *Blossoming Beyond the Desert* are intended to enhance the Passover Seder, elevating it from a rote ritual into a spiritual service that is meaningful and relevant. Illuminating the story of the Exodus in ways that can help us connect to its enduring truth and focusing on each of the ritual's formal "steps" creates a space for the ancient wisdom of our tradition to radiate its light in deeply personal as well as universal ways.

Blossoming Beyond the Desert is a compilation of readings, personal reflections, original prayers, poems, and *midrashim* (interpretations on biblical themes) that explore freedom, the essential theme of the Seder. This compilation, presented through the eyes of women and through the lens of Healing and Wholeness, addresses the sense of brokenness with which too many people struggle. To illustrate these challenges, I have included many case histories of psychotherapy clients with whom I have been privileged to work and learn from. Some vignettes are composites; all names and some personal information have been changed to protect their identities.

I also include many memorable moments of my own journey, the strands of my life that have been woven together to form the tapestry I am today. All our stories are, in fact, one united story, different threads in a universal tapestry. Because what we have in common is far more than what keeps us apart, perhaps some lost strands of your own stories will be revealed as well.

To further help you relate to the themes of Seder, I have included a brief section at the end of many of the readings called "Food for Thought." Since the Seder offers such fertile fare, too rich to be digested in one evening, you can consider this as a take-home "doggie bag" whose contents can be savored and pondered when mind and body are less full and thus more receptive.

What's *Not* Included in This Book

While the book is rooted in tradition, it isn't representative of a traditional Seder. It doesn't contain all the blessings and prayers; instead, it leaves space for guests to offer their spontaneous heartfelt blessings. And while it follows the order of the Seder ("Seder" actually *means* "order"), paradoxically, these offerings are intended to transcend the rigidity of the formal Seder structure. So rather than a "how-to" book, it gives you the freedom to celebrate and experience our heritage in ways that make it come alive for you with meaning and joy.

And while this book follows the format of a *Haggadah*, it is not one. (I've been tempted to subtitle it *Not-a-Haggadah*.) Yet I have taken to heart the sages' instruction for future generations to embellish upon the messages of the Seder to help make it a dynamic ritual that lends fresh insights to our ancient story. I trust that the sages' vision will be reflected in the readings and interpretations presented here. They are meant to contextualize the meanings and messages of the Exodus for you, to help deepen your understanding so that you can look at the familiar elements of the Seder in new ways. If some of them resonate with you, as I hope they will, feel free to use them at Seders that you're leading or attending. Many hosts welcome new material as supplements to the traditional Passover texts.

USING THIS BOOK AT A SEDER

If you are looking for material that views the Seder through a feminine lens, *Blossoming Beyond the Desert* will resonate with you. If you are seeking content that addresses the freedom to grow and change, to heal our sense of brokenness and separateness, to return to our "essential" nature as sparks of Divine Spirit, and to become more whole, then you may find many sections here that speak to you.

USING THIS BOOK AT ANY TIME (NOT FOR PASSOVER ONLY)

Your use of *Blossoming Beyond the Desert* need not be limited only to the time of the Seder; it can be read any time as an extended meditation on the multiple meanings of Freedom and Healing. It may be read at your leisure simply to expand and enrich your understanding of the holiday. Or it can stand alone, to be picked up at any moment when the need for words of wisdom, hope, or inspiration arises. Whichever way you decide to use it, I hope that *Blossoming Beyond the Desert* will help you connect to the richness embedded in our tradition and serve as a traveling companion to guide and support you on your own journeys.

A BLESSING

I trust that what I've offered here will help you feel more connected to and moved by our sacred texts; that they will nourish your spirituality, as writing about them has nourished mine. I am deeply humbled and grateful to think that my efforts may be experienced as another blossom on our eternal Tree of Life, whose fruit sustains us all.

Though I couldn't have known it when I first began writing this book, I was on a journey of healing and liberation—a meandering path that led me to find what I thought had been lost: my authentic voice. A voice that would allow me to speak of what I held precious and meaningful in my work and in my faith, in a language that others could hear. A voice that could finally tell the freedom-journey story to my children, as the Haggadah instructs.

Just as my journey began with a sense of brokenness and continues to arrive at a place of greater wholeness, so I invite you to read *Blossoming Beyond the Desert* with a sense of openness, allowing you to mend any broken pieces you may have found and make them whole, and, in the process, discover your Highest Self.

CHAPTER ONE

The Roots of Passover

No country can ever truly flourish if it stifles the potential of its women and deprives itself of the contributions of half of its citizens.

—Michelle Obama

BUT WHAT ABOUT THE WOMEN?

Like all spiritual traditions, Judaism has a narrative to help us to transcend boundaries, to feel a sense of possibility, to believe we are not trapped by the challenging circumstances of our lives. Our narrative is the *Exodus*, the chronicle of our ancestors' long journey from Egypt to the Promised Land, from slavery and degradation to liberation and freedom. This journey, which begins in shame and ends in triumph, is the defining story of our people. It tells of how, through a series of miracles—both human and Divine—an enslaved people emerge on the other side of darkness. It guides us across time and space, connecting us to the entire Universe, and to long-gone ancestors whom we have never met who suffered, endured, and prevailed. Our narrative is almost four thousand years old—yet also timeless.

The Exodus story is the heart of the Passover Seder. Retold every year, its roots run deep. The timeframe of the story begins on the eve before our ancestors were to leave Egypt, to flee for their lives. The tyrannical Pharaoh had decreed that all Hebrew males should be killed. As promised, God had instructed the Jews to sacrifice a lamb and paint their doorposts with its blood—a sign to the destroying angel not to take the male infants from their homes. "*And this day shall be for you as a memorial, and you shall celebrate it as a festival for the Lord; throughout your generations…as an everlasting statute.… And you shall keep this matter as a statute for you and your children forever.*" (Exodus 1–24)

Yet the traditional story has been rooted in the image of a *male* deity and male actors. Like most history, Jewish history has been centered on the actions and deeds, the trials, feats, and accomplishments of males. It has largely ignored the Divine Feminine, and has minimized the contributions of women, "half" of its citizenry, depriving us all of the fullness and richness of our history. And so I've chosen to tell the story through a lens that honors the roots and roles of the feminine in our people's flourishing.

A Ritual Rooted in Gratitude

Before the Exodus, when our ancestors were shepherds and farmers, dependent upon the rhythms and cycles of the natural world, the first full moon of spring marked the agricultural festivals celebrated by many Middle Eastern cultures. The first festival was *Chag Ha Pesach*, The Festival of the Pesach, which involved sacrificing a "paschal" or "Pesach" lamb to God in gratitude for the renewal of springtime. On the following day, *Chag Ha-Matzot*, farmers celebrated the Festival of Unleavened Bread in gratitude for the beginning of the grain harvest. Later, it also came to be known as *Chag Ha-Aviv*, The Festival of Spring, a celebration of the rebirth and renewal of the earth, the promise of new growth. And after the Exodus, it was also known as *Zeman Cheruteinu*, The Season of Our Liberation.

For me, Passover still holds the distant memories and meanings of its origins. I celebrate the return of color, indicating the earth's renewal as it emerges from the barren winter landscape. And more symbolically, I celebrate the renewal of spirit after harsh winters of discontent. I think of our ancestral family who could no longer bear to live in Egypt like tight, closed buds, and how they risked the pain and uncertainty of sea-crossings and desert wanderings to be free of their narrow, circumscribed lives to enter the Promised Land and a higher level of consciousness. *Zeman Cheruteinu*! And so Passover (which takes place in the spring) is the season of *our* liberation as well. The story of our liberation is at the heart of the *Haggadah* (meaning "the telling") At our Seders, we tell the story of our people's deliverance from slavery in Egypt (the Hebrew word for Egypt is *Mitzraim*—i.e., the narrow land that was reflected in their constricted lives).

And yet although we've been telling the story to each other and ourselves for thousands of years, the story today is not quite the same, because *we* are not the same—hopefully, with each passing year, we grow to a higher level of maturity—so *each re-telling* offers an opportunity to hear the original story in new ways. This spiraling perspective often expands our understanding of enslavement, including not only how *others* oppress people but also how *we oppress ourselves* by remaining stuck within our own *Mitzraim* and all the narrow passages that we traverse in the process of life.

We are stuck in *Mitzraim* when we cannot appreciate the complexity of the human experience—when life is viewed from a narrow, either/or perspective, rather than from a broader, integrated one where the paradoxical, contradictory aspects of life are understood as part of a larger whole. Historically, on the geographical level, *Mitzraim* referred to Egypt; but on the *spiritual* level, *Mitzraim*—narrowness—lives well beyond the desert. It is not limited to geography; it's everywhere—inside us, around us—wherever people are not free.

Giving Birth to New Parts of Ourselves

But the good news is that we don't have to stay stuck in our *Mitzraim*. As with plants that have the power to grow through cracks in concrete, there is a life force pushing us toward growth. We are works-in-progress, continually giving birth to new aspects of ourselves, continually seeking to expand out of our narrowness and grow toward our fullness. When we can recognize that we are living in emotionally tight spaces and begin to move beyond our familiar ways, beyond our fears and past conditioning into the mystery of the unknown, we evolve. When we take those first tentative steps to create new beginnings, new ideas, and new life, we expand. When we cope with disappointment, loss, illness, and death (even if we sometimes succumb to despondency, and lose hope and/or faith), somehow, we manage to go on being.

The Exodus story, encoded in our collective memory, reminds us that we may blossom again, beyond the deserts of our lives. Like the *karpas* on the Seder plate, the fruits of the earth whose seeds begin in darkness and push through the frozen soil to a place of holiness on our Seder table, we too can rise from the depths of despair and ascend to a place of holiness as we give birth to new aspects of ourselves.

What the Desert Experience Can Give Us

While leaving *Mitzraim* freed our ancestors from the dictates of the Pharaoh's ego, it did not automatically make them "free." What freed them was the experience of having to wander in the desert for "forty" (not a literal timeline) years with no Pharaoh to answer to. That was what allowed them to think for themselves and become responsible for their own choices. This is also where their true sense of self developed. This is where they learned to go beyond the noise of their personal opinions, rivalries, and needs, and—in the deep silence of the desert—hear their own hearts, their own voices, and the voice of their God. It was in the vast space of the desert that they reoriented their inner lives, redefined their self-identities, and moved from being slaves to being free people.

When we are wandering through our own internal wilderness, we assume that nothing is happening—that we are doing nothing to get where we want to go, that we are just marking time, like our ancestors in the desert, impatient for a better life. But when we are in those in-between places of uncertainty and vulnerability, it just may be that we, too, are more receptive to the new experiences, ideas, and possibilities that lie just beyond our awareness. It may be in what feels like the desert, in the seemingly barren ground beneath our feet, that miracles are stirring, seeds of change are growing, and that—rather than staying tight, closed buds—we are opening and blossoming. And so perhaps the desert is not a bleak, empty place after all, but a place of spiritual awakening, pregnant with possibility. Maybe "desert" is even another name for holy ground.

THE STORY BEFORE OUR STORY

About four hundred years before the Exodus, a young Jewish man named Abram heard the call from God, *"Lech Lecha"* (Go Forth)—to leave his father's house in the land of Ur in ancient Mesopotamia (what is now known as Iraq). What was it about Abram that he was "chosen" by God to leave? King Nimrod's astrologers predicted that Abram's birth would pose a threat to the king's rule, the Talmud tells us. So upon hearing this, Abram's father hid him in a cave. And when the child emerged from the cave at the age of three, we're told, he observed a powerful God *above* nature, a God who *created* nature—a singular Power above all others. Abram intuitively rejected the paganism of the culture into which he was born in favor of a supreme ethical and moral force insisting on compassion and righteousness. Maybe Abram had chosen God even before God had chosen him!

There is a Sufi saying that speaks of the Divine in this way: "I was a hidden treasure longing to be known, and so I created Creation and was known." The Divine's relationship to humankind also was put forth in a poem by Rabindranath Tagore, a venerated spiritual Hindu poet, musician, and artist: "I have loved you in numberless forms, numberless times, in life after life, in age after age, forever." Although the God of the Israelites was not warmly expressive, I sense that this God knew the longings of Abram's soul; that telling Abram to leave his father's house was an expression of Divine love.

And I can imagine God's delight in fulfilling Abram's destiny:

"Yes, Abram, I hear you. I hear how your soul longs to be known in all its multiplicity. If that is truly your desire, then go forth. Leave the land of your birth and all that is familiar to you. Go to a new place, to a land you do not know, to a self you do not know, where you will come to know who you will be. And there I will bless you. After all, I have been waiting for this moment all along."

The Beginning of our Wandering

Abram and his wife, Sarai, went forth from Canaan (which today encompasses Israel, Jordan, Syria, and Lebanon), and during their wanderings they entered a covenant with God, where Abram was promised to become the father of a great people. Further, if his descendants also worshipped God, they would receive God's blessings and protection. God then changed the names of Abram and Sarai to Abraham and Sarah (meaning they were exalted), signifying their transformation from an ordinary couple to the Father and Mother of multitudes.

Isaac grew up and married Rebecca, and they had twin sons, Jacob and Esau. It was Jacob and his wives, Leah and Rachel, and their sons, who went down from Canaan to Egypt.

And it was Joseph, Jacob's favored son, who revealed to his brothers a dream he'd had in which the sun, moon, and stars bowed down to him. I imagine that his brothers, already viewing Joseph as arrogant, experienced this as another display of Joseph's conceit, which stirred their contempt. In reaction, Joseph's brothers threw him into a pit in the desert to die, unbeknownst to Jacob, and told their father that a wild beast had killed him—a fabrication that sent Jacob into ceaseless mourning. Later, traders pulled Joseph out of the pit; but his deliverance was short lived, for they sold him into slavery with the Pharaoh.

But Joseph was able to use his God-given gifts wisely. By correctly interpreting the Pharaoh's dreams, he gained the ruler's trust and eventually rose to the position of Minister to the Pharaoh. When famine struck the land, Joseph's ability to understand the coded messages of God by interpreting the Pharaoh's dreams enabled him to save the lives not only of the Egyptians but also of the same brothers who once had betrayed him and their families. By forgiving them all, Joseph ensured their survival and softened their hearts. But this came at the expense of them not being able to live in their own land, having to live as strangers in Egypt.

The children of Jacob were also known as *Israel*, and they came to reside in *Mitzraim*, Egypt. What was supposed to have been a temporary sojourn over time came to be experienced as "home."

Time passed, and the lives of Joseph and his brothers came to an end. A new Pharaoh came to power, one who didn't know all that Joseph had done for the Egyptians. Projecting the view of the Israelites as a potential enemy from within who would rise against him in bad times, he decreed: "Every son that is born shall be cast into the river, while every daughter shall be kept" (Exodus 1:22). And the oppression increased. We learn from the Bible that the

Egyptians set taskmasters upon the Israelites to build stone cities for Pharaoh, imposing hard labor upon them.

But when our ancestors cried out to their God, *Adonai* heard their voices and remembered the covenant made with Abraham, Isaac, and Jacob—and spared Moses, the son of Amram and Yocheved, who would be chosen by his God to help redeem the Israelites.

Where Have All the Women Gone?

The Book of Exodus focuses on Moses's role in our people's liberation from Egypt. But our deliverance began even before he was born, with the help of the compassionate and courageous women who played crucial roles in his life.

Women like Shifra and Puah, the midwives, who defied Pharaoh's decree to "cast every son into the river" by creating and circulating stories that the Hebrew mothers were so strong and gave birth so quickly that the midwives never had a chance to help, and thereby to account for the Israelite males.

Women like Miriam, Moses's sister, who confronted her father when she heard that he planned to separate from her mother (his best solution to Pharaoh's decree, so that he would avoid bringing another child into their harsh world). But when he heard Miriam's reasoning—if he, as the head of the tribe, left, the rest of the men would follow his lead and then there would be no further lineage—he yielded to it.

Women like Yocheved, Moses's mother, who had the courage after his birth to swaddle him in clean linen, put him in a papyrus basket, and place the basket into the reeds of the Nile, praying for someone to find—and care for—him. She was unaware that after she and Miriam returned to their hut, Miriam went back to the riverbank, positioning herself so she could watch over her brother, and saw the Pharaoh's daughter arrive.

Like Pharaoh's daughter, who spotted the basket, lifted it from the river, and took the baby home to be her own, becoming yet another woman to defy the Pharaoh.

Where are *their* stories? These women are mentioned in the Bible and at Seders, but only in recent years have they been truly acknowledged and celebrated—mostly at Women's Seders.

The heroic acts of these women speak clearly about what it takes to mend a broken world; and surely, the world of our enslaved ancestors was broken. It took courage, decisive action, and risk-taking, and we can be certain that there were more than five women who filled that bill. Where are their stories? In his book *Creating Lively Seders*, David Arnow asks these same questions and provides some interesting answers. One is that responsibility for the Exodus belongs to God, not humans. True, God is the main actor, and Moses's role is minimized; but Moses is still God's co-star, and he shares the bill with a considerable cast of human actors—it's just that they're all males! Arnow also attributes the absence of women in the *Haggadah* to the cultural climate of the compilers, as well as a reflection of Hellenistic culture, where women's roles were confined to the private sector. Since the Seder was modeled on the Greek symposium, an intellectual males-only banquet, women were excluded—or more likely served the meal and the wine, but otherwise invisible.

Before the Bible marginalized and buried the veneration of feminine deities, their worship was commonplace. Our early ancestors lived close to the larger Canaanite society, with no walls to block the borrowing of customs or worldviews. Recently, archaeologists have been painting more complicated pictures of how the Israelites lived their religious lives; many homes had shrines and statuettes with the inscription of YHWH, the unpronounceable name of God, and his *Ashera* (Wife/Mother Goddess). During the time of the Second Temple (565–70 BC), household shrines, statuettes of male and female figures, inscriptions, and carvings all point to a regionalized religion that was practiced within families, beyond the boundaries of Jerusalem's orthodox elite. Biblical scholars recently discovered that goddess imagery was present in many of the Israelite homes even long after the biblical period had ended. They suggest—and I would agree—that what the goddesses represented spoke to deep human needs. They still do. Sadly, worship of the feminine was eventually displaced by male-dominated, hierarchical societies.

Years ago, several rabbis echoed the "party line" that women didn't need to study Torah because they are intuitively close to God, while men need extensive education. There may be more truth to this than intended. There is much to learn from the rabbis and their strict ideals, but there is also much wisdom gleaned from the complex, day-to-day realities of the peasants, the folk traditions, and the "family wisdom" that we inherit—not from books, but from centuries of the lived experiences of our mothers, grandmothers, and aunts and the Divine Feminine they worshipped. There's good reason to question why She continues to endure despite millennia of suppression. The light garnered from women, the keepers of our traditions, is no less bright than that of our earlier rabbis. In some ways, perhaps it is even more radiant.

This is the world we inherited. But true to one of the names of God, *YHWH*, "I will be who I will be," what "is" now does not have to remain so. It can change for the better, even if we have to take a few steps back before we can move ahead. But change does come incrementally, in small steps. After far too long, women's place in Judaism is being transformed from what it was, to what it "ought to be." Although our journey will be detailed in Chapter 3, I want to mention some of the women who played subtle but significant roles in our history—without which, as scholars attest, the Exodus might never have occurred. They need to be remembered, acknowledged, and celebrated, as well.

The Righteous Women of Israel

- Serakh bat Asher, Jacob's granddaughter, who was the only one who remembered long-forgotten information the Israelites needed to prove that Moses was the genuine leader sent by God. When they were ready to leave Egypt but had to honor the pledge to take Joseph's bones with them to be buried in Israel, it was Serakh who remembered where he was put to rest in Egypt, enabling them to leave.

- Shifra, Puah, Yocheved, Miriam, and Pharaoh's daughter—true heroines who defied Pharaoh and changed the course of our history.

- Tzipporah, Moses's wife, who is said to have saved her husband's life, another holy woman who is barely mentioned at most mainstream Seders.

- The women referred to in the Talmud: "In the merit of the righteous women, Israel was redeemed from Egypt, and in their merit the future generations will be redeemed." The Talmud cites the women who, as righteous women, refused to give their men gold to build a golden calf.

- The women who engaged in sacred seduction for the purpose of becoming pregnant. These are the women who secretly stole into the fields in the dark of night to bring their broken husbands food, drink—and more. I hope it brought them a sense of agency, solace, and pleasure to reconnect with their partners, even if the mission of the seduction was for the sake of continuing our lineage. They too should be remembered, acknowledged, and applauded.

How many more righteous Jewish women contributed to our history? Many of their stories are lost to us, so we will never know; but we can be assured that their number and their deeds are significant. We've learned about some of them because of their notable contributions: Emma Lazarus, Henrietta Szold, Hannah Senesh, Golda Meir, Anne Frank, Bella Abzug, Betty Freidan, Gloria Steinem, and Justice Ruth Bader Ginsburg, just to name a few; but there are so many more. What of *all* the women, of every religion and color, whose names never got into the history books, who were also agents of change, active in the suffrage movement, women's rights, workers' rights, civil rights, human rights…? Those who allowed their husbands to shine while they tended the hearth, focusing their energies on creating healthy families? And the single mothers who took on the dual parental roles alone? All the women who walked, worked, and marched alongside us? Righteous women, all.

These are the daughters of the Divine Feminine, often referred to as a symbol of our Torah and as the "Tree of Life." When we look at our roots, let us remember that the roots of the Divine Feminine run deep and wide. Their branches reach through history, from our beginnings, through the generations, reminding our daughters that, with vision and the courage to act, they can carry forward the tradition of all the righteous women before us. Our roots are as deep as those of the Divine Masculine. Eternally entwined, they, too, are the source of our strength, courage, wisdom, and compassion.

Finding My Way

*And the day came when the risk to remain tight in a bud
was more painful than the risk it took to blossom.*

—Anais Nin

For too many of my earlier years I remained tight in a bud, unable to take the risks that would help me change and blossom. Until psychoanalysis uncovered the source of the traumatic incident that shaped my life, when a doctor's careless words had rendered the words of my five-year-old self silent.

THE GIRL WHO COULDN'T BEAR TO HEAR HER OWN VOICE

Praying, talking, singing, laughing, eating, and drinking…these are some of the joyful sounds of a Seder. And my family's Seders filled the bill. They were lively gatherings of the clan, with all my grandparents' East Coast relatives sitting around tables that extended from one end of their modest-sized living room to the other. I can still taste my mother's Passover sponge cakes, those light and airy almond cakes with chocolate chip surprises in almost every bite, along with my grandmother's fruit compote.

Yet despite all these delicious and nostalgic memories, what stands out most was my being overwhelmed by anxiety when it was my turn to read from the *Haggadah*, the Seder text. Reading and speaking aloud in any setting produced similar reactions; I couldn't bear to hear my own voice, particularly at the Seder, where I was convinced that everyone in the room was watching me, hearing me. If reading in English wasn't difficult enough, imagine how I felt when I had to recite the transliteration of The Four Questions in *Hebrew*. My heart thudded in my chest as I struggled to speak the words aloud; my nervous laughter comingled with my sister's, culminating in a fit of uncontrollable giggling, causing me to be pink-faced and mortified. But there was nothing funny about this to anyone else, least of all my father. Knowing that this behavior upset him only heightened my anxiety, making the giggling feel truly uncontrollable.

In addition to my self-consciousness, the Seder text itself made me feel like an outsider. What did these parables and tales of a Pharaoh, the Exodus, and enslavement have to do with *us* here in Brooklyn in the 1940s and '50s? My grandfather and my father took it all with great seriousness, but me, *not so much*. Although the words of the Seder had been spoken for almost four thousand years and were at the root of who we were as a family and a people, I couldn't relate to them. I absorbed the Jewishness around me: the food, the stories, the culture, the songs, and the strong family values—all this made me feel unquestionably Jewish. But I had little knowledge or understanding of my heritage, and only a cultural rather than an emotional connection to it. If anyone at our Seder table tried to honor the *Haggadah's* instruction "to tell the story in a way that arouses the children's curiosity," my anxious state of mind didn't permit any awareness of it; I couldn't take it in. Nor when I was older, an adult, was I able to be part of "the telling" to the next generation.

THE INTERGENERATIONAL TRANSMISSION OF TRAUMA

My childhood family was a very close, somewhat enmeshed one. My parents, maternal grandparents, aunt, uncle, and cousins lived less than a stone's throw away from each other, with our larger extended family just a little farther away.

They were almost as close here as when they were in Holoskov, a small town near Odessa, in what was then part of Russia and now is in Ukraine—then the site of persecution and pogroms, now (as of this writing) a site of senseless slaughter and genocide.

My mother recalled how in 1921, my grandparents seized the opportunity to escape with their two small children in tow—my mother, who was four, and her two-year-old sister, Manya. They traveled under the cover of darkness from one town to the next, aided by local Christian farmers who hid them in their cellars during the day. My mother remembered exhaustion and hunger as constant companions and feeling responsible for keeping Manya quiet as she tried to comfort her, especially when her mouth had to be covered with cloth so her cries would remain undetected. My mother knew well the importance of silence. She too kept as quiet as possible until they finally made their way to France, where they boarded a ship bound for America, the *goldena medina*, the golden land. But this land of milk and honey couldn't erase the body memories of being bound, which left my aunt Manya (later Mona) fearful and claustrophobic for the rest of her life. Nor did it erase my mother's intense discomfort with crying, screaming, or other loud and messy expressions of need.

As research suggests, parents who suffer trauma are often less able to respond optimally to their children's developmental crises, such as when according to family lore, I began to have bouts of long and loud screaming just before my sister was born. This must have been my response to the looming change I felt was happening in my family, an intuitive knowing that I would have to surrender my privileged position as an only child and the first grandchild. But my mother was not able to make this connection and found my loud screams deeply disturbing. They must have triggered in her the trauma of fleeing Russia, being hidden, silenced, and having to silence her sister's crying. It's only been in recent years that *I* made the connection between the trauma that my family suffered and what would come to be my own trauma. This is what happens with the intergenerational transmission of trauma. The unprocessed traumatic experiences in one generation find their way into the next generation. When parents' traumas are reactivated, their ability to process their children's distress is often diminished. This was the case with the trauma of my mother having to be silent to survive—that robbed her of the opportunity to respond to me in a way that would have helped me understand what was happening in my changing, soon-to-have-a-sibling world.

An Unintentional Trauma

When my screaming continued, like any concerned parent, my mother, alarmed and frightened, sought medical attention for me. The elderly doctor examined my throat, chest, and neck. Finally, he drew back, gave me a rather stern look, and announced: "If you don't stop screaming, I'll have to cut the tonsils out of your throat."

(I retained only a vague memory of this, which was confirmed my mother.)

I didn't know what tonsils were or that I had them in the first place. But I got the message that this was serious. His pronouncement scared the screams out of me; from that day on, they stopped. But what also stopped was the development of a healthy sense of self: the innate knowing that feelings can be expressed, needs can be met.

Ironically, my tonsils *were* removed a few months later, which had a profound impact on my young psyche and my later development. The presurgical preparation and the implication of the elderly doctor were more traumatic than I can recall, but I do remember growing increasingly withdrawn and compliant after that.

By the time I reached high school, I had grown self-conscious and lost at sea. But as I was never one to rock the boat, the waters of my existence appeared to be calm. Few people were able to see the turbulence beneath the surface. With no sense of self, I lived by going through the motions—a wind-up doll that moved in the direction in which she was pointed, a paint-by-numbers project.

I filled in the blank spaces of my self-portrait by imitating the language, style, and behaviors of the girls around me. I learned to smile knowingly, when in fact I was clueless. When my friends and I went to a distant park, hoping to meet non-Jewish (aka "cool") boys, I followed suit and pretended to be a cool Italian girl named Joanie Ferrara! I don't know what ignited that spark of self that was strong enough to defy my parents' commandment: "Thou shall not date non-Jewish boys." But that incident was the exception, not the rule. Perhaps more extreme, but like many other "good" Jewish girls growing up in those years, I was charged with the task of living up to my parents' expectations. And like so many other young girls who felt little sense of agency, I was barely aware of my own needs and desires.

One of my saving graces came, as they often do, from a teacher: Mrs. Kleinman, my high school Spanish teacher. Although she recognized my fear of speaking in class, she had hoped to find a way for me to sing "Kitty Conga," a Spanish song, for an assembly program. However, when she realized the depth of the challenge, she didn't force the issue. Instead, like a horse-whisperer, she gently and masterfully coaxed me to lip-synch the song. And to my own amazement, I agreed. I rationalized that I wouldn't be using *my own* voice; I would be hiding behind someone else's; no one would hear *me*. Unconsciously, I was allowing myself to give voice to my unacknowledged yearning to be seen and heard, to discover my own self and truth.

Mrs. Kleinman's perception of my brokenness had the paradoxical effect of helping me feel somewhat more whole. Through her creative use of illusion, the lip-synching somehow made me feel a bit more real. She had planted seeds of healing. Although it would take many more years for them to blossom, her compassion was like a healing light that seeped in through the cracks of my dark inner world, nurturing those seeds.

REDISCOVERING MY VOICE AND A LONGING FOR SOMETHING MORE

What also warmed my heart was the love and attention of a warm, expressive, and out-going young man I met while in college, who was able to give voice to many of my unspoken feelings. In my receiving this crucial attention, both my heart and the blocked energy choking my voice began to open. Soon after Stan and I married, our first child, Robin, was born. Three years later, while I was still in college, we brought our second daughter, Karen, into the world. Gratefully, I was becoming more connected to my own yearnings and aspirations; I knew that I wanted to be at home to raise my children, *and* I was determined to graduate. Though it took close to ten years, I proudly graduated, with my two daughters cheering me on. Had it taken any longer, our son, Michael, would have been there, too.

Like so many of our contemporaries, our family left the city and moved to the suburbs. Life was good. I became more in touch with my own needs and felt a growing sense of agency. I loved raising our family in the "country," with nature in our backyard and a community college nearby where I took classes to learn about and feel part of the world beyond my home. My love of learning continued, and in time I would come to earn graduate degrees in Clinical Social Work and Psychoanalysis. But that would happen only many years later.

In this spacious new world of lush lawns and cul-de-sacs, religion was largely a backdrop to our secular lives. Our children mixed easily in a diverse stew with others from different backgrounds; the old world of religious homogeneity from our childhoods was left behind.

But was it, really?

A part of me felt empty, as if something central to my being were missing. I made several attempts to find a niche for myself; I found enough of my voice to sing in the choir, as well as edit the temple's newsletter. But neither was sufficient to fill the soul longing that stirred inside. I needed something more. I became increasingly aware that my *cultural* attachment was not enough to sustain my Jewish identity, nor would it sustain the next generation. As they grew older, my children's connection to our religion was a fragile one; they were disturbed by what they felt was narrow thinking and a tendency toward divisiveness. I understood their feelings well, but I wasn't sufficiently schooled in our people's history to pass on all that was rich, wise, and good in our tradition. I could not, as the *Haggadah* itself proscribes, "tell it to your children." Not when they were young or later when they were adults starting families of their own.

This is when I had the dream that changed the trajectory of my life, the dream of our heritage being lost to my family because the "elders" were no longer with us to connect us to our tradition.

FILLING THE VOID

My father, the quiet keeper of our family's tradition, died unexpectedly about a year before the dream. Mourning his death cracked my heart open and helped me understand what he had tried to teach—not with words, but through the example of the simple, dignified, and honorable way he had lived. He was a gentle, compassionate, non-judgmental man who was deeply devoted to his family—both his family of origin and the one he had created with us. His reverence for our religious heritage was clearly felt, if not communicated verbally. It was painful to imagine how he must have felt at those Seders—sitting at the table, noble and grave, reading the sacred texts as my sister and I tried to stifle our giggles. Not one to use his voice to express his feelings, he didn't reprimand us. He didn't have to. We only had to look at his face.

Perhaps because he died with his deep, mostly unarticulated feelings about our heritage still contained within him, unconscious thoughts of using my *own* voice to express my father's longings as well as my own began to stir within me. The void created by his death was an invitation for me to take my place in the chain of generations and carry our tradition forward. But without knowing enough about our tradition—or like my father, not being comfortable using my own voice—how was I to do this?

My next teacher appeared in the form of my granddaughter. At seven, Emily was already incredibly in touch with her feelings, and she expressed confusion and sadness about her Jewish religious heritage. Her Christian friends went to after-school religious instruction, and when they talked about the holidays or Bible stories (which she didn't understand), she felt left out. She needed to know: "Why don't Jewish people have things like that?"

When she asked me that, I turned away from the task at hand and looked at her. In her sweet face, I seemed to make out so many different aspects of our family, all melded together: long-gone grandparents, aunts, and uncles… and my father. I felt a pang of love at the thought of my quiet and unassuming father, who, I'm sure, had prayed that his family would continue our tradition. I couldn't let go of the thread of spiritual sustenance and tradition that he'd tried to hand down; I *had* to pass it on to my grandchildren and provide them with a meaningful sense of how our heritage resonated in our lives and in the world today.

But how? I found a clue in the *Haggadah* itself.

As a child, I was unaware that a central aim of the Seder is to appeal to children, to arouse their curiosity and interest so they can learn of their heritage. We adults are commanded, "You shall tell [the story] to your children" (Exodus 13:8) so they can identify with the Exodus as the foundational story of our people, and proudly pass it on to the next generation.

But something had gotten lost in translation!

Putting Together a Children's *Haggadah*

The search to find what I thought was lost became enough of an incentive for me to leave the only kind of Seders I had known for something unknown, like a Seder for kids that would allow them to grasp the spiritual messages of the Seder, the themes of freedom, perseverance, courage, growth-enhancing risk-taking, the importance of kindness, faith, and trust, and the belief that things can change from how they are to how they should be.

I would have to be mindful of the Parable of the Four Children, which addresses the different temperaments of children, their levels of understanding, and their openness or resistance to learning. I would have to meet them "where they were."

I cast the story in a historical context, to help them understand that this was not just a story about what happened to our ancestors but one that can help us live good lives today. And in a generational context, it was a story that was told to us (the adults) by our parents and grandparents and would someday be told by them (our children) to their children. We reenacted the story in the form of a play, with dialogue, songs, and characters from kid culture that they could relate to that were engaging, fun, and familiar.

In researching the many different aspects of the Seder, I also found myself understanding many elements of the ritual for the first time. So did my adult children and their friends. It was as though a door opened, and we were now standing inside the room instead of outside.

The seeds of these joyful and meaningful Seders blossomed into a true appreciation of the holiday. My heart filled with satisfaction when my granddaughter Becca spoke warmly at her *Bat Mitzvah* of how meaningful and fun our Family Seders were; when my wise-beyond-his-years grandson Ben named "narrow-mindedness" as a contemporary plague; and my son-in-law Bart expressed warm words of appreciation that meant so much to me. And while I cannot take credit for the insightful commentary on Moses's character that my granddaughter Hannah offered at her Bat Mitzvah, or the way my wildly expressive youngest grandchild, Ava, read from the Torah at her Bat Mitzvah and gave our people's Story wings, I like to think that our family Seders nurtured some of the warmth and pride that they have come to feel for our tradition.

Putting Together a Family *Haggadah*

My friends and my family's appreciation of my efforts gave me the confidence to push the envelope even further; I wrote a *Family Haggadah*, adding thoughts and ideas from other texts that resonated with me, as well as more original passages. Each year, I updated this *Haggadah* to express my evolving spirituality and my growing family's needs. I took pleasure in knowing that the many friends and contemporaries with whom I shared my ideas at our family Seders and later at Women's Seders felt a sense of pride in learning that our tradition held more meaning and relevance than they had imagined. I take pleasure now in sharing these thoughts and ideas with you, and hope that you will feel similarly.

OPENING AND BLOSSOMING

It is said that we teach what we need to learn. In teaching my grandchildren about Passover—about our beginnings and our heritage—I wrested meaning from the very ritual that I once couldn't relate to. No longer was I lost in a spiritual wilderness, in search of a path to nourish my fraying connection to Judaism. It turned out that my exploration of the Seder ritual *was* the path that would lead me toward what I was seeking, provide me with a deeper connection to our history and to the sacred, and help awaken a sense of holiness in me. I wrestled with some of the issues in our texts that had plagued me—such as the patriarchy, and the judgmental and vengeful aspects of the Divine—until I was able to relate to them in a more personal way. As a result, I felt more at home and engaged in my own tradition. Re-digging its wells, turning its soil, bringing light to its teachings, I discovered new meanings in the old symbols.

To reach this point, I had to put one foot in front of the other (much like my ancestors before me as they wandered through the desert), not knowing where my journey would lead me. As I traveled the path, with its unpredictable unfolding of events, sparks of longing emerged in me, igniting a passion to reclaim my heritage. No longer content to be a "closed bud," I was experiencing the sacred process of Opening and Blossoming that I sensed the true meaning behind Passover might be pointing to, the meaning that was missing from the family Seders of my childhood. But there was more wrestling to be done before I could truly open and blossom.

Healing the Shadow Side of Religious Experience

First, I would have to heal the "shadow" side—my (unarticulated) negative attitude toward religion. Initially, learning more about my tradition only confirmed for me its rigid, narrow, patriarchal aspects, and left me feeling that the God of our foundational story was an abstract concept to which I could not connect. Even saying "God" felt uncomfortable because I couldn't relate to this omniscient, all-powerful sky being. At this point, though, I understand that we *can't* name what is ineffable; and I often use terms like Spirit, the One, Divine, and *Sh'khinah* interchangeably, which feel more evocative of this wordless state of being and loving presence. Learning about my religion instilled in me a profound respect for its fundamental values, imparted much of the knowledge I lacked, and gave me a more solid sense of being grounded in my heritage. Yet it was the *spiritual* dimension to which I felt pulled.

But what would allow me to *feel* a connection to a presence that creates a sense of expansiveness, inspires us to live justly, compassionately, and graciously, and moves us to feel moments of intimate communion with others? I began to appreciate Rabbi David Cooper's concept of "God-ing"—that maybe, as his book of that title suggests, *God is a Verb*. A process, an action we bring to the world to make love, joy, and goodness known. An action we take that helps us reach beyond our limited selves, toward our best selves, and closer to the realm of the Divine.

I'm aware that many people's spirituality may not include a belief in or relationship to God. Their spirituality may be about those awe-inspiring encounters that somehow transform the sense of self—revelations that may arise within the silent spaces of meditation, whether from a sense of wonder, or from a connection to nature, music, or art, or from those spontaneous moments when our whole being comes alive and we feel moved to unimagined heights and depths. The spirituality that *I* was seeking would embrace all the above, including a relationship to an all-encompassing Spirit.

Caught between these two apparent irreconcilables of Religion and Spirituality, I was thrown back into the internal chaos of not knowing. But amid the confusion, the teachings of Rabbi Shefa Gold shed clarity and pushed some of the shadows away. I learned that—with some practice—Religion and Spirituality *could* be reconciled. That it was possible to integrate both perspectives. As a member of a "tribe," I'd have to confront and work through the accumulated "shadow" of my people—the negative experiences, memories, and emotions built up over millennia—before I could appreciate the hidden treasures in Judaism that could connect me to the universal consciousness of Oneness.

As I worked with this shadow, I found that I was ashamed of the wrathful, vengeful aspects of my tradition, which seemed to lack the very mercy and compassion it avowed. Its judgmental and exclusionary features furthered a sense of separateness instead of connection; and the patriarchal lens through which all was filtered rendered the wisdom and experiences of women almost invisible, relegating our gifts and strengths to the dustbins of history. I would have to empty myself of my *own* wrath, not just God's, before I could create an inner space to consider Judaism's mystical tradition—the more spiritual philosophy that would help me take this almost four-thousand-year-old heritage written in my bones into my heart.

As often happens, exploring other spiritual traditions helped me to appreciate and embrace my own. For me, this was Buddhism.

Cross-Pollination

Opening myself to Buddhist philosophy, I learned how its practice centered on looking into the self and finding ways of becoming more mindful in everyday life—to acknowledge and work with the different parts of our selves without attaching to any of them as the *true self*, and to focus on eliminating suffering and finding paths of peace and calm.

I was envious of the Buddhists' spiritual philosophy, the way my granddaughter was of her Christian friends' spiritual enrichment: *Why doesn't Judaism have a philosophy like this?* I complained. But to my surprise (and embarrassment), when I explored my own Jewish roots further, I discovered a similar spirituality in my own tradition, hiding in plain sight—*Jewish mysticism.* This is an intense path, based on ritual and knowledge that seeks to understand the Divine realm and to achieve an intimate, mystical union with God. It also seeks to effect change in this world and the world beyond by fostering goodness, by eliminating evil, by healing and mending the world. While not easily accessible, I found it mystically appealing, with its promise of an unmediated, direct experience of the Divine and being a part of the world's healing. But the study of this path was beyond the scope of my current concerns.

Another reason why I had neglected to explore my heritage before this time was because I was ashamed of the regressive Chasidism that we know today—its wisdom, like its followers' outward appearance, was cloaked in old-world garb and felt inaccessible. Yet beneath the dark, concealing garments of early thirteenth-century Chasidism (whose mystical approach had shed a spiritual light in the fifteenth and sixteenth centuries) was an enlightened philosophy.

I had never imagined that the spirituality I longed for was part of my very own heritage. But with the cross-pollination of wisdom from other spiritual traditions, particularly Buddhism, I was able to see how much seemingly divergent spiritual paths can have in common, and how they can complement each other. Indeed, the leaders of two great mystical traditions—Judaism (Rabbi Zalman Shacter-Shalomi) and Buddhism (the Dalai Lama)—met to learn from each other and share their spiritual wisdom, as Roger Kamenetz described in his book, *The Jew in the Lotus*.

The Dalai Lama appreciated learning how the Jewish focus on family, education, and adaptability were crucial ingredients in the preservation of our religion, especially in the face of exile and near annihilation. And our spiritual leaders welcomed the Dalai Lama's thoughts on how our own rich Jewish mystical tradition could renew, revitalize, and rejuvenate Judaism in a way that would speak to a younger generation, which Judaism's more rational approach did not. This mutual recognition of each other's experiences, successes, and vulnerabilities, and the willingness to learn from each other all serve as an ideal role model to achieve the noble goals of both traditions.

Deepening Religious Roots

Discovering the enduring wisdom of the Jewish mystics gave me the opportunity to re-visit an important aspect of the religion from which I had felt disconnected. And the more I learned, the more I could sense those religious roots deepening. It was gratifying to discover that like the Buddhists, Jewish mystics were *also* concerned with self-transformation. The Jewish mystics *also* used contemplative and meditative practices to achieve more highly focused states, in which they could not only pay attention to what was happening in the moment but also look at life from a larger perspective. They also developed a philosophy for dealing with life's suffering: impermanence, the inevitability of pain, loss, and disappointment, and the ability to "go on being" in the face of unspeakable pain. They appreciated how compassion could transform suffering into wisdom and cultivated a fierce belief that our grief would ultimately be transformed into joy, our "mourning turned into dancing."

And like the Buddhists, they too spoke of the *illusion* of duality and separation, and the *reality* of connection and interdependence. In Jewish mystical thinking, no gesture is without meaning—not a falling leaf, not the call of a bird, or a baby's cry. Our smallest acts impact the world. As single strands in an exquisite and complex woven web, every thought we have, every action we take, becomes part of the collective energy, with the potential to heal or harm our own lives and that of the planet. Like ripples in a pond, our openhearted awareness and compassion reverberate in ever-widening circles, touching everything around us: our families, our communities, and our world. It is my belief and my prayer that as we heal ourselves—as we grow in wholeness and freedom—our healing will extend beyond our individual lives and contribute to the healing of the world. The mystics have always known that, at the deepest level of being, we are all connected. Rabbi Lawrence Kushner describes it so elegantly: *throughout all Creation, just beneath the surface, all our beings are joined in a luminous organism of sacred responsibility, in invisible lines of connection.*

Seeds of Healing

Mystical Judaism created a space for me to explore the spiritual dimension, with its understanding that we are all sparks of the divine, connected to the Source of All Life, to a whole greater than and beyond ourselves. This Source no longer felt abstract to me. I was connecting to this Whole and felt a mystical bond to this Presence that I couldn't explain with words. But I could sense the seeds of healing growing in me; the negative feelings I had harbored for so long toward my tradition were softening, giving way to a sense of pride in my people.

The deep spirituality of these Jewish mystics—who were less bound by the parameters of the material world than many—most likely helped them cultivate a more spacious consciousness that could nurture their growth and compassion. And I imagine that their relationship to God helped them through their darkest times by expanding the boundaries of consciousness.

Perhaps in this realm, they could more easily understand that things are not always as they seem to be, that blessings are often buried within pain, that seeds of healing are hidden in heartbreak, and that there is *always* the possibility of healing and growth. Perhaps in this more tranquil space they envisioned a world of greater possibilities—where things could change from how they *are* to how they *ought to be*, a world where our inherent sense of dignity and freedom would belong to all.

My heart expands when I think of how our people—whose origins were rooted in such challenge, deprivation, and limitation—evolved into a people for whom *Tikkun Olam*, the healing of the world, is essential. Considering the psychic energy that needs to be expended in moving away from the known, narrow world of automatic self-protection and preservation, it is remarkable that we could maintain an expansive worldview, see beyond our own needs, and feel more compassion for and connection to others. This generosity of spirit fills me with pride and deepens my connection. Learning that these ethical principles were bound up with *Sh'khinah*—the feminine face of God, who softens the Bible's wrathful, judgmental sovereign—helped mend my religious/spiritual split. Her unifying presence is spacious enough to hold all our conflicted convictions.

As we will see in the next chapter, *Sh'khinah* is moving beyond the gendered attributes of passivity and nurturance assigned by a patriarchal culture to a power in Her own right, with qualities of courage, compassion, and strength.

Food for Thought

- How has religion/spirituality impacted your life?

- How has it strengthened and empowered you, or disillusioned and angered you?

- What shadows do you need to expose to light, wrestle with, and transcend?

- What is at the heart of your seeking?

CHAPTER THREE

Sh'khinah: An Indwelling Spirit

She is the indwelling Presence that calls us to fullness of being.

—Rabbi Lynn Gottlieb

Imagine having a Goddess-like, compassionate, maternal spirit, a presence that dwells in the innermost chambers of your heart, who is with you wherever you wander. A Divine Mother with the "feminine" attributes of wisdom, compassion, nurturance, and strength, who inspires you to be all you can be. Discovering the Jewish mystics' enduring innovation, the concept of the *Sh'khinah*—the feminine counterpart to the biblical God's "masculine" persona—opened my mind and my heart.

THE MOTHER OF ISRAEL

It was only when I began my spiritual quest that I came upon the concept of *Sh'khinah*. The notion was, historically, the province of the scholars who wrote the Talmud (rabbinic law) in the second to fifth centuries to convey God's closeness or immanence, the One who dwells within. The sages believed that this Presence dated back to the Garden of Eden, where it accompanied our people as they fled from Egypt. It was the *Sh'khinah* that manifested in the Sea of Reeds, in a cloud of glory, in a pillar of fire, and in the provision of manna in the wilderness. Not yet a feminized concept, *Sh'khinah* began to move toward this designation after the prophet Jeremiah had a vision likening Her to our foremother Rachel, who wept for all her children in the wake of the First Temple's destruction. *Sh'khinah* then became known as the "suffering Mother of Israel," because of her protective connection to Her people.

Almost immediately, I related to this Presence and wanted to learn more about Her. Rabbi Lynn Gottlieb, in her book *She Who Dwells Within*, and Rabbi Leah Novick, in *On the Wings of Shekhinah*, each followed Her journey as She moved through history, thereby providing nourishment for mine. As they traced the arc of Her evolution, they found that She had gone through many iterations before She came to be considered the feminine face of God, the mother of all beings who embodies the qualities of the ancient goddesses. *Sh'khinah* personifies love, compassion, fairness, justice, and healing. She is powerful, fiercely protective, but also capable of fury, destruction, and Divine retribution—especially toward those who persecute Her people.

The Israelites who worshipped Her at the First Temple in Jerusalem must have experienced its destruction in 586 BCE by the Babylonians as a searing trauma, with an immense loss of life, land, freedom, and the most sacred institutions and practices that had been connected to the temple. After the loss of Her home and the sense of national unity that it provided, *Sh'khinah* was said to have gone into exile with Her people, accompanying them wherever they went in their wanderings. In the absence of the Temple, the home from which *Sh'khinah* could bind the people together and preserve their collective memory, the rabbis and sages chose to make the observance of Sabbath—with its focus on community and ethical behavior—the centerpiece of Jewish life. Since Jews were considered conduits between Heaven and Earth, our actions could attract or repel *Sh'khinah*'s presence. Prayer, study, and good works could bring Her near; ego, self-importance, violence, and the sins of humanity would drive Her away.

Until the early Middle Ages, the ideas, beliefs, and thoughts about God had more to do with distance—immanence and transcendence—and less to do with gender. *Sh'khinah* was often considered a formless archetype from another realm, Who would appear in a recognizable form to convey messages to humanity.

KABBALAH AND THE DIVINE FEMININE

It was with the first mystical text, *Sefir Ha Bahir*, *The Book of Illumination*, attributed to a first-century sage that *Sh'khinah* began to be thought of as mother, sister, daughter, and bride. And in the thirteenth century, the early Kabbalists developed a complex formulation, *The Tree of Life*, otherwise known as *s'firot*, in which human qualities—including, perhaps most significantly, sexual dynamics—were mapped onto the schema. The concept of reuniting the Divine Feminine and the Divine Masculine in sacred marriage was formally introduced, with *Sh'khinah* emerging as a captive princess separated from her divine partner, waiting to be rescued from the forces of evil. Her exile is a metaphor for the world's disharmony. And once again, it was thought that prayer, charity, and study could restore the Divine couple's permanent sexual union, ensuring the harmony and balance of the universe.

As the Kabbalah continued to develop through the later mystics in the sixteenth century, the Divine Masculine and Divine Feminine were believed to be in permanent connection in the *spiritual* realm; it was only in the *material* dimension that the Divine Daughter and Her consort were separated. According to Kabbalah, they came together every Sabbath, but their union as *Bride and Groom* required deeply ethical human behavior in the human realm. Because the Sabbath was a time when work and time stopped, this provided more opportunities for humans to act in ways that would unite the Cosmic Lovers in sacred marriage. The Sabbath came to be known as the *Sabbath Bride* or *Sabbath Queen*, and during this time lovemaking was elevated to the realm of the holy. If the men were to access *Sh'khinah* energy, they would have to make their own needs secondary and focus on giving their wives pleasure. (Is *this* why there are still so many men with underdeveloped feminine sides?)

EARLY CHASIDISM AND WOMEN

Although the culture was still profoundly patriarchal, the focus on *Sh'khinah* elevated women's roles as wives, mothers, and homemakers, especially by the early Chasidic mystics of the thirteenth century. Just as the Sabbath became truly sacred time after the Temple was destroyed, so the home became a miniature sanctuary, "a palace in time," as described by Rabbi Abraham Joshua Heschel. A time devoted to acts of prayer, for joyous meals, and time spent with loved ones. A time of deep spiritual communion, when women became the conduits for welcoming the Sabbath in a manner befitting a queen. Being responsible for creating an aesthetically pleasing household—which included special foods, wine, music, prayer, and a peaceful, loving ambience—all helped to heighten the value of women's work. Chasidism envisioned bringing *Sh'khinah* back to Earth through joy, music, dance, and piety.

Besides attending to the essential Sabbath rituals, many women also wrote Sabbath prayers *(techinot)*. Though most of these women were not literate in Hebrew and wrote the prayers in Yiddish, the rabbis still recognized the women's capacity for holiness, prophetic abilities, intuitive and healing skills, and inherent connection to *Sh'khinah*. Although the times and the culture did not allow for gender equality, being given the role of ushering in the Sabbath helped the women feel like priestesses, ritual leaders, keepers of tradition, and vessels of sacred energy—if only in their homes for one day a week!

Although women of the time were not widely educated, early Chasidism produced some revered women saints who were valued for their piety, wisdom, and insights. They were felt to be messengers of *Sh'khinah*. While the movement could not bring women fully into synagogue life, it helped open the gates of recognition that they were living carriers of *Sh'khinah* energy.

EXILE AND RETURN

After the French Revolution opened the doors to secular education in the eighteenth century, many Jewish students moved away from the more insular religious lifestyle that had become the standard. Mysticism was relegated to the realm of superstition, and *Sh'khinah* went into exile once again. Only when the more liberal-thinking Jews spread to other parts of Europe in the nineteenth century and then to the Reform movement in America did She make a slow return to liturgy and culture.

The idealism of the concurrent *Haskalah* (Enlightenment) movement also impacted Jewish life and eased *Sh-khinah's* return to Her people in the physical realm. This movement, with its strong connection to Zionism, envisioned a path for Judaism that was rooted in Hebrew prayer, in nature, in social justice, in harmony, in greater equality for women, and in the creation of a homeland where Jews could live according to their ethical values. The spirit of *Haskalah* ignited a spark in many women within the movement and beyond, liberating them from old gender roles and attitudes; many insisted on working in the fields of the *kibbutzim* (communal farms) as well as in the kitchens. It also released long-suppressed creative energy, which birthed a considerable number of poets, writers, and activists. They became engaged in peace and social justice work that focused on addressing women's poverty and sexual exploitation, both in what became Israel and in the West. The religious fervor of the movement, like early Chasidism, was infused with ecstasy and joy, mirroring the positive energy of *Sh'khinah* as well as being an active prayer to bring Her back to Earth.

And they *have* brought Her back. She is a ripple on Her way to becoming a wave. Today, though She is still not widely known in "mainstream" culture, She is thriving among many of Her people in those spiritual communities, offering seekers a broader range of experiences and opportunities to express their spirituality, devotion, and *Sh'khinah*-consciousness. Her energy is returning to the earthly realm.

THE WOMEN'S MOVEMENT

Although we may now take it for granted, the expanded presence of women in Jewish leadership positions since the latter part of the twentieth century is remarkable, particularly the ordination of women rabbis and cantors in all streams of Judaism except for the Orthodox. The feminist activist groups that formed and flowered in the 1970s accelerated their long-awaited acceptance as clergy. These included the revival of New Moon groups, which wove ancient goddess culture into Jewish ritual; the groups of women who advocated for the use of feminine God language in our liturgy; and all those who pressed, pushed, and petitioned for the ordination of women rabbis. It was a struggle, but nevertheless they persisted! And synagogue life was transformed from the limited singular perspective of male clergy to a more egalitarian, balanced rabbinate, which would provide new role models; a greater focus on family issues; more diversity in Jewish life, especially for gay and lesbian seekers; and a greater connection to the hopes, desires, and concerns of women congregants who sought to be more engaged in their tradition but hadn't been able to find a place.

Restoring the Planet

The growing openness to *Sh'khinah*-consciousness blossomed beyond the walls of the synagogue in the fields of art, music, poetry, and the study of Jewish meditation and mysticism. In the Kabbalistic *Tree of Life* schema, *Sh'khinah* is the *sephira* (i.e., chakra, energy center) that connects us to all living things on our planet—an energy that helps us experience Earth as a living organism, which then gives rise to contemporary concerns about sustaining the life and health of our planet. This confirms the Talmud's teachings that *Sh'khinah* cannot tolerate life on Earth when there is pollution, degradation, violence, or any manner of abuse. Humanity's role is to attract *Sh'khinah* energy with mindful deeds of loving-kindness, prayer, and generosity. This is the energy that we need to restore the balance of our planet and its inhabitants.

THE DIVINE MOTHER IN THE HUMAN MOTHER

Sh'khinah's energy and qualities—Her unconditional love, compassion, creativity, and receptivity; her gentleness and patience; Her accepting, forgiving, nurturing, and healing capacities; Her intuition, courage, and protectiveness—make it easy for us to imagine Her as the Divine Mother, sheltering us under Her wings. The mother we all wish we had and aspire to be.

Although in our own ancient Jewish history, *Sh'khinah* was conceptualized as the glory of God, the Biblical era had marginalized and buried the worship of deities. Worship of the Feminine was displaced by male-dominated, hierarchical societies whose rise seems to have coincided with the development of written language. Although Supreme deities of many religions are cast in the masculine image, Judaism's mystical tradition created a place for the feminine aspect of the Divine, especially in the sixteenth century, when *Sh'khinah* was reimagined as a mystical embodiment of the feminine, earth-centered presence of God, with similar attributes to the Goddess. In more recent history, contemporary feminists and theologians such as Rabbi Jill Hammer have been reclaiming the *Sh'khinah* as a unified deity in Her own right, Who dwells within living things and the Earth, healing brokenness, seeking peace, and nurturing connection.

It is ironic that the feminine energies have been suppressed for so much of our history and that the masculine approach has been privileged, when we consider that our ancestors' deliverance came only after *the women* of the Exodus resisted a tyrant's decree and refused to accept injustice as the norm. Or was it *because* of their creative, courageous, out-of-the-box thinking that men—both then and today—felt the need to keep women in their place through a patriarchal system?

But women are once again reclaiming their inherent dignity and strength, their inventiveness and autonomy, their power to create positive change. The feminine attributes of wisdom, compassion, connection, and much more are once again ascending. They are challenging the prevailing patriarchal patterns of entitlement, power, and prerogative, standing up to the men who try to keep them down.

Can you imagine what it might be like to feel the presence of a Divine Mother Who is all that our own mothers aspired to be? Although they tried to care for us as best as they were able, our very human mothers—with wounds of their own—may have fallen short of their own ideals. Perhaps the Divine Mother is the repository of all their dreams for us, a soothing presence Who provides us with what we need when our own mothers cannot: the embodiment of patience, able to delay the gratification of Her own needs so that She can attune herself to ours, whose innate capacity for connection nurtures our own. She is the one who teaches us to understand the cycles of nature and time, cultivates an appreciation of silence and stillness so we can connect to our deeper selves, and inspires in us the freedom and confidence to give birth to the beings we are meant to be. She carries the energy of our mothers, who want to move Heaven and Earth to protect us from harm but often cannot. And when we're feeling separate and alone and our own mothers are not available, She is the healing, loving presence to whom we cry out and reach out, giving us the strength, wisdom, and courage we need to go on being.

How different would your life be if you were able to hold the countless attributes of *Sh'khinah* in your heart? If you felt guided and protected by an abiding sense of love, compassion, and wisdom as you made your way in the world?

In the Arms of the Divine Mother

This expansive, female-centered perspective helped me connect to the God of my Mothers—*Sh'khinah*, the wise and loving, strong and tender Presence within us and all around us, a Presence that holds us in a womb of compassion. I experienced her as a Divine Mother Who dwells in earthly places and earthly beings—in the human body, particularly the life-giving, nurturing female body. I needed Her to be in the physical realm as well as in the spiritual, and through this I began to connect with my body in new ways, paying attention to its sensations, its expressions of pleasure and pain, and becoming aware of the tight places, the constricted muscles and narrow channels that blocked the flow of energy. And I became aware of the almost constant drone of chatter in my mind. As I practiced releasing tension from my body and quieting my mind, I heard *Sh'khinah's* soft voice in the silent spaces of my heart.

The first time I felt held by Her was the night I attended the Shabbat service following my father's death. More than just experiencing comfort, I felt a brand-new connection to the liturgy—to the point where I thought we were using new prayer books! But in my vulnerable and receptive state, what I was experiencing was Her empathic presence, as though She were sitting beside me—singing, praying, and crying with me. And I felt myself held in Judaism's loving arms, an invisible web of continuity and security.

The energy of *Sh'khinah* was becoming inscribed upon my heart. My connection to Spirit was no longer an empty concept. It was a relationship in which I sensed Her calming, loving, open, and protective presence—the way my ancestors had felt so many years before. This relationship somehow made me feel more connected to our people's symbols and stories, and to those who came before me. Like the shepherds and the farmers who were so connected to the rhythms and cycles of nature, my own life was becoming part of an ancient pattern of ebbing and flowing, darkness and light, stillness, and creation; I began to connect across the generations to other times and other lives. I saw my father as a bridge to those other lives that came before us; *I* was a bridge to those who would come after. I had no idea how long that bridge would be or what shape it would take, but I had a clear sense that I was part of the pattern, and that I would somehow create something meaningful from the stillness.

ROSH CHODESH GATHERINGS: A SPACE FOR *SH'KHINAH*

Connecting to women's experiences—real, remembered, and imagined—inspired me to take my connection to Judaism to a deeper level. *Rosh Chodesh* groups and my involvement in them became a significant step on my journey.

Rosh Chodesh (meaning Head of the Month) is a minor holiday on the Jewish calendar, the first day of the new month, in which women gather to celebrate the new moon. Moon worship, with its association to fertility, was prevalent in the Near East in biblical times; and since our people lived among other nations, more than a few Hebrew women followed the custom as well. We can imagine how this was a source of controversy between the religious establishment and the women who designated it as "sacred time." Since a compromise was needed, the rabbis of that era deemed the holiday a reward for the women who had refused to participate in the building of the Golden Calf by withholding their jewelry. Over time, the new-moon gatherings evolved to become a holiday for men as well as women, but with the emergence of feminism in the 1960s and '70s, it was reclaimed by women.

These gatherings had a distinctly feminine energy. More than pouring old wine into a new bottle, this ancient ritual of celebrating the new moon was the perfect medium for contemporary women to explore their physicality and their spirituality. Like the moon, women's bodies and spirits go through cycles of waxing and waning, filling and emptying, ebbing and flowing. And like the moon that goes into "hiding," women too need to retreat, to create some space from the demands of life, to feel renewed. Characteristically, if women were going to explore their Jewish identity, they were going to do it their way. They met to study texts relating to the month to learn about female ancestors and contemporary role models through meditation, chanting, creative dance, and storytelling.

How I wish I had been part of that!

Then in the 1990s, a group of women rabbinical students sought to transform Jewish education through the lens of feminism, and so they created "*Rosh Chodesh*: It's a Girl Thing!" This program brought Jewish values and practice to bear on the deepest concerns of adolescent girls: identity, peer relationships, body image, family, and sex and gender issues. And I wanted to be a part of this.

I offered to lead a group for high school girls at my temple and was trained to do so by the parent group. And though I felt somewhat intimidated—these young women were far more knowledgeable about Jewish education than I was—I took the plunge. But it turned out that I needn't have felt tentative: having a safe, nonjudgmental space to have fun and be real with their peers in the context of Jewish ethics was something that these girls were hungry for.

This mutually fulfilling experience inspired me to start a *Rosh Chodesh* group for women, who had cravings of their own. They were hungry for more spirituality, for deeper connections to their inner lives and to the rhythms and cycles of nature, and to find what was holy within them and in the world. Our gatherings felt like monthly islands of calm. We shared our stories, we learned from our traditions, from each other, and from the deep wisdom within through discussion, meditation, song, dance, laughter, and tears. These were also safe female spaces that allowed women to speak of how they had been moving away from their religious roots; how they had been distancing themselves from their heritage or denying it; even to speak of the possibility of choosing different spiritual paths. Yet most of them wanted to return to traditional sources to *reinforce* their Jewish identity, not break away from it. They wanted something more from their religion, something less focused on laws and doctrine and more on finding a sense of the sacred in their lives.

As Gayle, one of the participants at the gatherings, put it, "Where's the compassion, the concern, the love?" Questions like Gayle's frequently emerged in the discussion group. Many of the women felt that her question echoed their own.

Gayle continued: "The services are formal and distant. I don't speak that language—and I don't mean Hebrew. The words don't touch me; I can't feel them. I don't hear talk of how we experience God in our lives, about the ways we treat each other. How different is our world from our ancestors' world? There's still so much cruelty, so much narrow-mindedness, and so much brokenness. Why don't the rabbis talk about how, underneath the fancy holiday clothes, we're all the same; we all love and suffer, life knocks all of us down. Why don't they talk about what it is that helps us get up again?"

From the nodding of heads, it was clear that Gayle's comments resonated with many others.

Although by this time in my life I no longer felt the sense of disconnection that Gayle described, her and others' stories resonated with me. I remembered being at religious services where the liturgy and the rabbi's sermons left me empty. Instead of being lifted, I felt admonished by the rabbi's words and tone. And then there were the memories of childhood Seders where I couldn't *feel* the words.

Something was happening inside me. I felt the familiar blend of excitement and anxiety that took place in me when a creative spark was ignited. I realized that I could counter these early experiences by creating *Haggadot* where I *wrote* the words.

INVITING *SH'KHINAH* TO THE SEDER

I took a leap of faith and I thought: *Why not create a Women's Seder inspired by Sh'khinah energy? A Seder designed to bring Her out of exile, to bring out of exile women's previously denied ability to shape Jewish culture and welcome our creative expression? A Seder that would not only reawaken some of the sacred aspects of the ritual but also illuminate our distinctly feminine sensibilities—our compassion, courage, and creativity, our capacity for connection?* I could hear *Sh'khinah* saying in response, "You go, girl!"

It wasn't long after my inspiration that I found myself standing at the podium, in front of a group of about one hundred women at my community temple, leading the Seder! The women, most of whom were Jewish but many who were not, were of all ages and stages of life—young girls, young mothers, grandmothers, and silver-haired women who were deep in the reflective years of midlife and beyond (as I was). They looked up at me with attention and respect. They were as hungry as I was for a spiritual experience that they could incorporate into their own lives to offer them unique and personal sustenance.

And I had to ask myself: How did I end up there in front of this group, leading a Passover Seder—I, the voiceless Brooklyn girl, once so shy that I panicked at the thought of calling the "Information" operator to ask for a telephone number? How did I ever become a spiritual elder, when I spent so much of my life feeling disconnected from the religious rituals of my tradition?

In speaking of our achievements, it is often said that we stand on the shoulders of those who came before us. I stand on the shoulders of my fore-mothers, my ancestors, all the women throughout history whose words and deeds have paved the path toward equality. And I stand on the shoulders of all the feminist activists, especially the Jewish feminists, who created the Jewish Women's Movement in the 1970s and inspired a different consciousness—bringing to light the historic discrimination faced by women in the Jewish community. Traditional Seders were prime examples of how women were kept from being full participants in this sacred ritual. They were the keepers of tradition, the ones to prepare and cook the festive meal but not partake in the ritual in any meaningful way. Certainly, women weren't creating or leading the Seders.

These Women's Seders, particularly those created by *Ma'ayan*, a feminist group in New York City, evolved over the years into such joyful, meaningful, and powerful affairs that they became a model for Women's Seders. I attended several of them in the 1990s, when Debbie Friedman, the gifted singer, song-writer, performer, and transformer of Jewish music, made the Seder come alive. Debbie, who died in 2011 after a long illness, was more than a presence. She was a force, a passionate soul whose music spoke to our emotions and our intelligence and left an indelible mark on so many of us.

After that Seder, I felt like the woman in the diner in the movie *When Harry Met Sally*, who overheard Sally's ecstatic moans (she was showing Harry how easy it was to fake orgasm) and told the waiter, "I'll have what she's having." I wanted to have a Seder with that *Ma'ayan* spirit. So I brought the idea to the Women's *Rosh Chodesh* group at my temple, and we made it happen.

While Women's Seders were springing up like wildflowers all over the country, I hoped to create one that would touch hearts as well as minds, one that would nurture the spirit and feed the soul. I wanted a Seder that would reveal what many others were missing—a feminine sensibility, a ritual that reflected our experiences as well as men's. As a psychotherapist, I listen to what my clients say and what they do *not* say. In this process, I've learned from women what they hold sacred and meaningful, what has been painful, and what has been healing. And I learned from many of the women who attended the Women's Seders I created and led that traditional Judaism had not nourished their spirituality. Not only did they want a ritual that would reawaken Judaism's *sacred* aspects, but they also yearned for a deeper connection to their Jewish heritage. Women's limited roles in our tradition felt like broken-off pieces of our lives that we only just realized we had been missing.

I wanted our Seders to acknowledge women's many contributions to our history, to infuse the participants with a sense of confidence that we could use our wisdom and creativity not only to contribute to and participate in Seders, but that we could also lead them. I wanted to demonstrate how our feminine energies and attributes could bring to the Seder a sense of softness and strength, connection and compassion that was largely missing. I hoped to show how a Seder could be meaningful, joyful, beautiful, and relevant to our lives today. And I wanted *Sh'khinah* to be our honored guest, to sit among Her people and smile, sensing that those who have been touched by Her energy and spirit will touch and inspire others. Like ripples in a pond, Her message of compassion, love, justice, and fairness will spread far and wide.

More than a few women echoed the feelings of the words of the participants who, afterward, commented gratefully:

"When I leave the Seder, the energy stays with me. It not only finds a place at my own Seder, but in the way I see the world."

"Putting the Seder into a broader global context gave me a deeper sense of connection; it makes me want to carry it into all my relationships."

"This Seder is for *me*. I'm not hosting, I don't have to worry about how the evening flows or deal with the comments if it doesn't. Here I can just 'be,' I can take in the beauty and the spirituality, enjoy the music and the food. Hearing our story told in the voices of women feeds my soul and it has helped me to enjoy feeding others at my Seder—and not just with food. ..."

And in the words of another woman: "It's a place of sweet respite where we gather, cry, laugh, dance, and return to year after year."

Sharing my own journey through this book—from the dread of reading at Seders to the joy of leading them—is meant to highlight *our* human capacity for change: *our* ability to go from being closed buds to blossoms, to heal from brokenness and grow more whole. *Sh'khinah* consciousness is infusing us with the energies of compassion and healing, nurturing our gifts, and inspiring in us a sense of freedom and confidence to become who we were meant to be. There is a Talmudic saying: "Every blade of grass has an angel that bends over it and whispers, 'Grow, grow, grow!'" *Sh'khinah*'s is the voice that whispers to the grasses and to each of us.

It is this consciousness, this sense of inclusiveness, this compassionate feminine spirit that we invite to our Seders.

Food for Thought

- How might your life be different if *Sh'khinah* energy was a significant part of your development?

- How might the world be different if it was suffused with *Sh'khinah* consciousness?

- Which qualities of The Divine Mother touch you most deeply?

- What is the impact of having a feminized deity complementing, walking alongside, Her male counterpart? Does it feel different for you?

CHAPTER FOUR

The Invitation

Let all who are hungry come and eat.
Let all who are in need come and celebrate Passover.

—Haggadah text

A STORY FOR ALL OF US

The Passover story is more than a Jewish story; it is for all of us. Each of us is hungry for nourishment and inspiration. Each of our souls yearns to be freely expressed, to connect to others and to the sacred. But we often feel imprisoned by our internal Pharaohs, our memories of past wounds, and the fears that keep our hearts closed. The iconic "Let all who are hungry…" quote from the Haggadah goes beyond welcoming the poor and the hungry to our Seder table to partake in our bounty. It's an invitation to all who are hungry for a *meaningful spiritual experience* that offers personal sustenance; it's an outstretched arm saying, "There is a place for everyone at the Seder table." It's an invitation to go deeper into the Seder, to allow the spiritual energies of our ancestral past to be reawakened and help us move closer to our own liberation.

The Seder ritual is a retelling of the ancient Israelites' exodus from the "narrow straits" of *Mitzraim* (Egypt) and a celebration of their freedom from oppressive lives of constriction. But *Mitzraim* isn't limited to geography. It lives beyond the desert. Narrowness is everywhere—inside us, around us, wherever people are not free. It's in all the ways we oppress ourselves by staying stuck in our own narrow ways—knowing, sometimes consciously, sometimes not, that we are not living our one and only lives with a sense of freedom, meaning, or joy.

This timeless ritual can help us see with clarity and compassion the narrow places we have constructed in our lives and in the world because of our fear, shame, or sense of lack. The Seder can be an invitation to reflect on what is important and meaningful in our lives, what we value, what good we have created, and the responsibilities that come with our freedom. It encourages us to consider the pain of people who don't know if they will be able to provide the next meal for their families, to ponder what poverty and isolation do to the human soul. And it encourages us to ask ourselves if there is one commitment we can make to help end all that is unfair, unjust, and painful.

This chapter is meant to provide an overview of what to expect at a Seder for those who are less familiar with it and to help you feel more comfortable at a Seder even if you *are* familiar with it. The mandate, "Let all who are hungry come and eat," has often been interpreted to mean Jewish people who are poor, hungry, or alone. Families might invite long-lost relatives who may be looking to be part of a Seder. A friend of mine who grew up in a town near an army base recalled with fondness how every year, her father would invite Jewish soldiers to their family Seders.

I'm heartened to know that many people today expand the meaning of "hungry" to include *spiritual* hunger, extending the directive even further to include friends or neighbors who are not Jewish. Because religion has been used by too many, too often, to create cultures of divisiveness, I relish the opportunity to share the beauty, joy, and relevance of our tradition with those who follow different spiritual paths. I also appreciate the opportunity to learn from them and integrate what resonates with me into my own thinking.

This is equally true for our Women's Seders, where many women invite non-Jewish friends, some of whom travel from the outer boroughs and counties to join us year after year—a "pilgrimage" that nourishes their spirituality and their connection to other women. We have often tried to also include women from the churches and the mosque in our community. While our event is not an Interfaith Seder, our intention has always been to be inclusive, to make all women feel comfortable: non-Jewish women; single women; young and not-so-young women; and gay women, who, for too long, have been made to feel there was no place for them in the Jewish community. What could be more healing, especially in these polarized times, than sharing the commonalities within the differences that connect each of us to the family of humankind?

An unintended benefit in the effort to help women of other faiths feel at ease in unfamiliar settings has been to awaken some of the sacred aspects of this ancient ritual for many *Jewish* women, for whom much of it has been lost or never fully understood, given our historical place on the fringes.

What has been especially gratifying is having my children's Jewish friends come to our Seders with their young families. They've often arrived a bit skeptical, with few expectations, and have left feeling surprisingly appreciative of our tradition. The seeds I planted to convey the essential meanings and messages of the Seder, as well as to make it particularly child-friendly, bore fruit for all.

I think of this book as a private Seder to which you, dear reader, are invited. So, whether you're familiar with this ritual or you're new to it, I hope these offerings help you feel more comfortable. They're intended to make you feel like an important part of the Seder. In the end, it is *your* presence and what *you* have to offer that makes a Seder the wonderfully varied family or communal event that it is.

DIFFERENT STROKES FOR DIFFERENT FOLKS

As with all people, there is tremendous diversity in the ways Jewish people celebrate Passover. While all the elements (and more) described below may be found in many traditional Seders, only a few of them may be present in others. More observant Seders are led with great seriousness and care to enact all the directives, passages, and songs in the Haggadah and last for hours. Other Seders highlight its essential aspects, with kids darting around the room or hiding under the table and move quickly through the Haggadah toward the festive meal. I'm reminded of the joking way in which some less-observant folks enact the Seder:

We were slaves. We were freed. We were persecuted. We survived. We're here. Let's eat!

Some Seders may be simply a warm gathering of family and friends, a time to eat and drink and enjoy each other's presence. And others are experienced as opportunities to create beautiful, joyful, and meaningful rituals.

I find it fascinating to learn of different traditions within the larger Jewish communities here at home, and especially those of the diaspora, the dispersal of the Jewish people around the globe. For example, there's the North African custom of placing a basket of Seder symbols above the heads of each participant as a reminder of how precarious freedom is. Or the fun moment for kids at Persian Seders to run around the table with scallions, whipping easy targets like the Seder leader—who is intensely focused on the Haggadah, a reminder of how Pharaoh's taskmasters whipped the slaves. There are probably as many variations of the Seder as there are people who celebrate the holiday.

Likewise, there are probably as many varieties of the favored charoset dish as there are women preparing it. Since the diaspora, women have been making charoset with whatever ingredients were available to them. This recognition is a great way to honor women's ability to adapt to where they live, while at the same time preserving our history and our culture. It's also a beautiful model of what it means to share and appreciate our diversity.

SOME RITUAL ELEMENTS

The Seder is a festive celebration of the Exodus, a ritual organized along an ordered path of fourteen or fifteen steps (some are combined). Each step marks the transition from slavery to freedom and is a key to open the doors of limitation and confinement. Here is a brief outline of the steps (these are elaborated upon in later sections of the book):

1. *Kadesh* – Sanctifying the evening, blessing the first cup of wine

2. *Urchatz* – Washing the hands

3. *Karpas* – Reciting the blessing over a green vegetable

4. *Yachatz* – Breaking the Matzah

5. *Maggid* – The Narrative

6. *Rachtzah* – Second Handwashing

7. *Motzi/Matzah* – Reciting Blessings for the Bread and Matzah

8. *Maror* – Reciting the Blessing for the bitter herb

9. *Korech* – Eating the Hillel Sandwich

10. *Shulchan Orech* – Eating the Festive Meal

11. *Tzafun* – Finding the Afikomen

12. *Barech* – Reciting the Blessing after the meal

13. *Hallel* – Songs of Praise

14. *Nirtzah* – Completion of the Seder

The Seder Plate

The Seder Plate is a sectioned plate with a place for each of the symbolic foods. It mirrors my thinking that just as there is a place for each item, there should be a place for each person at the Seder—a place for everyone to feel welcome and important, regardless of their differences. Just as the variety of customs vary among cultures—Ashkenazi (Eastern European Jews), Sephardi (Middle Eastern Jews), and Mizrahi (descended from Middle East, Central Asia, and North Africa)—so the diversity of guests also makes for a richer experience.

Although there may be some variation, most Ashkenazi Seder Plates are comprised of:

1. *Karpas*: A vegetable, the fruits of the earth. Parsley or another green vegetable symbolizes the coming of spring. It is traditionally dipped in salt water.

2. *Maror and Chazeret*: Bitter herbs, usually horseradish and Romaine lettuce represent the bitterness of slavery. It is typically eaten on a piece of matzah.

3. *Charoset*: A sweet mixture of chopped apples, walnuts, cinnamon, and red wine. It represents the mortar that was used by the Jewish

people to build the storehouses when they were slaves in ancient Egypt.

4. *Z'roa*: The shank bone of the lamb. This serves as a reminder of the Passover sacrificial lamb offered at the Temple in Jerusalem before its destruction.

5. *Beitzah*: An egg. The egg is a symbol of life.

6. *Salt water*: A symbol of the tears of the Hebrews when they were slaves in Egypt.

7. *An orange*: A more recent addition, a symbol of Judaism's ability to adapt to diversity. Its presence at the Seder comes with an interesting backstory (discussed later).

Other Elements of the Seder

It is worthwhile mentioning the many other elements of the Seder that are not listed as formal steps but are integral aspects of it. They are:

The Four Cups of Wine: The four cups of wine are enjoyed during the Seder, two before the meal and two afterward, with a long break between the first and second. Each cup is related to God's four promises of deliverance and their significance: "I will take you out from under the burdens of Egypt and I will deliver you from bondage; I will redeem you with an outstretched arm and with great judgments; and I will take you to me as a people."

The first cup is either poured before the Seder begins, ready for participants to drink, or is poured at the time of this first step. In traditional Seders, the custom is to drink all the wine in the glass, making it ready for the wine that follows. However, this varies from Seder to Seder: some finish the wine, and some use the same wine but raise their glasses for the blessings and drinking that follow.

Many contemporary Seders dedicate each of the cups to an aspect of the Seder to which they would like to give more attention—something that speaks to its host, and hopefully, to the guests. The cup may be in honor of the season, of someone who has been an inspiration, or of someone who has resisted tyranny or oppression. At many Women's Seders, the cups may honor our foremothers or women who are making changes in Judaism. In this book, I have dedicated the four cups to aspects of spiritual development: Awareness, Healing, Connection, and Wholeness.

The Four Questions: This phase forms a platform for the telling of our story; it introduces the Maggid. The Four Questions are usually read aloud by the youngest child and are meant to encourage the children's participation.

The Parable of the Four Children: In this book's context of spiritual development, these parables address the different learning styles and temperaments of children, the "child" in each of us, and what helps or hinders our learning.

Miriam's Cup: This is a cup or glass filled with clear spring water, to represent the water from the wells that sprung up in the desert in Miriam's honor. It is a more recent ritual, honoring the role of women in our history.

The Ten Plagues: The afflictions that God brought upon Egypt; the precursors of our escape are enumerated during the Maggid section.

Dayenu: A favorite Passover song, *dayenu* means "It would have been enough." This is a joyful, hand-clapping song of gratitude for all that we've been given.

Opening the Door for Elijah: This ritual is a symbolic welcome for the prophet to enter and announce the coming of the Messiah.

PREPARING FOR PASSOVER

For some, particularly the more observant communities, the preparation for Passover can be a "search and destroy mission." It challenges us to search and clean our homes of any trace of *chametz* (leavened products), removing, burning, and destroying them—an act of remembrance and solidarity with our ancestors who had to seize the moment of their liberation and leave their homes with just flour and water, the raw elements of the flat bread we know as *matzah.* For the eight days of the holiday, we are to eat no bread, grain, or anything that smacks of leavening. Homes are to be scoured and must conform to the various rules of making them "kosher" for Passover; everyday dishes, utensils, pots, and pans are to be changed to those used for Passover only. This preparation often functions as a spring-cleaning, but with the intention of clearing out any traces of what is considered *chametz*. In my experience, except for the men who lift the cartons containing these items from wherever they were stored, the women seem to do most of the work.

Perhaps there *were* some women who abided by these (and even more) directives and still had the time or energy to experience some of the sacred aspects of this work. But I don't know of them. I've often wondered if my mother or my grandmother felt any sense of sacredness in the preparation period. It didn't seem so, but I take heart in their knowing that they were the keepers of tradition, the memory makers.

But this process can be experienced as more than a burden. The cleaning can be experienced as a meditation to examine what is essential in our lives; an exercise to explore and rid ourselves of that which "leavens" us, puffs us up with arrogance, power, or pride; that fills us with anger, envy, or fear. It can be a time to clear the clutter from our homes and hearts, asking, "Do I really need this?" "Does it serve me or burden me?" "Can I let it go and let it free me up so something new can enter my life?" Even for Jewish women who are more secular than religious, who don't follow the strict directives, these questions and the actions accompanying them can help create a spacious way of being, allowing for the unknown to enter our lives.

I try to look at the preparation period as a refreshing pause that allows me to think about what is meaningful for me, to choose how I will expend my energy: will I use it to do what is prescribed but doesn't hold much meaning? Or will I devote it to what moves and inspires me? Years have passed; times have changed. Unlike my mother and my grandmother, I don't keep a kosher home, change dishes, or search for chametz in the physical sense. Now that I'm the keeper of our tradition, I am free to keep Passover in a way that is meaningful for *me*. While I've created many new rituals, I still hold on to some of the Seder traditions of my mother and my grandmother, who had held on to those preserved by those who came before them. It links me to generations of women I have never known, who are all long since gone, but in some ways, I feel, are here.

I love seeing how those links keep expanding, when—in some years—the mantle has been passed on to the next generation. Though my children's Seders can be very different from mine, it warms my heart to know that they are just as meaningful, bringing new concerns to light. While I once feared that our tradition might be lost to my children and grandchildren, I now feel confident that our family Seders will continue when I'm no longer here. I wonder what they'll look like. Who will lead them? What will be discarded, forgotten? What will be remembered, cherished? What will serve as inspiration for what is most meaningful for them? How I'd love to be the proverbial fly on the wall to see how this timeless ritual continues to evolve!

Behind the Scenes

In recent years, in the few months before the Seder, my body/mind has set aside a time for early morning musings—usually between 3:00 and 4:00 a.m.! No matter how much time I spend preparing for the holiday during waking hours, there's always some waiting-to-be-discovered idea that must present itself around that time. For me, it's less about what I forgot to buy at the market, or what to serve (although that's always a part of it), and more about refining a reading so that it touches us more deeply or helps us relate to it more easily or finding witty words for a parody of a popular song just for fun. I'm always trying to keep the ritual fresh, meaningful, joyful, and relevant. And beautiful! I never fail to feel filled up when all the work is behind me and I look at the table I have just set—crowded with porcelain plates, silverware, too many sparkling glasses, candles, flowers, matzah, wine, the Seder plate, other ritual objects, and *Haggadot*. I want it to reflect the sanctity and festivity of the holiday. And my heart swells when it does.

This is obviously very important to me, but so is the meal, with all the preparation that goes into it. If you could peek into any home before a Seder, I'm sure you'd see other women just as frazzled as I am, knee-deep in chicken/matzah ball soup, *tzimmes* (a mixture of carrots, raisins, dates, figs, prunes, lemon, and maple syrup), and more. The word tzimmes means "a big fuss," likely connected to the many ingredients in the dish. Some serve mostly traditional foods, some serve new versions of old familiar recipes, and some introduce new dishes that please today's more sophisticated palates along with the familiar ones. Some women do all the cooking themselves; others have husbands, children, and/or friends who help. And because it's not possible to make a "bad" charoset, many assign this task to the younger children.

While I do a lot (not all) of the cooking myself, I have help with the serving and clean up. Even though my husband had been suggesting this forever, it took me years before I gave in. Looking back, I don't know how I ever managed without that help. Now I have the freedom to lead the Seder, reassured that someone else is on top of heating and serving. And my guests and I are free to sit and enjoy the meal because we're not jumping up and down to serve it. Nor do we have to clean the tower of dishes, pots, and pans. What we do is help the servers put them away and put the leftovers in containers (for my children and friends to take home), all the while enjoying that old-fashioned, women-in-the-kitchen experience of talking, sharing, and laughing in that intimate and nourishing way that women have with each other.

LET ALL WHO ARE IN NEED CELEBRATE PASSOVER

I hope that this overview and the pages that follow will feel like an invitation to all of you to celebrate Passover in ways that feel comfortable and meaningful for you. Whoever is seeking a sense of family, community, or spirituality; whoever is in need of nurturing, healing, liberation or inspiration—come, let us celebrate Passover together. Anyone seeking a deeper connection to what is authentic in life, to what is eternal in our tradition, a connection to our people, to the family of humankind—come let us share this Festival of Freedom together. If you're making a Seder, attending one, or just seeking a deeper understanding of one of Judaism's most celebrated rituals, I hope these offerings will help make the Seder experience a truly more enjoyable and enriched one.

Food for Thought

- What about the Seder evokes a sense of hunger for you?

- How has your level of familiarity with the ritual elements of the Seder affected your comfort and participation?

- What would make the preparations for Passover more spiritually satisfying for you?

- What symbolic *chametz* would you like to remove from your home or your life?

CHAPTER FIVE

Creating a Sacred Space

Let there be light.

—(Genesis 1:3)

THE ART OF THE SEDER

As artists create on canvas, so Seder leaders/hosts create an ambiance in the opening moments of the evening, even before the ritual begins. As guests take in the ceremonial objects, the candles, the music, and the festive table, they are made to feel that this night is indeed different from all other nights. The feeling that something sacred is happening sets the tone for the rest of evening. They will enter the spirit of the Seder, open and receptive to remembering our past, being rooted in the present, and sowing seeds of peace, healing, and freedom to flower in the future.

The distance between the living room where guests are finishing the appetizers and the dining room is not far, but the transition can be a long one. It takes more than a few minutes before everyone finds their seat. The energy is still lively and animated: some conversations are being finished while others are just beginning. In the Seders that I lead, I wait a few more minutes, and then ring the soft meditation bells. The shift of energy is palpable. The chatter fades, and the room grows quiet.

In welcoming everyone to the Seder, invariably I get a little emotional as I think of families all over the world who will be singing these same blessings, telling the same story. This especially feels palpable when I look at the beautiful faces of my family and friends sitting around my table and imagine the faces of those who once sat here but are no longer with us. In a moment, we will light the holiday candles; but before we do, I take a deep breath and ask everyone to close their eyes and imagine loved ones whom they wish were here with us at our Seder. Then the candles are lit, a blessing is recited, and the soft sound of Debbie Friedman's words and music fill the room. A quiet chorus sings "Light These Lights" along with her.

Before the music stops, I feel the energy changing again. Now I'm not the only one who is emotional. Eyes are misting; the singing softens. When the song ends, stillness fills the room. The lilting melody has carried the poignancy of the words of the song into our hearts. We see images of those we love; we see those who are suffering, in need of goodness, mercy, and peace. And we see those who are no longer here, but who are with us in spirit.

Lighting the Candles

With the first commandment of the Torah, "Let there be light," we are commanded to be bringers of light in whatever we do, wherever we go. Most Seders begin with a candle-lighting to bless the evening and to create a moment of warmth, stillness, and reflection. It's a ritual that connects the Light of Spirit to each of us, inspiring us to carry our own light into the world, creating a bold and beautiful flame that will inspire others. The ritual may include a song, a prayer, or blessing to bring in the energy or spirit of those whose light has inspired us. It sets the tone of the Seder and helps us to settle into the sanctity of the evening. I usually invite my granddaughters to light the candles, and we all join in the traditional blessing.

In this section of my family Seders, I alternate between the feminine version of the blessing (the first one, below) and the masculine version of the blessing (the second). The subsequent blessings that you will read here are all in the feminine form. These changes are more than grammatical; they are spiritual and psychological as well. They acknowledge the shift away from the masculine imagery and energy of our tradition to the understanding that God energy is both masculine and feminine. The word change from *Adonai* to *Ruach* is also significant, in that it moves away from the image of Ruler to that of Spirit or Soul of the world, a much more feminine perspective:

> *B'ruchah at Yah, Eloheinu Ruach ha'olam, asher kid'shatnu b'mitzvoteha vitzivatnu l'hadlik ner shel Yom Tov.*
> [Feminine form of the blessing]

> *Baruch atah Adonai, Eloheinu Melech ha Olam, asher kid'shanu b'mitzvotav vitzivanu l'hadlik ner shel Yom Tov.*
> [Masculine form of the blessing]

> Blessed are You, our God, Spirit/Ruler of the world,
> who sanctifies us with *mitzvot* [commandments]
> and calls us to kindle the lights of the Festival Day.
> May the light of *Sh'khinah* dispel the darkness
> in the lives of all those who suffer.

Lena's Story:

Lighting the holiday candles took on special significance for Lena, a young woman with whom I worked in therapy, who grew up in a family of Holocaust survivors. Lena, her parents, her sister and brother, her grandmother, and her aunt and uncle all lived together in a spacious apartment in New York City, with high ceilings and large windows. However, the emotional space was dark and dreary, anything but light. Heavy curtains hung over the windows; small lamps barely lit the rooms. The heaviness hung over her family as well.

"It permeated the house," Lena had told me in an early therapy session. "You could feel it as soon as you opened the door. It felt oppressive."

The only sense of warmth that Lena felt was when her grandmother lit Sabbath or holiday candles. It wasn't until Lena began to visit schoolmates' homes, and then later when she left the family's apartment to live on her own, that she realized how the anxiety and darkness permeated her life as well.

One spring morning, she came to a session particularly depressed and angry. She had gone on yet another job interview that didn't go well. The interviewer intimated that the job wasn't a good fit; her style and energy didn't match the high energy that the position demanded. "My anxiety and depression are dead giveaways," Lena lamented. We stayed with her feelings around this observation, and I then asked her if she was up to doing a short meditation, as we often did. Within a few minutes of beginning, I noticed a slight softening in her face.

She explained: "I had an image of my grandmother lighting candles. I remembered the smell of the melting wax, and how I used to sit on her lap while she sang the blessings in Yiddish in this quiet voice. It was as if she was protecting her little pocket of peace. This was the closest I've ever come to hearing singing in my house. But I remember how her voice wrapped around me, and even though I didn't understand a word, I felt safe and soft in her warmth. I guess my own stuff started to melt."

When she realized that Passover was almost upon us, she capitalized on these tender feelings coming up with the thought that this year, before she went to her family Seder, she would light candles at home.

"It's time for me to get out of my own *Mitzraim*. Maybe lighting candles on Passover is a good way to start moving out of the smallness. Remembering my grandmother's quiet strength is making me feel that I can try to bring some light into my life. It's like she's reaching out to me from the other side, like I'd be honoring her as well as maybe healing myself."

When you light a candle for a holiday, or any day, and you gaze into the flames, what does it evoke in you? Does it inspire a prayer? Does it bring up a memory, perhaps of a long-gone loved one? Is there a shift in your mood, a change in the way your body feels? Is there a candle-lighting ritual you might create for yourself that will honor what you need in your life?

A Reading for the Candle-Lighting

As the doors of night begin to open, we kindle the Seder lights.
In the mind's eye, a wave of flickering candles
connects across time and space,
a giant ribbon wrapping the world in light,

marking, once again, that terrible night of darkness
in which our ancestors discovered freedom.

The strike of a match, a prayer said with intention,
and the ordinary is transformed into the holy.
Let us be open to this sacred moment and savor it as
dancing flames warm us, memories soften our hearts,
and muted embers of desire burn and turn into smoldering sparks.

Suddenly, all we want is to be like stars in the night sky,
piercing the Darkness with the Light You kindle in us,
carrying the light of freedom forward from generation
to generation, for all who are yet to be.

It is not just the evening that has been, or can be, transformed!

Invocation

An invocation is not a traditional element of the Seder. Yet I felt moved to
write one to invoke the presence of those who came before us, who live inside
us, and from whom we draw inspiration.

Dear ancestors:
You—who came before us, whom we can never know,
whose bones have long since turned to dust—
we are grateful to you for trying, for almost four thousand years,
to live your lives according to the enduring values of Torah,
under conditions we cannot begin to fathom.

We have come to learn just fragments of what you had to bear—
how, sometimes, you lived these values openly,
sometimes, in secret, under pain of death,
keeping them close to your heart.

But still you passed those values on, from generation to generation,
as best as you could, shaping our lives,
helping us find ways to live with courage and integrity,
compassion and justice,
tending, for thousands of years, our Tree of Life,
so we could be nourished and sustained by its fruit.

Dear ancestors:
I wish your names and faces were in our family albums.
I long to touch the place of your birth,
to know how you lived, who you loved,
to feel the earth where you rest.
How I would love to tell you that
the goodness of your lives has been a blessing
that continues to live on in all the lives you touched.
Your individual stories may be lost to us,
but you will always be part of who we are,
our past, our present ... and our future.

Let your mind's eye wander backward over time and then forward again. See if you can sense even a wisp of those who came so many generations before you, those from whom you are descended. You don't know them, but you do know that there are invisible lines of connection running between you. You have lived in different times, on different continents, had different challenges, dreams, and journeys. Perhaps you would like to talk to them, ask questions about their lives, learn from them. You can; they are part of you, they live on in you. The Native American Hopi tribe has a beautiful way of reminding us of who we are in relation to our ancestors: "You are the result of the love of thousands."

Shehecheyanu

Shehecheyanu is a two-thousand-year-old blessing recited at the beginning of Jewish holy days and on special occasions. You may feel moved to say it whenever you do something for the first time, or for the first time of that year, like celebrating another birthday, landing your first real job, or celebrating another Seder. *Shehecheyanu* is an expression of our gratitude for being kept alive, sustained, and able to experience another season. It's also a reminder *not* to take things for granted. So much can happen in the space of a year that can be life-changing: a new life is welcomed into the world, your once-helpless infant takes his first steps, or she says her first words and a whole new world opens before her. Yet we all know how life can change on a dime in ways that we hoped would never happen: an accident, a dreaded diagnosis, the loss of a job, the loss of a loved one. ... Yes, *Shehecheyanu*! We thank You God, Spirit of the Universe, for keeping us alive, sustaining us, and bringing us to this season so we can celebrate cherished moments which we are not guaranteed, but with which we are blessed.

As much as I appreciate the meaning of the *Shehecheyanu*, another reason why I love to include it in my Seders is because it's an endearing connection to my father. I can see him clearly leading us to recite it along with him, in a way that was somehow different from the way he led other parts of the Seder—with more confidence and a particularly joyful energy. The way I like to remember him.

Here is the traditional blessing that may be recited, or as in many families, sung with the joyful energy I heard in my father's voice. When it is sung, it ends with a melodious chorus of "Amen," often in harmony:

> *Bruchah at Yah, Eloheinu, Ruach ha'olam.*
> *Shehecheyatnu, V'ki'matnu, V'higiatnu lazman hazeh.* Amen.

Let us bless the flow of life that renews us, sustains us, and brings us to this season.

Another Blessing

> We thank You for bringing us to this moment
> so we may celebrate once again
> the gift of our freedom,
> to do what is right in Your eyes,
> to live authentically.

according to our values and ideals,
with the freedom to live lives of meaning and purpose,
and work toward a just and peaceful world.

Each of us has made many revolutions around the sun. And it's easy to lose track of time, to not notice how the years often blend into one another, blurring the boundaries between them. Some years stand out because they hold milestones for us: our first day of school, our first friend, our first love or loss…. Others slip by, with moments of significance lost to us because we didn't pay attention: the first time we felt vulnerable, lost; or maybe when we finally felt like we're "good enough," or when we looked at something familiar as if for the first time.

I'm not aware of when it happened for me—it was one of those moments that slipped by, unnoticed—but I find myself saying *Shehecheyanu* to myself far more often than I ever did before. It gives me pause; I stop to say thank You for these small but significant moments and to savor the warm wave of gratitude that flows over me.

Invoking the Spirits of Elijah and Miriam

To heighten the sanctity of the Seder, we invoke the spirits of the prophets Elijah and Miriam by placing two cups on the Seder table to honor each of them. Elijah's Cup (which will be used for a ritual later in the Seder) has long been a part of the Seder. The placement of Miriam's Cup on the table is a more recent innovation, intended to bring to the Seder Miriam's spirit and contributions to our history. Miriam, the sister of Moses, was a prophet in her own right. Legend has it that an abundant well of fresh water followed her as she wandered with her people throughout the desert. The well was a fountain of living water that sustained the people while she was alive. However, upon her death, it ran dry.

Pausing to bring the cup to our attention, explaining why it is now part of the Seder ritual, and/or reading a poem all add to the sacredness of the evening. This tribute to Miriam is an inspiration for women and a role model for all. In her honor, the cup may be unadorned, or it may be one of many artistically designed goblets, in keeping with the commandment of *Hiddur*

Mitzvah, the act of beautifying a ceremonial object to elevate its sacredness. Or it might be one that was proudly made by young girls at Hebrew school—perhaps glasses adorned with faux jewels, sparkles, and stars that help the girls identify with a strong and beloved heroine.

Many Women's Seders begin with a ritual to celebrate Miriam's role as a leader, prophetess, and inspiring foremother, whose spirit illuminates and clears a once-darkened path for women to walk and shine their own light.

I continue to be grateful that the sages of old had the foresight to instruct that the Seder should not be a static ritual, but a living, breathing one—a wellspring that can renew our heritage for each generation; a sacred space in which to make its concerns, visions, and insights relevant.

Having a Miriam's Cup on the Seder table honoring both Miriam and the life-affirming contributions of women in our history, we bind our present-day concerns with the life-giving waters of our faith and tradition.

A Reading for Miriam's Cup

Miriam, you were just a child yourself,
but you seemed to know from the moment Moses was born
that you would not let your brother die before he had lived.
With compassion, courage, cunning, and trust, you transformed
the Nile, waters of despair, into waters of hope.
Leaving childhood behind, you blossomed into a woman
bearing the gift of prophecy,
inspiring such trust as you led our people through the depths.
With confidence, fearlessness, spirit, and faith,
you transformed the Sea of Reeds into waters of redemption.
In your honor, wells of living waters holding Divine powers
to heal and renew sprang up in the desert,
sustaining our ancestors on their journey.
And we, carried by the winds of time to distant shores,
are still seeking your sustenance,
still drinking from your deep wells,
still looking to you for inspiration for our journeys,
still saying, "Thank you, Miriam."

The Impact of Sacred Objects

I am always amazed to see how something small—a gesture, a comment, an object—can have a big impact. At our first Women's Seder, we created a separate table to hold the traditional ritual objects, and then asked the women to bring something meaningful to them to add to the sacredness of the evening. Some brought photos of loved ones, others of trailblazing women. One woman read a poem that her aunt had written, and another brought her father's reading glasses. I remember the loving tone of that poem, and the wire-rimmed glasses still evoke the sense of warmth I felt as I pictured them on her father's face as he read the newspapers, Puccini arias playing in the background. I never met him, but because his daughter remembered him with such love and reverence, his presence was palpable. As was the sense of sacredness and connection felt in the room.

Think of yourself as an artist, and of the Seder—especially its very beginning—as a canvas upon which you can create meaningful, beautiful sacred space; it will resonate with others as they enter the Seder. And like the ceremonial objects on the table, the candles, the music, the blessings, and the festive table all create a mood that blessedly sets the evening apart from the hectic pace of our everyday lives. You are creating a sense of sacredness that will clearly be felt, and an evening that will inspire your guests and link them to a wordless, timeless realm that can connect us all to one another and to something beyond—to something truly holy.

Now you can enter the spirit of the Seder, open and receptive, to whatever the evening ahead brings. May you feel grateful for being able to reach this moment. *Shehecheyanu!*

Food for Thought

- What helps you to shift your state of mind from the mundane to the spiritual—candles, music, the aroma of familiar foods, a glass of wine, a prayer or blessing?

- What do you feel when you think of your ancestors—can you draw strength from them, inspiration, a sense of gratitude? Can you feel those invisible lines of connection?

- What are the *Shehecheyanu* moments in your life that make you feel grateful to be alive?

- What objects or rituals can you bring to the Seder table to help create sacred space?

CHAPTER SIX

Kadesh: Sanctification, Blessing the First Cup

*Slavery is merely an exaggerated version
of the reality endured by most human beings.*

—Rabbi Irving Greenberg

SANCTIFYING OUR LIVES

Kadesh, from the word *kedushah*, means "to separate," referring to the separation between holy and profane. To *sanctify* is to set something apart from its ordinary context: to make it holy. Just as the many sacred moments in our lives—such as weddings, baptisms, Bar and Bat Mitzvahs, and funerals—are imbued with a sense of holiness, so we sanctify the Seder ritual by blessing the first cup of wine.

The First Cup

The first cup represents God's promise that "I will bring you out from the burdens of the Egyptians." We raise this cup, recite the blessing for the fruit of the vine, and drink the wine. The healing message for this first step comes from *Chabad*, a Hasidic movement focusing on spiritual needs: "True spiritual freedom begins with sanctification, when we transcend the mundane world and introduce a higher purpose into all the things we do."

> *B'ruchah at Yah, Eloheinu Ruach ha olam, boreit p'ri hagafen.*
> Blessed are You, Ruler/Spirit of the world, who creates the fruit of the vine.
> May we be aware of all those who yearn for deliverance
> from whatever form their bondage takes.

As we leave ordinary time and enter the sacred space of the Seder, we have an opportunity to become aware of aspects of our lives that keep us small, that constrict and enslave us. It's a perfect moment for a new journey toward freedom to begin. During this part of the ritual, I often feel a shift in my awareness: I am more mindful of my one and only life. I find myself pondering questions that normally escape me as I go from one day to the next. Yet these questions are essential to my life: "What is the higher purpose of my life? Am I free to live my life in a way that reflects my values? What is my place in the world? What are the world's pressing needs? Am I contributing to filling those needs?"

What about you? What questions arise for you, as you focus your awareness on the gift of your life?

The Cup of Awareness: I call this first cup "The Cup of Awareness." This first cup addresses not only our ancestors' beginnings, including their need to become aware of the challenges of physical and psychological entrapment (since our story begins in a narrow stretch of land and a constricted state of mind). It speaks of the longing to be free from bondage, to heal those aspects of our lives that keep us living in small, constricted ways—the habits and behaviors that keep us from feeling vital, whole, true to ourselves. Until we are aware of our pain, we are powerless to heal it. Until we acknowledge our own distress (whether substances such as drugs or alcohol have become addictive, our relationship is abusive, or our physical pain has its roots in psychological stress), we cannot change our situations. At the same time, until we become aware that our suffering may *not* be caused by our own personal shortcomings but may have more to do with others' limitations and/or an oppressive system, we will continue to feel isolated, shamed, and powerless. Becoming aware that others struggle with similar issues reduces our shame and sense of isolation and helps us feel part of something bigger than only our individual selves. Such awareness connects us to an energy that empowers us to take those first steps toward breaking the cycles that keep us enslaved.

When the Israelite slaves became aware of the depth of their pain, they cried out to the ineffable force within them and beyond them that they called God. This Presence infused them with the courage they needed to take that extraordinary leap of faith toward freedom.

A Reading for the First Cup:

Why is this night different from all other nights?
Because tonight, we speak of Your ongoing Presence in our lives,
inspiring us to grow in freedom and in awareness.
You, Spirit of the Universe, Source of All Life,
have been with us always.
We've been through so much together:
joy and pain, beginnings and endings,
creation, destruction, and re-creation.
Because You loved us and wanted so much for us,
You parented us with all Your heart, Your might, Your soul,
commanding us to do Your will —
sometimes lovingly, sometimes harshly.
While some obeyed you freely, others reluctantly,
still others had to push You away.
Yet as we evolved, You evolved with us, growing and changing,
tempering Your judgment with compassion,
Your commandments as inspiration.

Like the new moon, Your feminine energy, often hidden,
was revealed as an illuminating source of light
helping us to grow

in softness as well as strength,
in love and understanding,
in caring and kindness,
in wisdom and courage,
in integrity and responsibility,
in justice, peace, freedom, and wholeness.

Your ability to evolve, to expand Your awareness,
embracing *Sh'khinah* into Your Oneness,
inspires us to expand our awareness of the narrowness in our lives.
May Her light illuminate the dark places in our lives,
reminding us that things can change if we have the courage
to acknowledge them, the courage to change.
May it be so.

Readings for Awareness of Enslavement

The following readings may help you become more aware of the different ways in which we may be enslaved. The first reading discusses our ancestors' physical and political enslavement and the rest relate to the often less recognizable psychological forms that may subjugate us.

The Exodus as a Journey of Freedom: The foundational story of our people concerns our ancestors' long journey from Egypt to the Promised Land, from slavery to freedom. It is the myth of the Jewish people—our collective story, memory, and experience.

According to Rabbi Irving Greenberg, the Exodus was a specific incident concerning a small Middle Eastern tribe, so small that there was no record of it except for the chronicle of this people—that is, the Bible. More than simply a movement toward liberation by a single tribe, it later inspired (many believe) other historical movements—such as the French Revolution, the Federalists, and the Civil Rights movement—and continues to this day in the protests all over the globe, as people revolt against oppression.

Our tradition teaches that we are created in God's image—unique and equal beings, endowed with dignity and infinite value. When we feel cut off from that spiritual bounty, we experience a *psychological Mitzraim*; when we live in chronic poverty, hunger, and illness, we experience a *physical Mitzraim*. When we're degraded or denied basic human rights, we often come to accept our condition as the norm, rather than as a distortion of our creation in God's image. We become passive and accepting of our political reality. This is the "reality" that was overthrown by our ancestors in the Exodus.

Yet the transition from a slave mentality to that of a free person does not occur in a single sea crossing. It can take many such crossings. The inner slave-mentality keeps trying to lure us back to the safety of the known; the path to liberation is accompanied by uncertainty, fear, and doubt. Although our ancestors were strengthened by their discipline, perseverance, and faith, it still took them *generations* to feel a sense of possibility where little had existed before—to weave a new consciousness. Staying on the path toward freedom involves:

- Moving ahead one day at a time

- Taking three steps forward, two steps back

- Accepting setbacks and celebrating progress

- Creating meaning and memories

- Building community

- Designing a way of life

- Learning to live together as a people.

And it took them generations to understand that freedom did not mean life without pain or suffering—that insecurity and impermanence were woven into life's very fabric. They had to learn that life's inevitable difficulties, challenges, and frustrations were part of an ancient pattern that was bigger and older than any of their concerns.

They had to explore the silent spaces of their hearts to hear the voice of the God in whom they were beginning to put their trust. They had to become still…see beyond their habits, fears, rivalries, egos, and opinions…and keep their hearts open to receive the deep wisdom of the One. And so do we.

The Exodus as a Journey of Healing and Transformation: The Jewish mystics saw that healing and transformation were at the heart of the Exodus. They viewed this epic event as a journey in which human consciousness evolved from constricted thinking, where we are disconnected from God to the more expanded consciousness associated with the Divine.

To be a slave in *Mitzraim* is to become so entrenched in the limited world we know, where the often-enslaving ego is in charge, so that we lose our connection to the mystery of the Unknown. To be liberated is to attain a more expansive state of consciousness, where the Higher Self is at the center of our being and we are connected to the energy of *YHVH*—one of the Hebrew names for God, translated as *"I will be who I will be."* While this energy connotes an unknowable essence, it seems to be pointing to an active, dynamic Divine Being Who can bring things into being—like creating a cosmos from chaos, or a new nation from slaves.

Being connected to this energy implies a need to be in the present, open to mystery and not-knowing. It implies an appreciation of how fluid our identities are, how we are always engaged in the process of unfolding—that we are always works-in-progress. In this state, we understand that the *freedom to* change—to become who we want to be—is possible only when we are *free from* the fixed beliefs of the past that lock us into believing that who we have been is who we will always be. Being connected to Divine energy—a spacious, expansive state of mind—suggests that each of us, made in God's image, has the power to evolve, to create ourselves anew, to grow into our potential to become all we may become. But first we must let go of our limited sense of self and become aware that our roles and dramas are *parts* of our experience, not the *whole* of who we are.

I often think of the teaching of philosopher/Rabbi Michael Lerner that *God is the healing force that lies at the heart of all creation and transformation*—a force that can slowly help us change our personal and political realities from where they are to where they ought to be. When some aspect of our lives is begging to be transformed, maybe our first step is becoming still enough long enough to become aware of the God/*YHVH* energy stirring within, whispering to us, "*Change is possible.*"

Though we may not be able to live in *constant* connection to *YHVH* energy, there is tremendous freedom in being aware that we can shift from what Jewish mystics call *mochin d'katnut*—our familiar, everyday "small mind"—to the more expanded consciousness of *mochin d'gadlut*, or "big mind." In this more open internal space, we are more receptive to God's Oneness, and see ourselves as part of a larger cosmic history—spiritual states of unity in which everything is connected.

And when we can locate our personal journeys within the context of the foundational epic journey of our people, our view widens even further. Then we can more readily understand that the challenges we face are necessary, inevitable stepping-stones along the path of growth and awareness. Then we remember not only the ruptures in our relationships but also the experiences of repair. And we recognize that the most difficult parts of our journey may ultimately become our greatest source of growth.

Dwelling in "big-mind," we experience moments of seeing not only what is in front of us—who and where we are *now*—but also the bigger picture of how things *can* be. As though Spirit, like a Mother Eagle, is lifting us up from our everyday lives, showing us a vast world of possibilities. Settling into this expansive interior space can be transformational.

Anna's Story:

Anna was not on a spiritual path seeking Divine guidance. She sat in my therapy office in silence because she couldn't bring herself to do anything else. Except for a faint memory of crying out for help to "someone or something out there." When the ending of an affair broke her heart, once again, she fell into a state of despair and numbness. She didn't have the energy to drown her sorrows in drink, as she tended to do whenever her pain felt overwhelming. She just sat in a somber stillness.

After several days, the numbness gave way to a vague sense of calm in which she felt less isolated and alone. Whatever that "someone or something out there" was, it comforted her, quieted her. In this unfamiliar state of stillness, memories emerged. Ordinarily, the pain of these memories would have consumed her with anger. But this time, Anna found herself weeping, wondering why all her relationships had ended the same way, why she felt such a profound sense of grief with the loss of each one. Was she so damaged that she didn't have the capacity to process these losses differently? Was the idea of dealing with things differently even possible?

Without realizing it, Anna was not running from her pain; she was sitting with it, observing it, exploring it, just as the Buddhists and the Jewish mystics counsel. Although she was unsure of the source of this newfound "strength," she was determined not to let alcohol cloud her mind. As Anna and I worked together in her therapy, over time she became able to connect her emotions to the physical sensations in her body. She began to feel the harsh stabs of self-judgment, the sting of shame, the heat of rage. Even though her romantic partners triggered these feelings, she was gradually able to take responsibility for her own reactions and explore their origins. She began to weave connections between old feelings experienced in her relationship to her parents, particularly her father, and how they came to shape her present-day reactions. She was developing the capacity to *bear* her feelings, rather than identify with them. Instead of *reacting* automatically, she was able to *respond* with greater clarity and a softer heart, facing her feelings with compassion.

The expanded perspective of "big-mind" consciousness helped her slow the downward spiral that had always turned into suffering. It helped her face her sorrow without sinking into bitterness or blame; she began to experience her emotions as discrete moments in time, as one small story within the bigger picture.

Anna came to experience that "someone" or "something" as a "sacred presence"—a Godlike Mother Eagle who could lift her from her limited perceptions and help her to grow into her fuller, higher self. She felt the depth of the words of Psalm 118:5: *"From the narrow place I called out to You and You answered me from the spaciousness of the open field."*

As I witnessed Anna's unfolding, I felt profound gratitude to see how she was able to find blessings hidden in the pain. Fear and suffering evolved into a deeper understanding that allowed her to relate—both to herself and to her circle of family and friends—with greater kindness and generosity of spirit. For Anna, seeds of sorrow were blossoming into flowers of compassion.

One of the central messages of the Exodus concerns the risks that our people took in their courageous journey from physical and political enslavement to freedom. Less adventurous but equally ennobling is the message gleaned from the mystical perspective: *the journey of humanity's constricted ego-consciousness into the more spacious Promised Land of Spirit.* This too entails risk: to leave the small, known world of habitual functioning, and move into the big world of the unknown. Moving into this more expanded consciousness requires us to suspend engrained beliefs and dwell in the mystery of being, unsure of anything, trying to trust in Spirit, the larger Self. Yet for our ancestors, this realization was the source of inspiration, courage, and transformation. It is for us as well. This, too, is the message we want to keep alive, to keep telling from generation to generation.

THE PAIN OF THE PAST

In thinking about the first generation of our people and how the pain of their pasts shaped their lives, I envision Abram living in his father's small, idol-making world as his father molded meaningless shapes of clay into "gods." I imagine him thinking, "This can't be what I was meant to do with my life!" He was seeking a deeper calling, the fulfillment of a need to be engaged in something more purposeful. A *midrash* describes him as being so angry and discouraged that he smashes the idols in his father's shop to demonstrate their powerlessness—and in so doing, incurs the wrath of King Nimrod, who has him thrown into a flaming furnace. While Abram survives the experience, he emerges scarred—not quite the same Abram, and not yet Abraham.

How *could* he be the same? The wounded part of him had been hidden away, rendering him incapable of paying much attention to either his external form or his internal trauma. But he is aware of the nagging feeling in his gut, and of the voice of his God telling him that change is in the air. To this, he pays attention. And soon afterward, with his wife Sarai (not yet Sarah), who is also his half-sister, he leaves his father's house for a land he does not know, for a life he cannot imagine.

Pressured to avoid the famine in Canaan, the couple make their way to Egypt. Though Sarai is known for her beauty, this does not necessarily turn out to be an asset. We see how in our own history, women are objectified, having little agency of their own. And so Abram, fearing that Pharaoh could kill him and take Sarai into his harem, has Sarai pose as his sister. When the princes of Egypt recognize Sarai's beauty, they ply Abram, her "older brother," with gifts (as is the custom) to gain Sarai's hand in marriage and have her become part of Pharaoh's harem. But God intervenes, and Pharaoh realizes the truth. He then restores Sarai to Abram and casts them out of Egypt, along with all the possessions Abram had acquired.

Abram and Sarai eventually return to Canaan. There the word of God comes to Abram in a vision, repeating the promise that the land and descendants will become as numerous as the stars. Abram enters a covenant with God, who changes the couple's names to *Abraham* and *Sarah*. Yet many years pass, and Sarah is still barren. Trying to fulfill their destiny, Sarah offers Abraham her handmaiden Hagar, who gives Abraham a son, Ishmael. But rivalry ensues between Sarah and Hagar, and Sarah has Abraham cast out both Hagar and Ishmael.

Many years later, deep into her old age, Sarah finally becomes pregnant and gives Abraham another son, Isaac. This is the son whom Abraham has longed for; this is the destiny finally fulfilled. And yet later, when Abraham hears God commanding him to sacrifice his son, he obeys. What numbs him to the terror of this moment? Is it because he has buried his *own* searing trauma? Is his gratitude to God for his having survived transformed into a routine, unquestioning, blind obedience—sealing off his suffering, deadening his pain? Unable to feel compassion for his child-self, Abraham is also unable to feel the horror of the trauma he inflicted on Ishmael, his firstborn son. Or the one he is about to inflict on Isaac.

And what of Sarah? She feels a sense of agency and uses it to protect herself and her son. But it is at the expense of another woman and child. Why did she insist that Abraham cast out Hagar and Ishmael? What made her act with unconcealed self-interest, with such a strong conviction that Ishmael should not, would not, share Isaac's inheritance?

Her life was not an easy one; she'd had more than her share of burdens to bear. She lived in her own *Mitzraim*, pushing down her own traumatic experiences: first as a young wife/sister who was almost sacrificed to Pharaoh, and later because of her barrenness. Perhaps too many long nights of anguish and self-doubt had shriveled her spirit, making her bitter, less generous, and overprotective of the child she finally birthed. Was this the beginning of the societal dynamic where women too often feel they must relate to each other in competitive ways to hold on to what they cherish?

We can understand and even justify her actions, but her casting Hagar and Ishmael out into the wilderness has left us a legacy of eternal enmity, and maybe a pattern of rationalizing and perpetuating overzealous self-interest. The thread of women's objectification and manipulation is woven into our history. After all, Isaac, too, passed off his wife, Rebecca, as his sister in a scenario like the one his father, Abraham, experienced. And Rebecca engaged her favored son, Jacob, in an act of deception to ensure that he received his father Isaac's birthright instead of it going to his (only minutes) older twin brother, Esau.

None of our foremothers escaped being manipulated in some way by the men in their lives. When Jacob flees to live with his uncle Laban, he falls in love with Laban's daughter Rachel and secures *conditional* permission to marry her. He then goes from the deceiver to the deceived, when Laban hides his older daughter Leah under the bridal veil, so that Jacob assumes she is Rachel. The rivalries and deceptions echo in the next generation, in the relationships among Jacob's own children, whose jealousy was kindled by Jacob's favoring his son Joseph. They react by selling Joseph into slavery and lie about it to Jacob.

Sadly, this unhealthy competition and sibling rivalry continue to mark too many relationships today. How different would our history be if women had the same options to determine their fate as men did! But that is another story, a *her*story to stand alongside *his*tory!

I wonder what would have made it possible for Abraham, Sarah, Isaac, Rebecca, and Jacob to have acted from their Higher Selves. Might they have made healthier choices if they had felt freer, more whole? And what are we to learn from this? *That we cannot feel fully free when we deny the vitally important events that have shaped our lives. There is too much psychic energy tied up in keeping the pain down. Only when that energy is released do we have the freedom to live more authentically.*

Nor can we feel whole when we use so much energy to deny aspects of ourselves that evoke shame. If only our foremothers and forefathers had had the psychological freedom to feel more compassion for their own painful pasts, they might have been more mindful of how their actions could impact the lives of their children and their children's children.

If they had been free enough to connect the disowned parts of themselves to their origins, aware of the enslaving hold that it had on them, might they have worked to free themselves from their personal *Mitzraims*, be kinder to themselves, and move on to find better resolutions to their dilemmas? They might have been surprised by the options that can emerge just by being engaged in this process.

If they had been able to listen to that still, small voice inside, they might have been able to experience the more expansive states of mind associated with the Divine—that spacious quality of mind in which creative solutions to seemingly hopeless situations arise.

CRACKS IN THE SHELL:
Into and Out of the Psychological *Mitzraim*

"With each new life, it is as though a new world is created." So goes the Chasidic saying. It's a comforting thought, assuring us that simply being born is an indication of so much love, so many hopes, so much promise for our lives. Yet the awe and wonder surrounding the miracle of birth eventually diminishes as infancy gives rise to toddlerhood, then to childhood, and our essence, spirit, pure being-ness becomes compromised. The child matures into the ways of the world and is part of a family. There are schedules to fit into, needs to accommodate. The child is no longer the center of the world.

When psychological development can proceed in a healthy way, a child constantly seeks, finds, and creates a balance between adaptation and autonomy, helped by parents who create the psychic space in which the child can grow as a separate being. But in less optimal situations, where the *parents'* needs take center stage, a child is often preoccupied with pleasing the parents to remain in their good graces and feel loved. Over time, this behavior can become the norm, and the child develops without a real sense of authenticity, a connection to his/her own needs or desires. Unaware of the Source and the inherent gifts of Spirit, such a child becomes someone whose innermost core is imprisoned in an outer shell—a "false" self. This is a psychological *Mitzraim*, as articulated by esteemed psychoanalyst Bernard Brandchaft.

Deep inside, many of us still carry childhood wounds of not being seen and honored for who we were. These wounds have left us feeling a sense of lack, of unworthiness; that we are not good enough; that we are unlovable, incomplete. Others' wounds come from feeling abandoned or having been abused. Trauma has many faces. In my own life, a surgeon's thoughtless comment was one of those potent early traumas. Whatever gives rise to these wounds, it's important to understand that *they are not one-time experiences that took place in the past.* They live on in us, deep in the cells of our bodies, unconsciously shaping our lives, subtly robbing us of our authenticity, our vitality—until we can do the inner work that lets us heal from them.

But until then, this way of being becomes the "norm." The wounds remain there, buried in our psyches. We live with the dawning realization that we don't know who we really are, that we're not truly "awake"—aware of our own deeper thoughts, feelings, hopes, dreams, fears, fleeting sensations, or aspirations. Until one day—maybe after hundreds of days of intuiting that something is wrong—we acknowledge our sense of brokenness.

Just becoming aware of the cracks in our outer shells is the first step of the painstaking process of healing. We learn this from the teachings of Rabbi Nachman of Brezlov, as well as from the late contemporary poet and song-writer Leonard Cohen: the brokenness is a doorway for Light to enter. This is the light of compassionate awareness. As author Pat Schneider sensitively explains in her book *How the Light Gets In*, it's what allows us to find a way to speak or express our truth by any means. It's what helps us understand that our abandonment, abuse, shame, or blame too often was not our fault but had more to do with the limitations of others. The light of compassionate awareness is what allows us to grieve our painful pasts and what we may have lost, what enables us to admire how we coped with and survived the suffering. It's what allows us to gradually shed the guilt, blame, and shame that have colored our lives. When we can understand who we are and why, a space is created in which we can envision who we can still become. And it offers us the potential for feeling more whole—the soul's deepest desire. I was touched to learn that in Japanese culture, when a treasured piece of pottery breaks, the cracks are filled with gold, and the cracked vessel is then more precious than it was before.

Sometimes brokenness can become a priceless gift.

Food for Thought

As we ponder our inner experience of freedom, let us also remember: retelling the Passover story reminds us of the possibility that as long as we are alive, there is the potential to become more aware, to grow, to change, and to become more whole.

- As you become more aware of the gift of your life, what essential life questions arise?

- What enslaving reality needs to be overthrown for you to live with freedom and ease?

- How can the light of compassionate awareness help you to understand who you are and to envision who you can still become?

- Reflect on how the expansive states of mind associated with the Divine can be a source of inspiration, courage, and transformation.

CHAPTER SEVEN

Urchatz:
The First Handwashing

When life places stones in your path, be the water. A persistent drop of water will wear away even the hardest stone.

—Autumn Morning Star

Considering that water covers so much of our planet, that it is so vital to every cell in the human body, so integral to our spiritual lives as a creative force and source of life (even a destructive force of death), and so essential to our daily lives, it's easy to contemplate its wide-ranging applications rather than focus on one of its primary functions—cleansing us from the impurities of the material world and purifying our souls.

All of earth's cultures have a spiritual reverence for water. More than being only a focus on removing pollution, water has been used to cultivate spiritual development. In the creation stories of most ancient cultures, water is the origin of life, and it is thought that healing water rituals existed millions of years ago in prehistoric times. The search for sacred water in which to immerse oneself and experience oneness with God has been present in all cultures since recorded time. This perspective has not abated. It continues to live on in contemporary religious and spiritual traditions as the basis of blessing and purification rituals, and of the ceremonies that mark the significant moments of our lives. As a giver of life, water connects us to the wholeness of life—birth, baptism, death—creating gateways to purification, transformation, and connection to the sacred.

Think of when the pandemic hovered over us, water—so essential to our physical existence—took on an almost ritualistic function for all of us. We were instructed to wash our hands multiple times a day, especially after touching anything that had been touched or breathed upon by another human being. Good medicine—for those of us who could turn on a faucet and wash with clean water. But my thoughts kept returning to those who didn't have access to this precious natural resource. Whether needed for physical cleansing or ritual purification, water is critical, its lack, catastrophic.

CULTIVATING AN APPRECIATION FOR WATER

For many people, clean water has long been in short supply. The ancient Israelites depended on rainwater for drinking, bathing, and feeding their crops, which would in turn feed their families. But rain came from Heaven, which they believed was controlled by God, on whom they were dependent. This was especially true after the Exodus, when they were bound by a covenantal relationship and rain was thought to be a Divine blessing contingent on their fulfilling the covenant. Still, because Miriam's wells supplemented water from the heavens, these desert wanderers took water for granted—until they lost it after Miriam's death. Upon receiving it again directly from God, they cultivated a profound appreciation for water and the One who provided it.

Although in contemporary life we have an almost inextricable bond to water, its lack is generally not experienced as a spiritual loss. Perhaps it should be. More than a hardship, its scarcity has created a water crisis that has led to a health crisis and become a leading cause of death. In much of the world, particularly Africa and South Asia, increased demand, pollution, and climate change have made clean drinking water more than just a scarce commodity. They have made it a spiritual crisis. Just consider the loss of life left in their wake.

Our planet cannot continue to sustain us in the face of so much abuse and misuse of our natural resources. We must stop taking water for granted. We must learn from our ancestors' experience to value and protect it before we lose it. Because we *can* lose it!

I'd like to extend this teaching to our human relationships. When we truly grasp the reality that we are not islands unto ourselves—that, as with our dependence on water and on the earth itself, we also depend on each other for our survival—we come to see each other in an altered way, less in terms of our differences and more in terms of how we need to work with, appreciate, respect, value, and protect each other. We too are precious natural resources.

WATER'S ROLE IN OUR LIBERATION

Water is intimately connected to the story of our liberation—even the story *before* our story—where the women in the Bible made their entrances at the well: a feminine, womblike symbol, and a hidden source of life. That was where Rachel met Jacob, Rebecca met Isaac, and Zipporah met Moses—a biblical watering hole!

According to some biblical scholars, water in a narrative implies the presence of God. So as we move from the waters of the well to the waters of the Nile, where Miriam and Pharaoh's daughter meet, we "know" that God will be involved in the encounter that allowed Moses to be carried afloat until found by the woman who would become his adoptive mother. It was this meeting that would ultimately lead to our redemption through the Sea of Reeds, the birth waters of our freedom. In fact, our story has often been told as a birth metaphor—with Egypt symbolizing the narrow birth canal; the Sea of Reeds, the amniotic fluid; and the splitting of the Sea analogous to the breaking of the water from which we humanly emerge.

LOOKING AT WATER THROUGH A SPIRITUAL LENS

For those who look at our tradition's stories and rituals from a spiritual perspective, God-as-water traditionally symbolizes flow, loving-kindness, intimacy, nurturance, transformation, abundance, and prosperity. We see this in the story of the Exodus, which transformed the Israelites from slaves to free people. Although the flow of the waters and God's loving-kindness allowed for our ultimate deliverance, water—like all of creation—has the potential to be a destructive force. In our story, the Sea of Reeds is also the site where the newborn Hebrew males lost their lives, the firstborn Egyptians perished after the last of the ten plagues, and where Egyptian soldiers who pursued the Israelites through the sea succumbed to its rising waters.

The absence of water in our narratives symbolizes disconnection from God—a disconnection manifested in the legend of the wells drying up after Miriam's death. We are not told why this happened, but some say that it was because neither Moses nor the Israelites took the time to grieve her death. Rather than mourn their loss—and surely the death of their prophet and leader *was* a loss—they charged at life with a sense of urgency, like many do today by rushing back to our normal lives. What if they had allowed themselves to experience the flow of life, be with their grief, and settle into stillness to mourn their loss while being held in the arms of *Sh'khinah*? What if we did the same? Might the waters of life begin to flow again, stronger, and sweeter, with the energy of those who we lost guiding our way?

WATER AS PURIFICATION AND TRANSFORMATION

There is a pattern of sanctification followed by purification that's performed at traditional Seders. The first formal step is to sanctify the evening; and the second, the ritual handwashing, is concerned with cleansing ourselves from the impurities of the materialistic world. The pattern is repeated later in the Seder, when the second cup of wine is followed by a second hand-washing ritual. Once a purification rite performed by the priests in the Temple in Jerusalem, after the Temple's destruction it was extended to the people to be enacted in their daily lives. Handwashing was to be done before eating; after waking from sleep, using the bathroom, touching one's shoes, and visiting a cemetery; before reciting a priestly blessing; and at the Passover Seder. Some of these practices still make sense for hygienic purposes, while others have been rendered irrelevant as a religious obligation, especially for the less observant.

And yet, there are some purification rituals that are enjoying a resurgence, because they are being imbued with spiritual meanings that touch our lives. *Tashlikh* is a symbolic casting away of transgressions that is performed on *Rosh HaShanah*, the Jewish New Year and a time of new beginnings. Tossing breadcrumbs, or to be environmentally mindful, stones or twigs, into a body of water—along with our desires to be rid of attitudes, beliefs, behaviors, or relationships that no longer serve us—can be both soothing and powerful. Standing at the shores of the sea or the banks of a river with our community, reciting prayers and singing songs of hope and renewal, watching what we cast away being carried away by the current, it is easy to envision the New Year as a clean slate from which we can begin anew.

And then there is ritual immersion, decreed in the Torah, to attain ritual purity. But rather than focusing on the Torah's long list of ritual impurities, I'm viewing water as a symbol of healing and personal transformation, which is also how ritual immersion was meant to be experienced. This immersion rite takes place in a *mikveh*, a ritual bath of living waters connected to a natural spring or well that's believed to be a manifestation of God's presence. Both observant men and women use it, but it is mostly associated with women, who undergo such immersion at the end of a menstrual cycle and after childbirth. Because of all the stringent laws connected to immersion in the *mikveh* regarding abstinence and the implication of women being "unclean," it has come to be seen by many as archaic, dirty, and misogynistic. But there is another side: the ritual has been transformed, particularly in Reform Judaism and in more spiritually oriented circles, both in its physical aesthetic and in its meaning and application. And yet its transformative essence is unchanged.

While historically the *mikveh* was used as a religious obligation, it has since been reimagined in terms of its power to restore and replenish our spiritual lives, and to wash away personal pain and spiritual stain. It has provided comfort for those facing surgery or chemotherapy, as well as for women who have suffered the violation of rape, the shame of abuse, or the pain of miscarriage, offering a private, elemental meditative space in which to commune with *Sh'khinah*. Today, people are encouraged to immerse in these living waters to mark meaningful moments: celebrations, transitions, crossing a threshold, beginning a new chapter in our lives, or coming to see ourselves in new ways.

Such is the healing power of water.

And such are its many points of connection to women. At our Women's Seders, one of the ways we think about water is to have this feminine symbol represent both purification and healing. A bowl of water placed on each table is imagined to be a healing well, the rose petals beside it a symbol of women's beauty and vulnerability and our power to heal the heart. We invite the women to pick some petals, to offer prayers of healing for someone in their lives, for themselves, or for the world, and to place the petals into the healing well.

This is one of the most meaningful moments people remember.

WATER: THE MEDIUM IN WHICH OUR LIVES BEGIN

We have looked at water as the medium in which the story of our *people* began. Let us now look at it as the medium in which the story of *our lives* begins.

Floating in our mothers' wombs, we draw nourishment and sustenance from her body, until her water breaks and we are birthed into the world as separate beings. With luck, most of us will continue to be bathed in the protective care of those who gave us life as we learn to make our way in the world. And yet loved as we may have been, we grow up capable of experiencing every emotion known to humankind: joy, love, desire, and delight, and jealousy, rage, grief, and despair. These emotions, which some describe as "energy in motion," flow through our beings much as rivers flow into the sea, often manifesting in tears of joy, tears of sorrow, and cathartic tears of release.

Like water, our emotions are fluid, dependent on our perspectives. We can be introspective, examine our own actions, and take responsibility for them; we can learn from our mistakes and feel humbled. Or we can blame others and feel angry. Although our emotions are ours alone to experience and process, it seems to be a human tendency to hold *others* responsible for what we feel: sometimes our happiness, mostly our anger and sorrow. While there may be some truth to our perceptions, *we* are responsible for how we react or respond to our own sorrow or pain. It's so easy to point fingers, to distrust others, and to separate and cut ourselves off from them—especially those whom we perceive as different from ourselves. And yet our perceptions, too, are fluid.

Our ancestors' tradition of welcoming strangers to their tents with a handwashing or foot washing is usually understood as an act of hospitality, of washing away the dust, dirt, and debris of the desert. But it also might be something more. Might our ancestors have had a heightened sensitivity to "otherness" because of their own experiences? Might this act of washing bespeak a deeper significance: a mindful moment in which to wash away all that sets us apart from each other? A moment to recognize our common humanity: the dreams, fears, strengths, and vulnerabilities we share, the Hebrew equivalent of the Eastern greeting *Namaste*, "I recognize the divinity in you"? Our interpretations are fluid as well.

THE "CONSCIOUSNESS" OF WATER

Interested in the *science* behind water's role in healing, I learned about the work of the late Japanese author Masuru Emoto, who discovered the "consciousness" of water. While it's too early to know whether his theory "holds water," Emoto's experiments—in which he and others "sent" specific emotions to containers of water, which then took specific crystallization forms (imagine a snowflake)—seek to demonstrate the influence of emotions over the molecular structure of water. Positive emotions and blessings sent into the water illustrate a harmonious, flowing structure; negative emotions, a more chaotic structure; and indifference, the most chaotic structure of all. This echoes Elie Wiesel's statement that the opposite of love is not hate, but indifference, and Rabbi Abraham Joshua Heschel's proclamation that the opposite of good is not evil, but indifference. The fact that we humans are made up of 78–92 percent water should give us pause. If every cell in the body is comprised mostly of water and its molecular structure can be modified by emotions and attitudes, we may want to be more mindful of our mental states and their impact on the body.

Recent research points to other factors that affect the water in our cells. The field of epigenetics studies how behavior and environment—experience, memory, culture, history, and tradition—can influence our genes, causing changes that affect the way they work. This information, which can pass through the membrane that surrounds the water in our cells, can activate the genetic material into the water. Consider the Jewish people's memory of enslavement or of the Holocaust; the enslavement of African Americans; the Armenian, Cambodian, and Rwandan genocides. Have these horrific events shaped the lives of the next generation, those who did not experience them directly? Most descendants would acknowledge that these catastrophes have made their marks on their psyches to varying degrees, leaving them vulnerable to emotional pain.

Several researchers have found direct effects of genocide on the survivors of atrocities, such as their compromised parenting styles, which can include maintaining silence about the trauma or offering fear-based "survival messages" that they pass on to their children and grandchildren. Messages like "keep your troubles to yourself, asking for help only brings more suffering," which earlier may have been critical to their survival, can become negative (though unintended) consequences for their children. Understandably, survivors may be rendered unstable, emotionally distant, or anxious, which further affects their relationships to their children. I imagine that my mother's trauma—being hidden and silenced—created enormous anxiety for her about my screaming, and inadvertently found its way into my life, leaving me feeling voiceless, invisible, hidden.

On the biological level, researchers have noted that trauma, like exposure to persistent stress or cold, can trigger metabolic changes and leave chemical marks on the genes, which then can be passed down to future generations. Although these studies suggesting that experience can alter biology are compelling, they are not conclusive. And because epigenetic changes do not alter the genes themselves, such changes are reversible. They may cause offspring to be more vulnerable, but they are *not* destiny. The waters can be calmed.

The confluence of ideas between some Buddhist practices and the field of neuroscience offers an escape route, a way out of the sorrow, anguish, or despair. As with the practice of meditation and mindfulness, neuroscience claims that one of the most effective means of stopping the flow of stressful neurochemicals into our bodies is for the mind to become aware of the body and its sensations. When we practice this type of mindfulness, the biochemicals that produce a sense of calm (dopamine and oxytocin) are released in the body, activating the brain's more evolved capacities to be *responsive* to stress rather than *reactive*. Over time and with repetition, new neural pathways are established that allow for the development of more optimal mental functioning that softens the suffering. A four-step process of *acknowledging, naming, focusing,* and *reframing* interrupts the cycle, facilitating healthier, more empowering ways of processing our experience, both behaviorally and on a cellular level.

Acknowledging the Pain

When we remember how painful experiences, historical and personal, have caused us to struggle, we are taking the first step toward living more liberated lives. Acknowledging how our experiences shaped our lives allows us to process their effects on our psyches and begin to heal.

Naming

When we're in the grip of negative emotions, naming them allows them to be registered as *sensation*. This prevents them from finding their way into the amygdala, the part of the brain that stores emotional experiences and memories. Naming the source of our reactions can help us to modify them and lessen their intensity. We can say to our overwhelmed selves, with love and compassion, with a hand touching our hearts, "You are fine. You may be feeling abandoned/frightened/angered/shamed…given your experience, but you are fine now, you are fine."

Focusing on Our Bodily Experience

When we shift our attention from the emotion itself to how it is being expressed in our bodies, we interrupt the cycle of reinforcing an old story. We do this by paying attention to the inner life of our bodies, with their varied sensations of heat and cold, the knots in our stomachs, a rapid heartbeat, our trembling limbs, and so on.

Reframing Our Experience/Transcendence

When we stop adding more layers to our stories, we create more space to *reframe* our experience—for example: how what we expect to happen is so often a projection rather than a reality; how our challenges have strengthened us; how our sensitivity may reflect some of our positive core values, such as compassion and our sense of justice; how what appears to be a crisis in reality may be an opportunity for growth. This is how we create space for a new narrative—one that can transform us from feeling imprisoned to feeling liberated, from feeling victimized to feeling empowered.

Over time, it may be possible to *change the molecular structure of the water in our bodies*, creating a shift from a more chaotic structure to one that is more harmonious. Imagine how this change may be experienced in your own body as the water flows through you, removing toxins from your cells, washing away narrow, constricting patterns. Just as water soothes and cleanses our bodies, it also heals us, purifies us, and carries us toward freer, more fluid ways of being.

 ## Carla's Story:

Carla is a sensitive, intelligent, compassionate young woman in her thirties who is anxious, depressed, and given to self-deprecation. She spent her formative years in one of the Central American countries from which so many of today's immigrants are fleeing. The gangs, drugs, violence, and corruption that we hear about in the news became the soundtrack of her life. She lived with her mother and her extended family, all hardworking people who struggled to keep the family fed, healthy, safe, and alive. Her father was never part of her life. As good as the family's intentions were, the enormous stress they experienced was too often alleviated by alcohol. Their method of discipline bordered on abuse. Carla felt loved by her mother and adored by her grandmother but was cursed at by her grandfather and hit by her older cousin who minded her while her mother worked outside the home. The mixed messages and conflicting attitudes of her family and the fear engendered by the larger culture shaped her life.

The challenges of Carla's early life were muted into distant memory after her mother remarried and created a stable and loving home in America. Life in this country afforded the family a decent lifestyle, which allowed her to feel normal, relatively secure in her family and friendships. She was blissfully unaware of how her early years had formed and influenced the woman she had become.

In the recent past, she experienced a deep disappointment in a relationship and problems with her job performance. More currently, an elderly relative with whom she is close was brutally beaten. Shortly afterward,

Carla suffered an injury during a workout at the gym that led to her not being able to compete in a competition for which she had been preparing. Her physical strength, developed from training as a gymnast, empowered her, allowing her to feel that she could defend herself and that she no longer had to be a victim. But when she had to stop training, she became more anxious, depressed, and filled with self-loathing. She knew that she needed help.

Early on in our therapy work together, she revealed an underlying fear of death—of her parents and of her own early demise. This created in her a sense of urgency to be successful and experience life while she was still healthy and alive. As she revealed her early history, my body language revealed the sense of horror I felt for what she had experienced. It took several months before she could acknowledge and absorb the sense of dread that she had experienced in those early years, how they were the source of her anxiety, depression, impulsivity, and of her fear of death.

In the safety of my office, she has been able to name her emotions and locate where they manifest in her body when she's in the throes of panic: the nausea, trembling, the rapid heartbeat, and the sensation that she's taking her last breath. As she speaks about what she experiences in her body, she stops the emotions from intensifying. Although it is one thing to be able to transmute the terrifying emotions into a calmer state in a therapeutic environment and quite another to be able to do this when alone and unsupported, Carla is beginning to do this in the dead of night, when many of her panic attacks occur, with no one beside her. She is still affected by anxiety and depression, but she is no longer plagued by these states.

What has been strikingly less present is the self-deprecation. She attributes this to having a clearer picture of herself, especially as we explore the ways in which she has been able to transcend those early experiences of victimization by owning her sense of empowerment. Though she was made to feel that she was bad because of the excessive reprimands and harsh discipline she received, she is coming to realize that her family's limitations don't have to define her. She understands that their parenting abilities may have been compromised by their own experiences of intergenerational trauma. This understanding has helped her stop adding layers to the story of her life, and to create a new narrative. Her sense of badness is being transformed into viewing herself as a "good person who treats others with the compassion and respect we all deserve, someone who also deserves to live a good and long life." She is leaving her own *Mitzraim* and heading for the Promised Land of being good enough. When we consistently challenge our familiar but flawed assumptions, we become like the persistent drops of water that slowly wear away the crushing stones of life, creating a path for us to move forward with a clearer sense of ourselves, of who we really are.

I don't know if the changes in Carla's emotional life affect the molecular structure of the water in her body chemistry. But I do know that Carla's life, once plagued by inner chaos, is gradually being transformed into a life lived with more ease, trust, and love—even of herself. Our sense of self is fluid, too!

MORE THAN PERSONAL PAIN

I've become aware that many people, both inside my office and out, have been distressed not only by their personal pain but also by the state of the world. It is hard *not* to feel overwhelmed by the tsunamis of disasters, shootings, bombings, and all manner of tragedies that fill the airwaves, newspapers, and other sources of information (or, too often, *mis*information). We can't stop the waves of violence, corruption, the starving children, or the refugees fleeing their homeland, but we can learn how to ride them by being attentive and awake, being still enough to be carried by their energy.

We can acknowledge our anxiety and name our fear that the next fire, flood, or school shooting could be in our community, or our overwhelming sadness at the sight of malnourished children dying from starvation. We can focus on the way these emotions are expressed in our bodies: the tightness in our chests or the sickening sensation in our stomachs. And we can transform our sense of helplessness by taking action to address the suffering; we can reframe our powerlessness by making donations, signing petitions, joining protests, and creating music or art to honor victims. We can write about these people, to let them know they are not forgotten. We can find ways to stop the pollution of our water, our land, our bodies, and more. And considering the recent manifestations of climate change, perhaps we also need to look within at our own human makeup deriving from the four elements—earth, our bodies; water, our blood; air, our breath; and fire, our spirit—and to question, "If these elements in me were to come into balance, how that might affect the fate of the planet?"

Imagine water running over your hands,
liquid velvet that soothes as it washes away
the parts of your life that no longer serve you.
Let your grief, your loss, your pain
be carried away by the current.
Exhale. Deeply. Let them go.

Imagine water running over your hands,
tickling your fingers, your palms, the backs of your hands.
Let the sensation wash over you, relax into it.
At this moment there is just silence.
And in the silence, there is remembrance, honor, and possibility.

Remember how the waters of the Nile were transformed
from waters of despair to waters of redemption.
Remember your own transformation, your own holy moments.
Honor them. Celebrate them.
Be grateful for the possibilities that flow like a river before you.

Now you can enter the Seder feeling cleansed, open, and ready to receive.

Food for Thought

- How do you cope when waves of anxiety, depression, fear, grief wash over you?

- What happens in your body when you acknowledge your pain, name your emotions?

- What helps you to focus on the sensations in your body instead of on your emotions?

- How do you reframe the experience, stop reinforcing the old story, and write a new narrative?

CHAPTER EIGHT

Karpas: The Fruits of the Earth

Those who sow in tears will reap in joy.

—Psalm 126:5

OUR JEWISH RITES OF SPRING

Rites of spring, performed in both religious and nonreligious communities worldwide, are associated with the awakening of both animals and the earth; they are celebrations of the new life that comes after cold, harsh winters, when the sun shows its face only briefly. Then comes spring. Darkness gives way to light, and there's a taste of sweetness in the air. With renewed energy we walk with a spring in our step, a restlessness that wants to be rid of old energy, and an openness to life's possibilities.

Thousands of years ago, when the Jewish people were farmers and shepherds, before Pesach was known as the Festival of *Freedom*, it was called *Chag Ha Aviv*: the Festival of *Spring*, celebrating new growth. Now, we acknowledge how intimately the two are connected.

This season of rebirth and renewal is symbolized by the *Karpas*, the first fruits of spring and the first symbolic food eaten before the festive meal that comes later…much later. Many people use parsley, celery, or a boiled potato for the ritual, placed next to a bowl of salt water for dipping. Some hosts have full plates of it on the table for nibbling and staving off hunger. At my Seders, for a decorative touch I put a large bunch of parsley in a vase and let its soft leaves hang over the edges like a flowering spring bouquet.

The *Karpas* is dipped into the salt water, symbolizing our tears, and is then blessed. In my version, as well as blessing the fruits of the earth, I add the hope for tears to be shed only in joy:

Bruchah at Yah, Eloheinu Ruach ha'olam, boreit p'ri ha'adamah
Blessed are You, Spirit of the Universe, for creating the fruit of the earth.
May we too sprout from the depths of the earth and arrive at a holy place.

Like the water in the handwashing ritual, the *Karpas* ritual goes beyond just blessing the first fruits. It also serves to remind us that opportunities for transformation abound—for transformation of the current political, societal, and environmental realities, and of the forces that keep us gripped in narrowness. Rabbi Michael Lerner's concept of God as "the Transformative Power of the Universe" comes to mind. Created in the image of God as we are, we are continually growing, changing, and evolving.

Our growth may not come easily; it is not a linear progression. We're inspired and overcome obstacles on our path—and then we plateau, unable to move forward. Until—like a warm spring day that comes after winter's chill—there's an opening that allows us to move ahead again. This is the healing message of karpas: *Like tender shoots pushing through the hard earth, opening beneath the warm rays of the sun, the frozen, buried parts of our authentic selves are reawakened, and push through those narrow patterns that keep us from blossoming into our fullest selves.*

Journeys of Growth

Perhaps because I work with many more women than men in my therapy practice, I am more sensitized to their journeys of growth. I have witnessed the swelling seeds and tender shoots of selfhood pushing through the frozen soil of accommodation. After long winters of lack—of self or of agency, or because of being overly skilled in the art of pleasing others—the journey is not an easy one. Yet somehow, with enough awareness, nurturance, and patience, spring comes—along with a sense of growth, newness, and possibility.

How do you acknowledge your *own* growth? Do you honor it, taste its sweetness? Or do you tend to minimize what you've accomplished? Practice owning the sense of pride that accompanies your growth. Tears of gratitude are like an oasis in the desert; they water a parched soul.

Although spring is a time for blossoming, not all buds—or beings—blossom. Just as there are sprouts that cannot survive the journey and wither in the dark earth, there are people who remain in the shadows: those who live in fear, oppression, hopelessness, and depression. We dip the *Karpas* into salt water to honor them as well as the tears of our ancestors' bondage—to honor all those who have not yet healed from personal pain—and to remind ourselves that *we are part of this ongoing liberation story*; to ask ourselves: "In what way can I be a part of the world's transformation?"

When you taste your own salty tears, do you stifle them, dwell in them, or honor them? Can you experience them as a cleansing rain, helping you feel a sense of sweet release and healing? Just as rain nurtures seeds, tears can provide nutrients for your own growth.

 ## Margi's Story:

My client, Margi, is a woman who suffers residual trauma from a childhood characterized by profound emotional neglect. Competent as she is in the world of work, she is often reduced to tears in her personal life. The lack of acknowledgment or regard for her opinions sends her into depression or rage.

Intellectually, she knows that her heightened sensitivity is evoked by childhood feelings and memories and is not necessarily due to the way she is currently being treated. Still, she can't quell the emotions or their physical embodiment until she goes into the bathroom and cries...and cries. The tears release the storm inside. Being able to honor her feelings—by expressing them in a way forbidden to her as a child—helps her to feel recognized, restoring a sense of worth and dignity. Only then is she able to process her subjective reactions with more objectivity.

Although Margi is not yet where she hopes to be, she feels that "being able to cry like a baby is what lets me process my feelings like an adult. I feel like a baby who needs to crawl before it can learn to walk." For her, the tears are rich nutrients for her emotional growth.

Like so much else in life, the *Karpas* offers us a paradoxical symbol—of sorrow and joy, grief and celebration. We mourn the devastation of so much of Mother Earth, yet we rejoice in Her renewal; the quiet reawakening hidden beneath the surface stirring with unseen possibilities for new life. In witnessing seeds reaching for the warmth of the sun, ripening and blossoming, we are grateful for Her blessings, bounty, and silent sustenance. And for Her wisdom—for all She teaches us on our journeys through life, on our journeys of growth.

We thank you, Mother Earth for teaching us:
The blessing of stillness, like the hush of grasses before dawn.
The blessing of patience, like seeds maturing in their own time.
The blessing of courage, like trees standing tall again after a storm.
The blessing of flexibility, like those who bend and do not break.
The blessing of limitation, like insects that crawl on the ground.
The blessing of freedom, like winged creatures taking flight.
The blessing of acceptance, like leaves dying in the winter.
The blessing of renewal, like buds blossoming each spring.
The blessing of forgetting, like melted snow forgets its life.
The blessing of remembering kindness, like fields weeping rain.
The blessing of caring, like mothers nurturing their young.
The blessing of resilience, as they teach them to rise after a fall.
The blessing of darkness, like wombs of creation.
The blessing of light, like hearts opening to wisdom and love.

* Adapted from Native American (Ute) prayer

After Winter, Spring

As I walk along the wooded path, the winter sun shines through the bare branches, casting an unexpectedly bright light on the moss and the shoots of grass peeking through the earth. Their spring-green youth creates a soft carpet that covers patches of the path. The ground along the marshland is hospitable and welcoming, neither hardpacked nor frozen. Even the reeds look happy. Their vibrant green has turned a light brown, like fields of wheat reaching skyward. They sway in the warm winter wind as if they're waving to the mountains on the other side of the river. What should seem bleak and barren feels very much alive.

This is not so different from us—those of us who have been beaten down; who have fallen but are still standing; bent over but standing. Like the seasons with their cycles of growth, decay, and regrowth, our divine spark may be diminished but not extinguished. We may despair, but we have not lost hope or heart. Something in us aches for change, for healing; and we push ourselves through buried, crusted over hope and reach for the light.

Mary's Story:

Confined to a wheelchair, my mother-in-law Mary was now living in a nursing home, in need of care that could not be given at home. At eighty-four, she appeared physically diminished—smaller and frailer than the imposing figure she had been—but the spark of youthful drive and passion was alive. Muted but burning.

Widowed two years earlier, after being married for sixty years, she had lost her will to live; unbeknownst to us, she had intentionally let an illness go untreated. We later learned that she had made a neighbor promise that he would not call my husband—a promise he kept until the morning he found her unconscious on the floor of her apartment. An ambulance whisked her away to the nearest hospital, where she underwent surgery for peritonitis and where she remained in intensive care for almost three months.

Kept alive by a ventilator and a feeding tube, she appeared to be in a semi coma until my husband made his weekend visits from New York to

Florida to see her. Then she pushed through the darkness that had become her world and her eyes brightened. When I came and joined him, I could see behind the lifeless figure, traces of the Mary I knew. And when our daughter visited from California, her grandmother tried to talk with her, and actively communicated through gestures.

Three months and three life-saving procedures later, she was taken off the ventilator and the feeding tube was removed. My husband and two nurses accompanied her on a small private plane to fly her back to New York to live in a nursing home within walking distance from our home.

Cared for by aides who became like family to her and with frequent visits by her family, Mary was nursed back to health. Like a wilting flower, she was slowly but miraculously coming back to life. Always a take-charge, creative, and productive woman, she navigated the halls of the home in her wheelchair to visit with less-able residents. Although I looked forward to visiting with her, I found it hard to walk through the nursing home's doors—until one day, when I passed a room and heard a familiar voice coaxing one of the residents to "chew carefully." There was Mary, spoon in hand, feeding a weak but smiling woman.

This was her new job; she fancied herself as a nurse's aide, and several of the nurses came to see her as just that. She bridged the gap between patient and staff, determined to be productive once again. If she couldn't be the weight-loss lecturer she once was, giving nutritional advice and motivational talks to a roomful of neighbors, then she would do what she could to help whoever needed help, and to make herself feel useful.

Being of service to others helped her leave the *Mitzraim* of her physically constricted world and live in a more expansive spiritual one. Her depression lifted and her spirit lightened. It lifted the spirits of some of the residents as well. There was a lighter energy in her section of the home. She lived for another year and a half with a sense of purpose. Her life had meaning again. She was like the *Karpas*, the fruits of the earth that sprout from the depths and end up in a holy place on our Seder table.

I don't know if she lived because her life had been supported by artificial means, or because it was not her time to go, or because my husband was not ready to let her go. I remembered all the times at the hospital when it seemed so clear that the life and the light had gone out of her.

But then she'd rally. I was grateful that those life-and-death decisions were not mine to make, and more than grateful to have had the privilege of witnessing the quiet reawakening of my mother-in-law's spirit. Even when she seemed totally broken, her spark did not die. The seeds of her life force were seeking the light, waiting to blossom . . . at least for one more season.

We mourn the earth's destruction and rejoice at its renewal; we grieve suffering and celebrate healing. The Festivals of Spring and Freedom are inextricably intertwined.

KARPAS: SEEDS OF A JEWISH PRESENCE IN POLAND

They were all gone: the intellectuals, the shopkeepers, the peasants, the pious, the nonreligious ... gone. Murdered. Barely a trace of them. As though they had never lived on Polish soil or breathed its air. Such was the fate of the Jewish communities of Poland in the late 1930s, when the Nazis systematically annihilated them.

A strange and discomfiting phenomenon befalls the droves of American Jews who go there in modern times, looking to connect to their roots: the old neighborhoods *(shtetls)* are all gone. But my husband and I hadn't come to find the wooden dwellings our grandparents lived in. We had come to find information about my husband Stan's grandfather, *Yisroel*, for whom he was named. We had begun the research at home, going through databases from all the Polish towns we thought could yield some clues. We knew it wouldn't be easy—especially because of some family lore that *Yisroel's* last name was not *Goldstein*, like the rest of the family who had emigrated to the United States, but possibly *Brzoza*.

Before we arrived in Poland, we hired a local guide and self-proclaimed ambassador/historian to help us. Krys was an intelligent, worldly man in his fifties, who sprinkled his charmingly accented English conversation with Yiddish.

Krys brought us to visit the town halls near—and finally in—Rzhon, where we were told *Yisroel* had lived. To smooth the way, he joked with and offered cigarettes to the clerks, many of whom looked like they were still living in Communist-era Poland. Older women wearing white blouses and gray skirts, the no-nonsense, comfortable lace-up shoes my grandmother had worn, and freshly curled ringlets with a hint of blue in the gray.

In the neighboring town of Pultusk, we climbed the stairs to the room where the archives were kept and pored through long ledgers with black-and-white speckled covers like composition notebooks, with Krys right beside us, translating and explaining. We didn't find *Yisroel*, but I did find a sense of awe as I touched the yellowed books and read familiar-sounding names and the shorthand life stories—births, marriages, deaths—entered in them. I drifted off into reverie, imagining their faces, their voices, their hardscrabble lives.

Then we drove to what had been the cemetery. As in so many other towns in Poland, the cemeteries were decimated. Gravestones with carefully carved vital information and loving sentiments, meant to be enduring markers of life, were hacked, smashed, used to pave rutted roads.

With Krys at the wheel, we drove through the countryside, past a forest of tall-standing majestic pines, where seemingly older women in flowered skirts and kerchiefs covering their heads picked mushrooms and placed them in buckets. We stopped for a few minutes so I could breathe in the crisp autumn air and walk among the pines with the women. But this pleasant pastoral respite quickly morphed in my mind into a different kind of forest, one where partisans hid, and prisoners were shot.

Finally, we came to Rzhon, a nondescript contemporary village. Here we were not permitted to look through the archives ourselves, so Krys and a clerk went through the records, line by line, page after page—until, miraculously, the name "*Yisroel Brzoza*" appeared, with the date of death that corresponded to our information, along with the date of his marriage to Stan's grandmother *Rivka*. The room went silent. Stan and I breathlessly looked at each other and then at Krys, whose eyes were as moist as ours.

The drive back toward our hotel in Warsaw was bittersweet. We were so grateful to have found *Yisroel*, even though we were left with many unanswered questions about his life and death. But our excitement was tempered by the intrusive reality of what became of the Jews in Poland in subsequent years, particularly during the Holocaust. I think Krys wanted to show us a better picture of his homeland, so we made a stop at a local community center, where children's paintings adorned the walls and bulletin boards were covered with schedules for countless activities. The director of the center was a bright young man who eagerly engaged us in conversation about contemporary Poland, somewhat apologetic for the Poland of the past.

The conversation led my husband and me to ask, naïvely, if the Holocaust was part of the curriculum in local schools.

It was not.

We both felt discouraged, yet pensive, and almost simultaneously we came up with a thought. We carefully broached the question of whether it would it be possible for this "progressive" community center to offer the local children and young adults a gentle, educational overview of the Jewish community that was once part of their village. A way for them to learn about their history and the people who lived amongst their parents and grandparents: people who lived, loved, prayed, worked, struggled, worried about their children, and tried to better themselves, just as their own families did. I've always felt that learning about those who are different from us—getting to know them as people with their own culture, customs, history, and belief systems—can go a long way toward building understanding, respect, tolerance, and hopefully a more peaceful coexistence.

Our idea was not met with enthusiasm.

On the drive back to Warsaw, we told Krys that we would be happy to fund the class as a gesture of appreciation for the gracious hospitality shown us by him and the director of the center. Krys attempted to return to his jovial self, but the car fell silent. A line had been crossed; we had pushed the envelope too far.

In retrospect, our gesture must have smacked of implicating him in something his country was not ready to acknowledge. It was a disappointing ending. We wished we could have left with a more hopeful feeling that Poland would take more responsibility in not allowing its Jewish neighbors and citizens to disappear from the town's collective memory, so that "Never Again" would resonate deep within the Polish soul.

Fast-forward seven years: *The New York Times* Travel section (Aug. 2, 2015) featured a story, "Return to Poland." A brother and sister take a "roots journey" to visit their parents' hometowns. They cannot find a trace of Jewry. But they do find a "new Poland," where Jewish expatriates have planted seeds of a reviving community in Warsaw and Krakow, aided by "an astonishing corps of Polish gentiles," whose mission was to rediscover the people whose lives had been entwined with their own. Today, there are Sabbath services at a synagogue, a Jewish school where half of the students are *not* Jewish, and a thriving Jewish community center.

This is not a movement of national reconciliation. It is a movement by some of its younger citizens trying to make amends for the marginalization and demonization of Jews committed by their ancestors, and by some impassioned Jews with a desire to reseed Judaism on what may be only slightly less inhospitable soil. No doubt some of this may be in the interest of tourism, as in other European countries that once housed significant Jewish populations. This reflection is not meant to glorify Poland, although I applaud and am deeply touched by these young people who are doing what my husband and I hoped to do. Rather it is to praise the Jewish soul, which—like *Karpas*, the fruits of the earth—sprout from the depths and end up in a holy place.

The Jewish mystics remind us that every sorrow and every loss carry within them seeds of healing. How good it is to see that from one of the darkest periods in our history, seeds of Jewish life are blossoming again. May the winds of change scatter these seeds to every village and town across the country and beyond.

Food for Thought

- What in your life needs to make the journey from depth to light?

- In what ways have you honored your own salty tears, your own growth?

- What do you need to do to make your own transformation possible?

- How can you contribute to the earth's rebirth and the world's transformation from its harsh realities to one where dignity, equality, and freedom belong to all?

CHAPTER NINE

Yachatz: Breaking the Matzah

How ironic that the difficult times we fear might ruin us are the very ones that can break us open and help us blossom into who we were meant to be.

—Elizabeth Lesser

THE HOLY REALITY OF BROKENNESS

The theme of brokenness runs like an unbroken thread through the teachings of the early rabbis, mystics, and Chasidic rabbis: brokenness is inevitable; it is embedded in Creation itself, part of the fabric of life that is woven into our human experiences. It is a universal state of being that arises from living and loving; no one is immune from it.

Who of us has not known the pain of loss—of a loved one, a significant relationship, our life's dream? Who has not had to struggle with illness, mental or physical—with problems of aging or addiction, be it our own or that of a loved one—or felt the sting of disappointment from personal failure and the self-loathing it can generate? We live in a world permeated by anxiety and despair because of the harm and violence we humans inflict upon each other—in war, in acts of terror and abuse. Because of the rise of hatred in both rhetoric and deed, and the prevalence of natural disasters such as hurricanes, fires, tsunamis, and earthquakes that arise from ignoring the perils of climate change, the world feels very broken indeed.

Although the rabbis had more than their share of worldly challenges, they focused more on helping the people deal with personal pain, the feelings of guilt, shame, or disappointment in themselves. They point to our ancestors' transformative experience of the shattered tablets and instruct us to do similarly: to cherish our own brokenness by giving it a place of honor in the ark of our lives, because it is an authentic part of who we are.

> Carved in stone, the Ten Commandments
> were not quite written in stone.
> Moses—in the heat of anger, having seen the Golden Calf—
> threw the Ten Commandments to the ground,
> where the shattered stones scattered into bits and pieces.
> Years later, they were placed in the Ark, alongside the holy text.
> We are still carrying both sets of tablets within us on our journeys:
> the truth of brokenness, and the hope for wholeness.
> Like the scattered fragments of the tablets,
> we can pick up the pieces of our shattered dreams
> and weave them into the tapestry of our ever-changing lives.

The Creation myth of the Mystics carries its own teachings:

> A Divine vessel shatters and scatters holy sparks over the earth:
> In blades of grass, grains of sand, and deep within the human soul.
> They come to teach that brokenness,
> like imperfection and impermanence,
> is woven into the very fabric of Creation.
> They teach that the path toward wholeness begins with brokenness,
> that every sorrow and loss carry within them seeds of healing,
> that we are all here on this earth because we have the capacity

to find those hidden holy sparks.
When we act from higher levels of awareness,
do deeds of loving-kindness,
and live in harmony with the universe,
 we become wounded healers,
releasing sparks, returning them to their Source,
restoring the wholeness of the world.

The Chasidic rabbis helped us to view the brokenness in our lives as "openings," because it is often when the heart is broken open that wisdom, compassion, and hope fall in. The heart is most whole *in* its brokenness. They would probably all have agreed that the only way *out* of our brokenness is by going *through* it: staying with the discomfort or pain and holding the tension in that space between the reality of how things are and our dreams of how things could be. They would have concurred that attention must be paid to our brokenness, that we must feel it, reflect on it, and then take some action to mend it so that we and the world we live in can become more whole.

A Buddhist Perspective

I love finding threads of connection among different spiritual traditions—for example, how Buddhist teacher Achaan Cha's words of wisdom mirror our own Jewish wisdom teachings. Cha would hold up a glass and say, "To me, this glass is already broken. Everything is like this, already broken." Then he would question why this was upsetting. His view was that when something is still whole, we believe we must protect it. Then when it turns out that we cannot protect it—that it breaks, or we lose it—like the glass itself, *we* go to pieces. We feel profound pain when we cannot protect what and whom we love; for us, the world is no longer a safe place. But, he suggested, if we realized that the *nature* of things—especially and most importantly, ourselves—is brokenness, and if we could learn how to embrace and accept this, we could then live happier lives. When we know that we may lose something dear to us, we appreciate it more deeply, softening the sadness of loss, deepening our gratitude for what we have had.

YACHATZ

This is the step in the Seder that speaks of *matzah*, the bread both of poverty and of freedom. A piece of *matzah* broken in two represents the brokenness that our people suffered when they were enslaved in Egypt and is a potent reminder of the brokenness in our world today.

The Seder leader holds up the larger piece, and explains, "This is the bread of affliction that our ancestors ate when they were slaves in Egypt." The smaller piece is wrapped in a napkin and hidden, becoming *the afikomen*, waiting to be found at the end of the Seder. It represents those parts of ourselves yet to be discovered and freed; the parts of us that feel broken and are waiting to be healed.

At this point, we all recite a version of *Ha Lachma Anya*, The Bread of Affliction:

> To all who are still enslaved—
> those living in poverty or fear,
> who are deprived of education,
> hungry for food,
> starved for freedom—
> You are not forgotten.
> Even as we celebrate our own freedom
> we will act on behalf of yours.
> We are with you,
> we speak out for you,
> we reach out to you.
> Next year,
> may the bread of scarcity and affliction
> be simply a symbol,
> with all people enjoying the bread of plenty,
> the bread of freedom.

Janice's Story:

Even though Janice was feeling less depressed than before, she still saw herself as "a sad and broken piece of humanity": a woman whose splintered identity—the successful biologist and the cold, unfeeling woman she'd become—caused her grief.

Brokenness is not a domain that belongs to women alone. But Janice felt that she, along with so many other women, had to bury one aspect of who she was to privilege another; she couldn't honor both.

Her mother was one of such women. She might have had a career as a talented, passionate musician, had she pursued her dream instead of giving it up so that her husband could excel in his own more lucrative field. Her mother had buried her feelings along with her aspirations. Denying her disappointment, she focused instead on her husband's success and what she believed to be her daughter's talents. In our sessions, Janice held on to the story of her life: "I grew up in a family without warmth or anything resembling caring or love. My schoolwork and my music lessons were what mattered to my parents, not *me*!" Her anger was directed mostly at her mother (what else is new?) and the belief that too many women become broken and bitter.

She recalled more than a few times, "I'll never forget when my piano teacher humiliated me because I couldn't play the piece he had assigned with enough feeling. Why couldn't he have just told me, and not shamed me into feeling worthless? When my mother asked how my lesson was, I didn't know what to say. But she kept pressing me for an answer and I finally found the words to tell her what happened. She rolled her eyes, letting me know how frustrated she was with me, telling me I was too sensitive, I was acting like a baby, I was almost ten, and if I ever wanted to be a success in life, I should just keep practicing and learn to master the technique.

"I shouldn't have been surprised at her reaction. My parents are the Jewish version of the film *Ordinary People*—they don't do feelings. But I was stunned, crushed. My spirit was broken. For years after that incident, I tried to hold it together, but I didn't know what to do with my feelings except to stuff them down with every variety of Dunkin' Donuts I could find."

After a year of a huge weight gain and continued shame, she reached her breaking point. Something shifted inside her. It was as though she had sunk so low that she didn't have anything to lose, and she refused to continue with her lessons. "I don't know where I got the courage to stand up to my mother, but I did. There was no arguing, just a firm refusal on my part and a cold belittling on hers." Janice had, on some level, come to feel that her life was "already broken," which helped her feel the preciousness of what she *did* have—a voice and the ability to make a choice. And once she stopped the lessons, she also stopped bingeing. "It was like someone flipped a switch. I didn't make a conscious decision to stop or diet, but within a year most of the weight melted away."

Until she got in touch with another source of deep distress and conflict: "I guess I've been living my life just going through the motions, trying to master the technique of whatever I set my mind to; but as much as I hated the piano teacher, I knew he was right, there was no expression of feeling, not in my piano playing, not in my life. The apple didn't fall far from the tree!"

But Janice also felt that her upbringing had helped her to be proficient in her studies. She believed that if her parents had paid more attention to her emotional life, she might not have become as successful as she was. That if she were to change the way she lived—stopped burying herself in her work, paid more attention to her feelings—she would lose her drive and determination. "That's what made me 'me.' I don't want to lose that!"

I worked hard at helping her broaden her perspective. I wanted her to see that she didn't have to give up the qualities she valued; that—like the broken stones kept in the ark—her perseverance and steadfastness would always be a part of her. But they didn't have to define her. That there were other parts of her as well—the lost or buried parts: the feeling part; her need for understanding, validation, comfort, and support; her healthy sensitivity—the parts that had been sacrificed, which she felt couldn't be retrieved. We spent hours together, working to help her identify and mourn the loss of her diminished capacity to be in touch with her emotions.

These were difficult sessions for her. She wanted to feel compassion for her child-self but was convinced that this would be at the expense of her professionalism and the accompanying attributes that made her proud of herself.

About two years passed before she began to let go of what had been an almost intractable inner narrative. This created a space for her to imagine the possibility of healing a self that felt broken in two into a self that felt more cohesive and whole. She reluctantly began to meditate, stopping and starting again because she couldn't do it "right." But because meditation gave her glimpses of feeling states that she learned to recognize and name, she stayed with it long enough to see how it could help her gain access to her emotional life.

And when she did, it was as though a dam broke.

The depth of her sadness first evoked tears, then gut-wrenching sobs. Although she was frightened by the intensity, the crying became a way to empty herself of tension, creating a sense of space—which she filled with things that brought her joy. She was opening herself to life; she worked at cultivating relationships and letting friends into her life, and she went to concerts, enjoying the music from which she had turned away. She even taught herself to play the guitar "just for fun"! Steps along the path out of the small, isolating confines of *Mitzraim* that she had lived in for too many years. It was gratifying to hear her say, with lightness in her voice, "I guess I should give my mother credit for forcing me to *practice*, because my meditation *practice* helped me to feel less broken and more whole!"

Janice's life now has taken on a softer energy. She is still determined and persevering, sometimes at the expense of being able to sit with her feelings and just "be." But her splintered identity is mending. She is transforming the one-dimensional professional into a livelier, more animated, *feeling* woman who is now trying to balance how much energy to give to her career and how much to give to herself and the people she loves. She is shattering her personal belief that women must bury one part of them so that another part can live in the light. I pray that her healing reflects a society in the throes of its own transformation.

Every sorrow and every loss carry within seeds of healing.

MUSINGS ON BROKENNESS, REMEMBRANCE, AND RESTORATION

The Jewish people have had a long history of sorrow and loss, and within them seeds of healing that have flowered into an unimaginable blessing. Yet, the State of Israel emerged from the from the ashes of the Holocaust into a homeland for its people: a place to gather the fragments of the broken Jewish communities from all over the globe and reweave them into a whole, the varied shapes and colors giving texture to the glorious tapestry that is Israel.

Yet Israel is more than a geographical State; it is also a state of mind, an identity, a people, a family. *Am Israel Chai*, an Eternal Nation.

Threads in a Tapestry

Years ago, on a trip to Italy, my husband and I found ourselves happily lost in Rome, unsuccessful at getting directions to a recommended Jewish restaurant in the area—until we met Marco, a souvenir peddler who wore a *chai* around his neck. At first, I assumed that he had just plucked this religious object, which symbolizes "life" in Hebrew, from his cart. But I was wrong; Marco wore it because he was Jewish, which somehow my husband had known.

Marco spoke only Italian and Hebrew. We spoke neither. But my husband brought forth a Yiddish word, one of the few he knew: "*landsman*," fellow countryman. This opened a door, bringing both smiles from Marco and an immediate connection among us. Once the door had been opened, somehow we made ourselves understood (between my hand gestures and some long-forgotten high school Spanish as a substitute for Italian). And before we knew it, instead of giving us directions to the restaurant, Marco—in beautifully broken English—offered us an invitation to his home for dinner.

A few hours later, we walked to his apartment in the Jewish ghetto, bearing wine, flowers, and my well-worn Italian-English dictionary. We rang the doorbell. When no one answered, we rang again. Still no response. We waited. Something must have gotten lost in translation. Maybe we *thought* he invited us for dinner! We were preparing to leave when we spotted Marco and his extended family walking from the market, down the hill toward home, each of them carrying brown paper bags. As we could see, some contained long loaves of Italian bread sprouting from the top. Another had fresh chickens with legs dangling from the bag's wet, torn bottom.

Once they brought their bags upstairs and onto the kitchen counter, they welcomed us with open arms and lots of gesturing. We had to rely on body language because no one spoke English, except for the few words Marco knew—not his wife, his brother, his sister-in-law, or their young children. I tried to wing it, with more gestures, some half-remembered high-school Spanish words, and by frantically finding words in the dictionary (a beloved companion).

And then Ambra, Marco's older daughter, opened the door, both literally and in terms of communication. She spoke high school English, which helped us connect to this gracious family. But our most meaningful moments weren't expressed with words at all.

Marco's bounty extended far beyond the table. After dinner, he directed all of us into his family's two old Fiats so that he and his brother could give us a tour of the Seven Hills of Rome, softly illuminated by moonlight. This was followed by a stop at a local carnival, where he bought us delicious gelato, and an alabaster marble cigarette lighter and an ashtray (assuming, like most Italians, that we were smokers—we were not), as souvenirs of our Rome journey.

Back in the car, amid laughter, talking, and more gesturing, Ambra started to sing a Hebrew song. I knew the words (I'd sung in my temple's choir) and joined in. Then, one by one, the others joined in, singing, humming, or clapping the songs of our people, one melody after another. Tears flowed. Here we were, total strangers only hours before, separated by time, space, language, and experience—and now we were "family," different threads in a brilliant multicolored Jewish tapestry! *Am Israel Chai*—the people of Israel live! Scattered seeds blown across continents, yet still blossoming.

Extended Family

My husband and I are visiting the World War II cemetery in Normandy, France. Endless rows of stark white crosses sprout from perfectly manicured green grass, almost numbing the magnitude of loss. But it is not possible to be unmoved by the sobering effect of this sacred place.

My husband wants to say the *Kaddish* prayer (to honor the deceased) in memory of a fallen Jewish soldier. We walk past endless rows of crosses and find some Jewish stars among them. But he is not ready to stop to chant the timeless, rhythmic prayer traditionally reserved for deceased immediate family members, even though his parents gave him their blessings to do so. The stars become more numerous as we walk on and on. ...

Finally, he halts, obviously moved now to say the prayer. I walk away to give him the privacy I know he needs. This will be an emotional moment. It always is.

I walk among the gravesites, trying to absorb the enormity of what has happened here, imagining the families who have traveled here often to talk to their dead sons, brothers, husbands, and fathers, to weep for them and honor them.

Turning the corner, I realize that we had been walking along the backside of the stones. And now I notice that they are not anonymous memorials. Each stone is inscribed with the name of the soldier whose body now mingles with the earth beneath it. I walk slowly toward my husband, who is still standing over the stone, finishing his prayer. I look down at the name he doesn't see— *Goldstein*, Abraham. His name. Our name. He is saying *Kaddish* for a family member after all. Another fragment of the whole, Israel… *Am Israel Chai.*

It is comforting and inspiring to see how compassion and connection can blossom from the deepest pain. After visiting the cemetery, we take a short drive to the World War II Museum in the neighboring town of Arromanches. Sobered by exhibits depicting the heroism, sacrifices, and the ravages of war, we leave the museum and walk solemnly to our car, along with two other couples. My husband exchanges some comments with the men who before long begin to tell us about their annual trip to visit their "daughter." The men are former American paratroopers whose unit had become dispersed after they parachuted into Normandy. Walking through fields trying to find the others, they found instead a young girl, dazed, wandering nearby. She miraculously had escaped from her farmhouse, which had been bombed, killing her family. The men could not leave her, nor did they know where to take her, but they took turns carrying her on their backs until they came upon a seminary where she could be tended to and cared for.

Several years after the war's end, they heard from her; she wanted to express her gratitude to them for saving her life and invited them to visit her and her new family, her husband and their first child. They accepted the invitation. The reunion had been so meaningful and deeply touching that they have been returning, together with their own families, to Normandy year after year ever since. At the time of our visit, the young woman has three small children; the men and their wives have become honorary grandparents. The family she knew and loved are gone, never to be replaced but from the ashes of her utterly broken life she somehow has found enough of a spark to go on. I imagine that her intense gratitude for the compassionate action of the two men and the care she received at the seminary opened her heart enough for her to love and trust again. I see her as a woman who has created a richly colored tapestry woven from threads of love, loss, compassion, and gratitude—images of the family she loved and lost but who live on in her heart, interwoven with the new family she has come to know and love. Together they provide a backdrop of love and support, allowing her, her husband, and children, to feel a sense of wholeness, complete.

The healing message of *Yachatz* acknowledges our brokenness as part of who we are. *We may be forever changed by our pain and loss, but we can turn these feelings into the wisdom that allows us to love and trust again.* They can break us open and help us blossom into who we were meant to be.

Every sorrow and every loss have within seeds of healing.

Food for Thought

- What will we do to break the shackles that bind us and blind us to the Wholeness of Creation?

- How can we feel free and whole when there are still so many who go hungry, who are still enslaved, who feel broken?

- How might it help us live with more authenticity and freedom if we could truly acknowledge that in some ways, we are all "already broken"?

- What can help us minimize the *excessive* energy spent on trying to protect ourselves, and make more energy available to work toward mending the brokenness and becoming whole?

CHAPTER TEN

Maggid: The Telling Reimagined

If history were taught in the form of stories, it would never be forgotten.

—Rudyard Kipling

Storytelling has been a powerful tool of communication since the beginning of human history. It still is. From the earliest cave drawings to the oral tradition, in which stories were passed down from generation to generation, storytelling has created connections among people and between people and ideas. They convey the culture, history, and values that unite us; they are ties that bind. Every spiritual tradition has its own stories. The Exodus is the foundational story of the Jewish people.

REIMAGINING THE EXODUS

Throughout our history, there have been those whose goal has been to silence the voice of the Jewish people. They have not succeeded. Every generation has woven its story into our larger Ancestral Story. Sometimes it's been told in hushed tones, for fear of being discovered. Other times it's been told with great flourish and pageantry. Many times it's been told with boredom because its power has not yet been revealed. But the story continues to be told. Our voices will not be stilled. We will tell the story as long as there are children who ask questions. And we are instructed, even if there is no child or no one else to ask, to tell it just the same.

The telling is the primary obligation of the Seder. In fulfilling it, we are creating a linked chain back through the ages to our ancestors who left *Mitzraim. Through telling and retelling our story, our families become the transmitters of memory; and with each new generation, we breathe new life into the meaning of the Exodus and our commitment to heal the world.* This is the healing message of the *Maggid.*

As the centerpiece of the Seder, the *Maggid* is a long step with many different aspects, which I have chosen to illuminate over the course of several chapters. This chapter explores some of the different elements of the Seder. Chapter Eleven, a continuation of The Telling, is told in the imagined voices of those "who were there," giving you as the reader a more intimate sense of your imagined experience. Chapter Twelve explores two significant teachings that while not formal steps, are essential elements of our celebration.

The *Maggid* opens with The Four Questions.

THE FOUR QUESTIONS

To preserve a sense of continuity and tradition, and because questions themselves signify our freedom and our desire to learn, the iconic question asked at every traditional Passover Seder is *Why is this night different from all other nights?* It is the first of the Four Questions, and usually is asked by the youngest person able to do so. To hear that young child carry our tradition forward is a sweet and pride-filled moment for parents and grandparents, but for the child, it is sometimes a source of embarrassment. So at many contemporary Seders, all the children and the adults sing it together.

The first line of each question asks in Hebrew, *Ma Nishtana?* Meaning, "Why is this night different from all other nights?" This first line then opens into the following questions:

- "Why on all other nights do we not even dip once, but on this night, we dip twice?"

- "Why on all other nights do we eat bread or *matzah*, but on this night, we eat only *matzah*?"

- "Why on all other nights do we eat all vegetables, but on this night, we must eat bitter herbs?"

- "Why on all other nights do we either sit or recline, but on this night, we must recline?"

The answers to these questions are not given in a straightforward way, but instead are woven into the narrative. We dip twice, once into salt water to remind us of the salty tears of slaves, and a second time into the *charoset* (a sweet nut paste), symbolizing the mortar the slaves used to make bricks. We eat the *matzah* to remind us of the night our ancestors escaped from Egypt. We eat *maror* to remind us of the bitterness of slavery. We recline to remind us that this is something only free people can do; slaves were not afforded that luxury.

A VERY DIFFERENT NIGHT:
PASSOVER IN THE TIME OF THE PANDEMIC

The Passover ritual, like the rabbinic tradition, values *questions* as much as answers. Yet sometimes the old questions, as well as their answers, leave us hungry for deeper meaning, encouraging us to ask our *own* fundamental questions about our lives, our culture, and our world. Beginning in 2020, the pandemic prompted us to ask many questions that no one could answer: "How will I feed my family if I can't go to work?" "Will my mother's neighbors look in on her?" "How can I let my father die without saying good-bye to him?" "How are those working on the 'front lines,' the healthcare and emergency workers, the food-market staffs, being protected?" This was Passover in the peak of the pandemic. Covid-19 was raging, keeping us all in relative isolation; after weeks of lockdown, people were hungry for connection.

A question on many a Jewish family's mind was: "How can we have a Seder without our families and friends?" Gratefully, for *this* question there was an answer. It came in the form of modern technology; we could have a *virtual* Seder on the Internet, and even could share it with those with whom we don't often celebrate because of geographical distance. For some, the Seders became less a sacred ritual and more like a family reunion, with relatives logging in from all over the country—temporary respites from the fear that hung over everyone like a black cloud, with videoconferencing apps our silver linings.

At the eleventh hour, I thought: "If my family and friends are willing to have a bare-bones Seder, with no communal festive meal and not much time for conversation and laughter, and if my son can help with the technology, I will put together a Haggadah." Like others, we would have our first Zoom Seder.

It turned out to be meaningful, relevant, and fun. With the specter of not being able to celebrate hanging over us, and by focusing on only what was essential—reflecting the mandate to stay at home unless the need was for something "essential"—the meaning of this ancient ritual was heightened, somehow making it all the sweeter. We remembered those who held secret Seders during the Inquisition and the Holocaust because the Seder, with its deeply rooted hope for liberation, held so much meaning for them. For them, the Seder was an expression of hope, defiance, and the freedom to do what gave meaning to their lives: to honor, celebrate, and perpetuate their tradition. And—under very different and, gratefully, far less threatening circumstances—so were we.

SAME STORY, DIFFERENT QUESTIONS—
FROM A FEMININE PERSPECTIVE

On this night, Jewish communities all over the world would be telling the same story in different voices. But their questions and answers might not be the same at all. And when those Seders are held by and for women, the questions and answers often focus on those issues pertaining to women. For example: "*Why is it this night different from all other nights?* At all other Seders, the stories of our forefathers take center stage, with those of our foremothers hidden in the wings. Now the voices, stories, courage, and heroic deeds of women will be heard and celebrated."

Women's Seders may highlight the stories of our foremothers Sarah, Rebecca, Leah, and Rachel, who were considered strong "administrators" of God's plan. They may include the story of Deborah, the only female "judge" and prophet. They may speak of Judith, who emerges as a heroine after beheading Holofernes, commander-in-chief of the Assyrian army.

Or they may speak of Tamar, who—according to Levirate tradition (pertaining to a widow's inheritance)—was supposed to marry her husband's brother after she became a childless widow. When Tamar's father-in-law, the tribal leader Judah, resisted this, she took matters into her own hand and tricked him into seducing her by appearing as a ritual prostitute. She became pregnant, was able to prove Judah's paternity by presenting personal sacred objects he had given her as a pledge, and the Levirate obligation was fulfilled.

These women are in the company of other strong-minded women in the Bible: our foremother Sarah, who offered her handmaiden, Hagar, to bear a son for her husband and then cast mother and child into the wilderness. Rebecca, who deceived her husband Isaac to secure his blessing for their son Jacob. Shifra and Puah, the midwives who deceived Pharaoh. And Miriam, who offered to find a wet nurse for Pharaoh's daughter who "mothered" Moses—in direct violation of her father's decree—but the wet nurse Miriam called in was the baby's own mother.

Women in the Bible had very little power, if any. Yet it's interesting to note that the Torah doesn't condemn the behaviors that might still be deemed inappropriate or even illegal today. It's as though we are meant to learn that when people *in power* fail to do what is right or fulfill their obligations, others—including those without power—may fill the vacuum and take matters into their own hands. In these stories, the women's actions are mostly for the greater good (although in other situations, this is not always the case). The takeaway here is that we must act on behalf of those without power so that they don't feel they have to act with whatever means are available to them, which often leads to greater harm than good.

THE FOUR CHILDREN WITH QUESTIONS OF THEIR OWN

Another traditional part of the *Haggadah* is the parable of the Four Children. The heart of this section is our obligation to teach the next generation about this powerful story in a way that allows them to be part of the conversation. It takes the Seder questions and puts them in the mouths of four children—not surprisingly, four sons. But because boys are not representative of all children, I have altered that here to portray the personalities, temperaments, questions, and abilities of young *girls* more fairly, as well as the approaches to learning they represent. Here the children may be daughters as well as sons.

This tale about four diverse kinds of children, each with a different level of understanding, is also about adults. The teaching conveyed by this parable parallels a classic tenet of the field of social work: *Meet the clients where they are.* This means that we don't expect people to be where we *think* they should be; we meet them—and our children, as well—*wherever they are* in their understanding and development. And on another level, the parable of the Four Children addresses the child within the adults: the approaches that we bring to the Seder and to life; the parts of us that are still curious, that want to know and learn in ways that make sense. It addresses the inner child in all of us, especially those who—for different reasons—have not been engaged in the Passover ritual but still seek to connect (or reconnect) to the ancient wisdom of our tradition.

Traditionally, the Four Children are identified as the "Wise Child," the "Wicked Child," the "Simple Child," and the "Child Who Does Not Know How to Ask." I find these designations judgmental, and I have changed some of them, as well as their interpretations, to reflect a more compassionate, psychological view.

The "Wise Child" knows that something vital is missing in our history—the women! How has the historic omission of women's voices impacted your life? What do *you* do when the need to know more bubbles up inside you?

The "Wicked Child" is recast here as the "Alienated Child," who has separated out from the community that has not included or engaged him or her. Have you felt like an outsider in your own faith? How have you reacted to feeling disengaged? Do you try to find a way in, or do you drop out?

The "Naïve Child" is sincere yet unaware of complexity and doesn't want to appear uninformed. How do *you* respond to not knowing what's going on around you? Do you ask for help, do you fake it, or just zone out?

The "Child Who Does Not Know How to Ask" is reframed, here, as the "Silent Child," who is overwhelmed by the suffering. If you have felt compassion fatigue, do you disengage or take the next small right action? If you have been silenced in your personal life, how does this affect your participation in the Seder?

From this understanding, we can open more fully into the rich reflections that the parable may bring forth for us. As women, we question ourselves in the spirit of the Four Children. I have often been disappointed in myself for not being *wise* enough to have adequately transmitted the deep spiritual wisdom of our people to my children and grandchildren. Like what some call the *wicked* child (but I call the *challenging* or *alienated* child), I, and many of you, have raged against a God who seems indifferent to the pain and suffering in the world and railed at a tradition that has cast women in secondary roles. We may have felt ashamed of our *naïveté* for not having been more aware of the injustices in our midst. Or of having remained *silent* for too long because we didn't know how to ask or where to begin.

The Wise Child

The Wise daughter asks:

"What place do women have in Judaism?
Why does the Seder not speak of our many contributions?"
She is the one who knows the stories of our foremothers:
Sarah, Rebecca, Leah, and Rachel.
They are etched in her being.
She is the one who knows what our ancestors
Miriam, Yocheved, Shifra, and Puah did in Egypt.
She is the one who knows of the heroic acts of
Deborah, Judith, and Tamar.
Of how Dinah's brothers avenged her "rape."
And she knows of the multitude of women, since,
who have contributed to our history
yet remain mere footnotes in our texts.

To her, we say:

"Your questions will help our own daughters
to reclaim their places in our tradition.
Awakened by your questions,
we will teach them the struggles and triumphs of our foremothers:
how they followed their hearts and their conscience,
planting seeds of revolution that would change the course of history."

The Alienated, Challenging (Formerly "Wicked") Child

This child asks:

"What does Passover have to teach me?
What does Judaism have to offer me?"
This child says "me," and not "us," because
she or he feels cut off from, and by, the community,
by those who could not, or would not,
welcome her or his questions and doubts.
This child is trying to understand and seek meaning in our tradition.
 Because these issues create anxiety and discomfort,
this child has been cast aside, made into the "other."

To the Alienated, Challenging Child, we say:

"We have often let you down
by staying stuck in our own *Mitzraim*,
in the narrow thinking that keeps us from recognizing
the 'other' as ourselves,
from seeing ourselves in the 'other.'
We have let down some of your sisters and brothers, as well.
In our zeal, we expected you
to have the same reverence for our tradition as we have
when your experiences have been so different from ours.
Rather than chastising and rebuking you,
we should have educated and inspired you.
To you, we acknowledge that we have much to learn."

The Naïve (Formerly "Simple") Child

The Naïve Child asks: "What is all this?"
She wonders why we follow rules and rituals that link Jews together,
but separate us from others.
She asks, in heartfelt naïveté, "Why can't we all just live in peace?"
She does not yet understand the complexities of multiplicity.
And, perhaps, neither do we.

We tell this child that the truths of the Exodus
were not limited only to our own people,
that the Torah was given in the wilderness,
in a land that belonged to no one, yet was available to anyone
willing to accept its teachings.
Just as Ruth did when she became part of Naomi's family.
Just as all those who convert to Judaism are part of our family.
We tell this Naïve Child that our God is One,
that our God's commandments teach us
how to live with each other,
how to care for each other and for the earth we all share.
We must keep her questions alive in our minds,
letting them inspire us to make this truth our answer.

The Silent Child
(Formerly "The Child Who Does Not Know How to Ask")

Then there is the Silent Child,
the one who does not know how to ask,
the one who can't imagine what relevance this ancient,
elaborate ritual has in our lives today,
how it could possibly heal all the brokenness in our world.
The Silent Child feels overwhelmed by suffering beyond words.
If we can remain silent and tolerate this child's confusion and silence,
and not run from moments of awkwardness and discomfort,
we may hear the beating and the pleading of the Silent Child's heart,
and the desire to be of service to a world so much in need of repair.

We tell this child, "You are the future of the Jewish people.
We will create a Seder that will help you taste the sweetness of freedom,
a Seder to help you move from helplessness to healing,
a Seder to help you feel more whole,
so your energy will reverberate in the world,
and inspire others to do the same."

THE EXODUS: LONG AGO—THIS NIGHT—THIS MOMENT

"The Lord spoke to Moses and Aaron, saying: This month shall be to you the head of the months.... Speak to the entire community of Israel, saying, 'On the tenth of this month, let each one take a lamb for each household. ...' And they shall take some of the blood and put it on the two doorposts and on the lintel, on the houses in which they will eat it. And on this night, they shall eat the flesh, roasted over the fire, and unleavened cakes, with bitter herbs. ... And this is how you shall eat it: your loins girded, your shoes on your feet, and your staff in your hand; and you shall eat it in haste—it is a Passover sacrifice to the Lord. ... I, the Lord, will pass through the land of Egypt on this night, and I will smite every firstborn in the land of Egypt, both man and beast, and upon all the gods of Egypt will I wreak judgments. ... And the blood will be for you a sign upon the houses where you will be, and I will see the blood and pass over you, and there will be no plague to destroy you when I smite [the people of] the land of Egypt. ...

What a night of terror this was for the Egyptians! On the night of our redemption, the darkness was pierced with screams. Pharaoh's people had already endured nine plagues, which had caused unbearable suffering. There was more to come. Pharaoh's heart was still hardened.

With awe and trepidation, under a black sky illuminated by luminous stars and a full moon, we did as Moses had instructed. We prepared the Pesach meal, ate in haste, and kept our shoes on our feet. We took our dough before it was leavened and wrapped our kneading bowls in the shawls on our shoulders. We would have to wait until after the tenth and most devastating plague, the slaying of the firstborn sons of Egyptian households, before Pharaoh would let us go. Then with the full moon as our guide, we walked to the shores of the Sea of Reeds.

The Ten Plagues

Reciting the Ten Plagues is a traditional ritual in which we spill a drop of wine after the mention of each plague, reflecting our ambivalence about this part of our story. It is hard to fully rejoice with a celebratory glass of wine, knowing that the Egyptians suffered such a huge loss of life. This is not the way we wanted to achieve our freedom.

And so it is not enough to just mention the Ten Plagues; we are to *feel* their impact in our own lives. In 2020, it didn't take much for us to feel the fear and terror of a plague; we were living in one. Covid-19 was claiming thousands of lives, leaving tens of thousands more languishing for weeks with dreaded symptoms. And this was just from the pandemic; what about all those who, like our ancestors, are fleeing today—not from plagues inflicted by God, but from those brought to bear by our own hands? Those who flee from oppression, terrorism, genocide…those who cross deserts and seas seeking asylum, whose destination is often confinement in refugee camps.

I reflect on these issues and feel plagued by a feeling of helplessness and the desire to flee from my powerlessness. But *am* I without power? Do I resist doing more because I believe that whatever I do won't be enough—that it won't matter, it won't change the world?

It has been suggested that the ancient Egyptian plagues symbolized the pain that arose in response to Pharaoh's stubborn resistance to change from the status quo. If only it were just Pharaoh who was so resistant! Might this resistance mirror *our own* attempts to change—when an internal alarm alerts us to potential danger, and we prepare frantically to do that which we've resisted—and then our wake-up call slowly fades into "snooze" mode and we go back to sleep, back into complacency, as if it were a dream? How often do we do "the three-steps-forward, two-steps-back" dance on our own journeys, in which each tentative step we take to express our longing to change is met by the urge to fall into familiar patterns. . .until—as author, psychotherapist, and spiritual teacher, Estelle Frankel, wisely suggests in her book *Sacred Therapy*—at last the self we are longing to be begins to emerge?

It would serve us well to remember the words of Charles Darwin: "It is not the strongest of the species that survive, nor the most intelligent, but those most responsive to change."

If only the plagues were limited to biblical times! But since they are not, at today's Seders we recite each plague—blood, frogs, lice...in Hebrew and in their English translations—as well as taking the opportunity to call out plagues of our own times: poverty, racism, sexism, ageism, natural disasters.... At Women's Seders, the focus may be on women who flee from domestic violence, rape, incest, sex trafficking, and more. It might be on how the rape and maiming of female bodies have become among the most depraved weapons of war.

If only there were just ten plagues instead of the countless others that cause so much pain and suffering.

Food for Thought

- What plagues you in your life? Anxiety, illness, addiction, a painful relationship, clinging to fixed beliefs that keep you trapped?

- How do you deal with this?

- Do you feel you have a choice, or are you so convinced that this is who you are that change is not an option?

- How might you lift yourself from a narrow perspective and shift into a more spacious consciousness so you can see your situation with new eyes?

CHAPTER ELEVEN

In Our Own Words

The world is not made of atoms. It is made of stories.

— Muriel Rukeyser

Every spiritual tradition has its own Creation myth, its books of beliefs and values to guide the generations that follow. For the Jewish people, it is the Torah. Our book tells of our ancestors—fully human, flawed beings whose vulnerabilities, strengths, victories, and struggles mirror our own. Their stories, which teach us how to live or how *not* to live, are part of the formal Torah.

But there is another Torah—The Torah of Our Lives—whose stories also mirror our own; they break our hearts open, validate our aspirations, and strengthen us. This book is written by all of us. Especially women—the mothers, daughters, sisters, partners, lovers, and friends whose lives and lessons are not part of the formal Torah. Women who write textured narratives of every facet of life: love, loss, parenting, infertility, aging, death. ... Many of these stories are guided by the values of our tradition, which have sustained them; others speak of how their tradition has failed them. But because they reveal our truths, they are valued.

Just as these stories help broaden and deepen our perspectives, yours can do the same for those privileged to read them. I hope our people's stories, below, told in their own words inspire you to speak your truth, write your stories. They, too, are part of the Torah of Our Lives.

HOW THE JOURNEY TO FREEDOM BEGINS

We know some of what the men's lives were like, because they are the ones who wrote the stories and preserved our history. But what about the women? All those whose names and stories were lost, never to be recorded, because most weren't prophets, leaders, or scholars; they were *just women*—wives, mothers, daughters, and sisters. To bring back the voices of those whose stories were lost to us, I have written *midrashim* (interpretations of biblical texts) weaving a tapestry of our people's beginnings from the threads of memory of the women I imagine were there.

The Wise Women

How does the Journey to Freedom begin? Ours began with *Sh'khinah* stirring the souls of *Shifra* and *Puah*, the midwives. Her silent power, strength, compassion, and courage moved them to defy Pharaoh's decree, and deliver those beautiful baby boys in secrecy, under the apple trees of *Mitzraim*—where the mothers labored to birth them, without knowing how to protect them. She transformed the mothers' prayers and dreams from fear into hope: "We will find a way!" they proclaimed. And they did.

Outside the tent, *Yocheved*'s daughter Miriam—herself a child—heard her mother's birthing cries and raced to her side. She glimpsed the new life emerging from her mother's womb, and in that very moment she knew that this baby would not die before he lived. Like those of the mothers, her dreams and prayers were transformed from fear into hope: "I will find a way." And she did.

She found a way in Pharaoh's daughter, who also reached deep into herself, listening to the still small voice inside, then reached into the water—to draw Moses out of the Nile and into her arms.

How does the Journey to Freedom begin?

With *Sh'khinah's* outstretched arms holding the possibility of change, moving the women to risk their lives, to choose life. It begins with moments of awareness, glimpses of vision, and small, scattered acts of courage, nurtured in the silent spaces of the soul.

Pharaoh's Daughter

I can still see Pharaoh's daughter bathing in the flowing waters of the Nile, her *mikveh* (ritual bath), where she cleansed herself of the spiritual impurities that permeated her father's house. She stopped when something beneath the water moved, and a muffled sound emerged from a grass basket. It was not the heart-wrenching, gasping sound of the Hebrew male infants being swallowed by water, but the cry of a baby who—miraculously—had escaped her father's decree. It was a cry that commanded her to let her eyes see the helpless infant before her; to let her ears hear his breath and the pounding of both their hearts; to reach into the river and to draw the baby, whom she named Moses, to her breast. Her courage and compassion fed his spirit as surely as his birth mother, *Yocheved*, fed his tiny body. The moment Pharaoh's daughter reached into the water her outstretched arm forever changed the course of history. She did more than reach into the river; she reached across boundaries of class and culture, recognizing the innocence, the Divinity of the other's cry, the other's soul.

Like so many of our sisters throughout history, Pharaoh's daughter had no recorded name. Then somewhere in time, the rabbis recognized the depth of her compassion and her courage, and called her "*BatYah*," Daughter of God.

Then we all breathed her name, remembering that naming is a sacred act, announcing to the world: "*You matter, you are unique, your being is a blessing.*" We kept repeating her name until it became part of us—knowing, now, that *BatYah's* name and being would become part of our history forever.

Memories of Moses

I knew Moses as a child, and always wondered how it felt for a child of slaves, decreed to be drowned, to turn into a prince, a prophet, a leader, and a savior. How was it that for someone who was raised in a palace, riches and royalty didn't have a hold on him?

I remember him as being different from the others. When he witnessed an Egyptian taskmaster beating a Hebrew slave (a commonplace sight), he was the only one who seemed to care, the only one to stand up, to intervene: he slew him. To escape punishment, Moses fled to Midian, married a foreign woman, and worked for forty years tending her father's flock, leading the sheep into the wilderness in search of new pastures, caring for their needs as he would later care for the needs of his people.

Was it all his years spent in the vast space of "God's country" that made him so introspective? Or did the guilt of killing a man weigh heavily on his mind? I am grateful to my granddaughter Hannah for illuminating Moses's complex and layered character. Preparing for her Bat Mitzvah, she struggled to understand how his character impacted his becoming the leader of his people.

But more than that, he also knew compassion, a gift from his adoptive mother, *BatYah*, who risked her life to give him his. Or did that compassion come from his birth parents, *Amram* and *Yocheved*, whose suffering seemed to blossom into compassion in all their children?

The forces of justice and compassion cultivated in him a strong spirit and a gentle soul. He seemed to be a prophet-in-training from the start. That may be why an angel appeared to him at Horeb, the mountain of God, in a blazing fire, inside a bush that was not consumed. But *Moses* was consumed—with the fire of injustice burning in his belly. In the depths of his being, he heard God call him: "Moses, Moses." And he answered without a moment's hesitation: "*Hineni*. Here am I." Spiritual Warrior, reporting for service!

And yet he was awed; he stood back. He intuited the Divine warning, "Do not come closer. Remove your sandals from your feet; the place where you stand is holy ground." Moses understood this warning. He knew the deep connection between the Hebrew words for *sandals* and for *lock*. Again, Estelle Frankel's book *Sacred Therapy* reveals the link between the Hebrew words for shoes—*na'a-laim*—which shares the same root as the word for lock. He understood that he would have to *unlock* what imprisoned him: the garments of his materiality, his self-consciousness, lack of confidence, and his temper, which still needed to be tamed before he could become who he would become.

Then when he let his bare soles touch the "holy ground" beneath him, he was given the gift of Vision, the ability to see through God's eyes. With tests, trials, and tribulations, Moses became who he was destined to become: the leader of our people.

Perhaps Moses isn't the only one who needs to shed his shoes to feel the holy ground beneath his feet. Maybe *every* place we stand is holy, and all we need to do is shed that which locks our spirit—so that we, too, may become all we are meant to become.

Miriam—Our Sister, Our Prophet

We were all in awe of Miriam. Even as a young girl, mature beyond her years, she saw things that we didn't. Like the time she chastised her father who, upon hearing Pharaoh's decree to drown our newborn sons in the river, prepared to separate from her mother. He explained, "It is wrong for us to be together and bring more children into the world," but Miriam wouldn't accept that. She knew that if her father—the head of the tribe—left, the other men would follow his lead. So with her characteristic *chutzpah* (audacity), she convinced him to return to her mother, knowing that love was stronger than fear, knowing that fathers don't "always know best."

She seemed to know that God had another plan for her family. And when a baby boy was born of her parents' love, she did what she had to do: she wrapped him in grasses and love, brought him to the river, then waited and watched for the source of his redemption to appear. And when she did, in the form of Pharaoh's daughter, Miriam suggested the perfect wet nurse – who just happened to be their mother, Yocheved.

And again, years later, when we fled the borders of our bondage, Miriam's fierce spirit inspired us. Her vision allowed us to see the bigger picture. Her faith helped us remember that change was possible, and that God would not abandon us. She infused in us a willingness to take the risk and leave the certainty of our lives for the uncertainty of the unknown, instilling in us the belief that something better awaited us on the other side of the river. Helping us manage our anxiety and tap into our Highest Selves, she inspired us to sing, knowing then what science knows now: our most creative and courageous moments often arise from the expansive consciousness of Spirit lifting us to a higher place.

So we sang, and the words we'd sung a thousand times before took on new meaning. They became songs of "letting go," chants of change, hymns to help us open our hearts to the possibilities that lay before us—possibilities we could not yet imagine. The singing calmed us and empowered us as we took those next steps. Following her lead, we put one foot in front of the other and walked to the water's edge, dropping our memories and burdens like pebbles; and the life we knew began to dissolve into the Sea of Reeds. Each step brought us closer to the realization that we just might make it.

The thought made us almost giddy; it felt like we were dancing our way through the water! Is that why she insisted we gather our timbrels and never said a word about bringing food—because she knew that God would provide sustenance, that there would be reason to rejoice—and that tambourines were exactly what we needed?

We all marveled at the spark and spirit that burned brightly inside Miriam, how they danced in her soul as she marched to the beat of her own drum! Miriam tasted bitterness but never swallowed it. She spit it out, letting the seeds scatter and grow into righteous rebellion! For all she had done to inspire us, nurture us, and sustain our spirits, God made life-giving wells of water spring up in the parched desert, in her honor. Wells of wisdom still flow from generation to generation; all we must do is speak her name, breathe in her spirit.

Avodim Hayenu—We Were Slaves

People always ask me the same question: "What was it like to let go of all that was familiar and risk what seemed impossible?"

It was not easy. True, we had shelter from the blazing sun and almost enough food, and we all looked out for one another. But our spirits were shriveling, like fruit left too long on the vine. Bondage had become part of our lives, slavery our identity. I hope you never know the pain of watching someone you love, lose their dignity, their sense of value, their will to live.

The backbreaking work was taking its toll on our husbands. They returned to us broken, as the sun left the sky—with blistered feet, their bodies tight and coiled; ashamed and withdrawn. Rage burned inside them. Degraded and humiliated, blaming themselves for being too weak to change things, they came to believe that life would never be different. No exit! Past, present, and future were fused. Defeated, they slowly drifted off to sleep.

At some point during the night, I lay down next to my husband, hoping that his warm body would soften the tension in my own. I could hear his heart beating and feel the tremor that lingered in his limbs. I became aware of the shallow breath struggling in my own chest, of the thoughts moving through my mind like dark clouds in the sky. And I wondered, what is the blessing of our becoming numerous? Are we birthing children just to see our sons turn into the once strong, now broken men their fathers have become, so our daughters will witness their despair, helpless to heal them? No! If the seeds of our love are to flower, *let it be for something greater than this. ...*

Then I, too, fade into the dark void of sleep, where I am connected to the Divine Mother. Rage rises in my belly, and I hear myself cry out, "If something has to die, let it *not* be our children! Let it be our fear: of Pharaoh, of speaking out, of daring to imagine that it doesn't have to be this way. *It doesn't have to be this way!*"

Later, somewhere between dreaming and waking, my mouth forms the words *Sh'khinah* and I cry again, "Eternal Mother, *Sh'khinah, Sh'khinah!*" And She answers with a promise: "I am holding you. I will deliver you from this darkness."

I awake before dawn, holding (just barely) a sense of possibility. The pattern that has defined my life is broken. I have just taken my first step toward leaving Egypt. I'd like to tell you that I, alone, had a revelation; that I inspired the other women. But the truth is all our hearts were broken. We all dreamed and prayed and cried out to the Divine Mother. Somehow, we each heard an answer that miraculously transformed our pain into hope. And we began to believe that it could be different. So we trusted, supported, and learned from each other as we thought about leaving the only lives we had known.

But I worry about you, my children—all of you who have come after me. You too know what it's like to feel so depressed, that you accept your reality as being how it has to be. *It doesn't!* Look, learn from our lives. Pay attention to what's happening inside you, to the parts you don't want to see: the anger, the shame, the fear. ...They're part of the One, waiting to teach you what you need to know. This is the first step toward leaving your *Mitzraim*, living your life fully, authentically, becoming who you are yet to be. As you go forth to places you do not know, we will be with you. *Lech L'cha.*

Leaving Egypt

The moon of Nisan rose in the dark sky. The last plague had descended upon the people of Egypt. Pharaoh, plagued by the deaths of so many Egyptian infants, promised to let us go. It didn't matter that he would change his mind once again and send his armies to follow us into the Sea of Reeds; we were ready to take the plunge. We didn't know how we would survive, only that we could not stay. Less a conscious choice and more like being pulled by a magnet toward the sea, we knew that we had no control over our own lives, and so we surrendered to this force.

Sure, Moses promised us that God would save us. But none of us fully trusted his promise. Yet somehow courage triumphed over fear and allowed us to push forward—not so much for ourselves but for our children, the next generation—believing against all odds that there would *be* a next generation!

Imagine how it feels to leave the only place you've known for one that you're not even certain exists, based on the word of a God you've never seen. Imagine your heart pounding as loud as the waves crashing around you, the panic bubbling inside you that can't be expressed but hovers at the edge of your consciousness, so you have just enough presence of mind to stay alert, awake, aware. How would we be able to cross, with Pharaoh's chariots in tow behind us? Or was it because they were right behind us that we mustered the strength to do what we thought was impossible? What was that small voice inside each of us that whispered: "Breathe…Breathe…Breathe…" that made our consciousness expand with each breath so that we could see one small opening in the sea, and then another?

This process kept repeating itself: our panic surfacing, then subsiding, our awareness constricting, then expanding, just enough to sustain the hope that we would make it to the other shore. Did we dare trust that this energy, rising from our collective being, was the Divine Mystery that Moses knew would deliver us? It was as though this Force was testing us, asking us:

"How much are you willing to risk for your freedom?
Are you willing to get more than your feet wet,

to face the possibility of annihilation,
and lay your lives on the line?"

We were! We had nothing left to lose. Maybe "freedom is just another word for nothing left to lose"!

And I ask, "What about you?
Are you willing to let your ego fall away and become "no-thing" as you're faced with your own sea crossings? Can you imagine hearing a voice that springs up from deep within, whose presence is so total and affirming that you are ready to surrender and push yourselves toward the edge, into a sea of uncertainty? Can you imagine yourself filled with fear, yet compelled to do what must be done because you know *you* must *be* the change you want to see in the world?

Are you willing to get more than your feet wet?

Going Forth to a Land We Do Not Know

Without knowing how, or if, we would reach the other shore, we plunged into the abyss, flooded with feelings—fear, gratitude, and unexpected sadness—knowing that our redemption might come at great cost to others. We hoped that the discordant voices could join in harmony, instead of being drowned out by the other. But when we took that leap of faith, the only thing we prayed for was to reach the far shore.

It felt like we had no choice. But we did, and we chose life—which doesn't come with guarantees. But we had no clue as to what was in store for us. For after the crossing, we were in no-man's-land, with nothing around us but burning sun and blistering sand in that wilderness. Was this a cruel joke—leaping from Pharaoh's frying pan into the desert fire: to be in this Godforsaken place with no grain to feed the children, barely a drop of water to quench their thirst, or wipe their brows? Watching them wilt like faded blossoms, we were almost immobilized by fear. Almost. But we hadn't risked everything we had to let our children perish. We believed that we had reached this place for a reason. *They* were our reasons.

Knowing that we had to find the strength to go on being, resisting all temptation to give in to despair, we reoriented our expectations. Holding it as no longer a question of *if* we would find food but *when*, we set out at daybreak to explore the unknown, putting one foot in front of the other wherever intuition led.

And before dusk covered the land in shadows, some of us found berries and grasses that would not sicken us. Others, following Miriam, found a well with enough water to fill all our bellies again. Some called it "manna from heaven," provided by the God of Moses. Others called it "luck"—being in the right place at the right time. But our bodies expressed the truth of our experience—by weeping tears of gratitude. And slowly, somewhere between our doubts and complaints, many of us began to believe that this God of Moses was not only a force beyond us, but also an energy that dwelled within, urging each of us to reach for our highest selves and beyond ourselves. A cosmic glue binding us together to help us do what we could not do alone.

Some of us believed that God was our reason for trying. It mattered less how we tried to understand this God, and more that we were experiencing a change in how we were, deep inside ourselves and with one another; we were more patient and kinder, slower to anger, treating each other the way we ourselves wanted to be treated. We were beginning to believe, to trust that we would be sustained on this journey to God knows where.

And we were.

We walked and rested, alternating between hope and confusion, until—weeks and weeks and weeks later—we found ourselves at the foot of a mountain. It felt as if we were surrounded by millions of people, yet the world around us was silent, as though someone had turned off the sounds of the earth. And there we were, standing at Sinai, in the desert, in a place that belonged to no one, a "placeless" place, pledging our faith to be a family, a nation, a people, experiencing a deep knowing of some primal breath that connected us all to each other and to a Power within and beyond.

The arduous journey changed us, as all true journeys must. It was more than a voyage of traveling from slavery to freedom; it was also a transformation of consciousness, from narrowness to expansion. Suddenly we were able to see possibilities that we could not have imagined before. Humbled, we began to acknowledge that the God of Moses was the unexplainable force helping us see that things did not have to be as they were but could be changed. And that we were the ones to make those changes.

Empowering us with a dimension of experience far beyond our usual functioning, the God of Moses became the God of Israel, the Great Mystery with Whom we entered an Eternal Covenant, joining our sparks into a collective flame, infusing in us a desire to be our best selves, inspiring us to do good, to live lives of meaning and purpose, bringing justice and truth, peace, and love wherever we go.

A Legacy for Our Daughters

We knew that there would be more unsettled times ahead, and we wanted our daughters to know that they had inherited great strength, fortitude, and courage, which would enable them to endure and prevail. We wanted them to know that they came from women who lived and loved with passion, compassion, unwavering determination, and wisdom; women who were the heart of our family and our people. And we wanted them to pass this knowing on to their daughters and their sons and to all the generations to come, so that the stories of their resourceful and resilient mothers and grandmothers (though not recorded) would be remembered.

And they have been. We may not know their names; we can't trace the features of their faces or put our hands in theirs—our mothers, aunts, and sisters—but their energy is a constant source of inspiration and courage. They live on in us…and we hope with you.

Imagining my ancestors' story, hearing their voices—not disembodied, impersonal voices, but in a way that makes them come alive—helped me to see the Passover Story as something that happened to real people. Escaping slavery, whether physical or psychological, is an ongoing existential experience, making this *all* of our stories because we are all so connected—if not by sharing the same experiences, then by sharing the same feelings. Understanding what our ancestors endured, how they coped, healed, and moved on can help us in our own struggles. Their stories are like markers on a path helping us find our way.

Food for Thought

In keeping with the Food for Thought questions at the end of many of the chapters, below are questions for you to consider culled from the sections above.

The Wise Women:

- What prevailing values of your group/tribe/family have you rejected to do what you felt was right?

- What compelled you to act?

- What were the consequences of your actions?

- How did they change the course of your life or another's life?

BatYah:

- In what ways have you felt invisible?

- What was it that made you feel recognized?

- How have your senses allowed you to see beneath the surface?

- How have you helped to draw someone out of the depths?

Moses:

- What limiting or unquestioned beliefs do you hold about yourself, your family, and your culture that create fear and doubt, excuses that prevent you from moving forward?

- What early trauma might be driving some of your behavior today?

- What do you need to say or do that has remained unspoken or undone because you were too inhibited, intimidated, self-conscious, or complacent?

- What do you need to unlock so that you can become the person you want to be?

Miriam:

- How does your name reflect who you are?

- How can you protect yourself from swallowing the taste of bitterness?

- How can you cultivate your spark, your spunk, a sense of holy *chutzpah*?

- How can you manifest the spirit of Miriam in your everyday life?

The Women of the Exodus:

- When in your life have you experienced a shift of consciousness so dramatic that you felt that your reality changed?

- In what way did it change? Was it something in your external reality, or was it more a change in your perception?

- What possibilities were you able to see that you couldn't have imagined before?

- To what do you attribute this shift of consciousness—a force outside you, a force within, both, something else?

CHAPTER TWELVE

Two Messages from the *Maggid*

*Stories have to be told or they die, and when they die,
we can't remember who we are or why we're here.*

— Sue Monk Kidd

Every culture has its own roots and values that demand to be preserved, especially when people leave their homelands to settle on foreign soil, and the next generation seeks to assimilate into the new culture. For the Jewish people who have wandered for generation after generation until they had a country to call their own, the stories and memories of those who came before us have been a source of sustenance and inspiration.

Dayenu and *B'Chol Dor V'Dor* are not formal Seder steps or ritual acts performed at the Seder, but they are essential and enduring messages that have emerged from the Exodus experience. They help us cultivate an attitude of gratitude, and preserve for all the generations the stories, memories, and values of our tradition that remind us of who we are and why we're here.

DAYENU: IT WOULD HAVE BEEN ENOUGH

One of the primary purposes of the Passover Seder is to keep the memory of the Exodus alive, to remind us of all that our ancestors endured on their journey toward liberation. *Dayenu* is more than a joyful, hand-clapping song whose fifteen verses describe each step of that journey. If we stop to think about each of those steps, it can feel like we're traveling with them and sharing their gratitude, as God

- brought them out of Egypt,

- slew the Egyptians' firstborn and gave the Israelites their wealth,

- split the sea for them,

- sustained them in the desert,

- gave them the Sabbath,

- brought them to Mt. Sinai,

- gave them the Torah,

- brought them to Israel, and

- helped them build the Temple.

And that is the point. To make us feel that each small step on our own journeys frees us from our own *Mitzraims*: our narrow, constricted, limited lives, bringing us closer to our dreams.

The refrain, *Dayenu*, means that each one of the blessings was sufficient, was enough. How do we view our *own* sense of freedom as we move toward more fulfilling lives? Do we take each of our actions for granted, thinking of them as a natural progression? Or are we grateful for each of the steps and missteps along the way, understanding that each one allows the next one to come into being?

While the Israelites attributed their liberation to a Supreme Being they called God, we may credit our good fortunes to our motivation, courage, wisdom, fortitude, patience, a force that empowered us and sustained us, or pure Grace. However we understand these blessings, sometimes we can only appreciate where we are by remembering where we were, and by being grateful for each step of our journeys that helped make us *who we are.*

Surely, when we live with a sense of gratitude, aware of the abundance of blessings in our everyday lives, we are living more fully. *Dayenu* takes this potent message a step further and brings us to a higher level of gratitude: to become more mindful. To consider *how* we're living our lives today, in a world where so many have so much…and so many more don't have nearly enough. Not enough food, water, health care, education, means of support. …It makes us think that how and what we consume matters. And beyond our individual experiences are global consequences, from income inequality to climate change, which affect us both directly and indirectly. Living in a land of plenty we often live with little sense of restraint, without regard for its impact on others or gratitude for the many blessings we enjoy.

That is, until we experience living in scarcity and constraint, as we did when the pandemic knocked at our doors and locked us in to a world of limitations. *Dayenu* had an immediate resonance. "If only we could remain in good health…if we could have enough food to eat…if we could remember that we are not alone…if we could live with a sense of trust instead of fear, *Dayenu,* it would be enough!" We are living in a time of enormous grief and loss, yet suddenly we are grateful for even the smallest blessings.

Can we remember to be present to and grateful for the small steps that bring us closer toward our ultimate goals, however distant they may be or however uncertain we are that we will realize them in our lifetimes? This is a blessing that allows us to press on, despite obstacles and obstructions. Think of how disappointed Moses must have been after all those years of leading his people toward freedom, pleading with Pharaoh, pleading with his God on behalf of the people—and then learning that he would not be allowed to enter the Promised Land with them. Yet he persevered in bringing them there. How can *we* prevent our disappointments and setbacks from draining us of the energy we need to keep trekking on our journeys? Perhaps by focusing on the incremental successes so crucial to the larger struggle, and on the gratification that comes from knowing that we are helping to clear the paths for those who come after us.

IS GRATITUDE ENOUGH?

Even as we're filled with gratitude and acknowledge the importance of each small gift, many of us tend to think of each gift as being one part of a greater whole, rather than being enough on its own. When our own journeys include the desire to right the wrongs of social injustice, it's easy to be disheartened and overwhelmed by the magnitude of suffering in the world. It's easy to believe that we can never do enough to transform our vision into reality and ask: "Is gratitude enough?" A good guide comes from a maxim found in "The Sayings of our Fathers," *Pirkei Avot* (2:21): "You are not obligated to complete the work [of repairing the world] but neither are you free to desist from it." Many Women's Seders express both gratitude for how far we have come *and* anger at the price we've had to pay over the centuries for what we have been denied. Similarly, many contemporary Seders make a point of both celebrating our progress and acknowledging how far we have to go to achieve *Tikkun Olam*, the healing of the world.

Another Meaning of Manna

As the concept of "enough" began weaving itself into my consciousness, I reflected often on Rabbi Shefa Gold's interpretation of *manna*—that miraculous sustenance given to our ancestors each day of their sojourn in the wilderness. Our ancestors were instructed to gather only what they could eat each day. Can you imagine gathering only what you need for that day and not worrying about tomorrow or the day after or the one after that?

The teaching here is "food for thought." The ancient sages must have known that if the people's will grew too strong, it would feed their ambition and they would try to gather more than they could use. They would want to have more and more *manna*, enough for a week…a year…a lifetime. And they would never feel they had enough.

It's as though the sages predicted what could happen in times of difficulty. What *did* happen in the face of the pandemic when many people gathered more than they could use, to feed not their ambition but their health and sanitary needs. Driven by fear of not having enough, their gathering more than what was needed turned into hoarding, and the unintentional consequences of their actions meant that friends and neighbors would have to go without. I must admit that when I shopped and found more than enough of what I needed, I was tempted to do the same. But the command to *gather only what the present moment requires* echoed in my head. This teaching helped me trust that I would be provided with what I needed as well as to be more discerning, mindful of others' needs along with my own.

This reinforced my view of *manna* not just as food but also as our desires. Are we satisfied with what we have, or are we destined to always want more? I recognized our culture's emphasis on "more"—more money, more toys, more ways to communicate, more time to do more things (with more speed). And I reflected on the need to slow down both personally and culturally, so that we can better grasp the reality that deep and enduring change comes in small steps, one moment at a time, so that we can come to know the importance of being present to the moment at hand.

To counteract the pace and effects of multitasking in preparation for my family Seder, I make sure to walk every day for some quiet alone time without distractions. On one of those walks, innovative words to the traditional melody of the song *"Dayenu"* found their way into my head—as if to teach me what I needed to learn. Simple and playful, this version and subsequent updated ones have become favorite Seder moments.

> iPads, iPods, iPhones, cell phones
> More and more apps for our smart phones
> When's enough stuff…just too much stuff?
> *Dayenu!*

> Texting, tweeting, never waiting
> Constantly communicating
> When's enough stuff…just too much stuff?
> *Dayenu!*

> CHORUS:
> *Day, Day, Dayenu, Day, Day, Dayenu, Day, Day,*
> *Dayenu, Dayenu, Dayenu*

What if we could stop the chatter
Pay attention to what matters
Life's so pleasant when you're present
Dayenu!

With the wisdom of a Moses
Let's take time to smell the roses
Life's so pleasant when you're present
Dayenu!

CHORUS:
Day, Day, Dayenu, Day, Day, Dayenu, Day, Day,
Dayenu, Dayenu, Dayenu

Being and Having Enough

In this culture of plenty, where it's sometimes hard to tell the difference between "more" and "enough," *Dayenu* asks us to remember all the ways in which we *have* enough…all the ways in which *we are enough*. Being "enough" doesn't mean that we're finished learning, growing, or striving to be our best selves. It means knowing that we are exactly as we were meant to be at this moment in time; that for this moment, we have all we need.

The trick is to find a balance that lets us straddle the two poles of *striving* and *accepting*. There is a Jewish teaching about a rabbi who kept two pieces of paper in his pockets. In one pocket was a note that said, "The world was made for me." And in the other was a note that said, "I am but dust and ashes." The first note has a grandiose tone; the second, one of deep humility. Rather than seeing them as contradictory, we can view them as opposite sides of the same coin. Sometimes the only limits for how much we can do in this one life are self-imposed; there are no limits on how brightly we can shine. Yet we also need to remember that in the end, we are mere mortals. Life as we know it will end, and we will become but dust and ashes. What lives on is how we lived, what we did to make the world a better place.

The legacy we leave may be connected to whether we believe we are "enough." It seems that those who feel they are "enough" live with more gratitude and generosity, giving of themselves with no strings attached. Giving money, attention, love, or a smile are all acts of giving that we can offer. And there are people all over the world who need just that.

So is gratitude enough? It may be, if it compels us to *act* so that *all* may feel the blessing of having, and being, enough.

 Joanne's Story:

I marvel at my client Joanne, whose intention now is to live a life of kindness and compassion. This was not always so. She lived most of her adult life trying to prove that she could be a success in the corporate world despite her "packaging"—her short, heavyset body that didn't fit the corporate image—or her difficult journey getting an MBA degree. And that's just what she did. She rose in the ranks of her company to heights beyond her expectations, earning more money than she needed to feel successful. And yet the emptiness that characterized her life never abated. It was as though she had a hole in her soul that could not be filled. Until the company she worked for underwent a major restructuring and she underwent several surgeries for a lifelong condition and had to retire.

Deprived of a source of competence and esteem, Joanne plunged into a depression that led her to seek therapy. Our work together uncovered her unloved, unworthy child-self, a feeling that was replicated as an adult in her marriage. She hadn't realized how much she longed to feel genuinely cared about. As she recovered from her medical issues, she experienced an unexpected sense of caring from friends and neighbors, who visited, expressed their desire to help, and brought her meals that nourished her spirit as well as her body.

And as our therapeutic relationship deepened, she also came to experience other longed-for needs—to feel understood, validated, and respected. This was a balm to her soul. She explained, "This is all I ever wanted: to feel acknowledged and appreciated for who I am, not for what I produce. I lived my whole life always reaching for more, but I was reaching for the wrong thing. For the first time in my life, I feel like I have enough—my physical health and now my emotional health. My cup runneth over. This is all I need." Maybe that's all any of us need.

When she set out on a new career of giving back, it was not to prove anything or get anything; it was because it added meaning to her life. These days she brings all the passion that she brought to the world of business to her new calling; she volunteers her time at a nursing home, goes out of her way to do random acts of kindness to strangers and friends. This is what brings her joy. "I'm just so grateful for all I've been given in this life," she said. "Not the financial reward I got when I was working, but my health and dignity, the feeling that I'm a valuable human being. If I can make someone else feel valued and cared about, I'll have done what I was meant to do in my time on this planet."

B'CHOL DOR V'DOR—IN EVERY GENERATION

Think of the deep wisdom in these words from Rabbi Nachman of Breslov: "The Exodus from Egypt occurs in every human being, in every era, in every year, in every day." Rabbi Nachman knew firsthand the pain of *Mitzraim* that we all experience—if not every day, then at some point in our lives—and how we long to be liberated from its grip. If we pay attention to the way we are living our lives, we don't have to imagine the Haggadah's mandate: "In every generation, it is our duty to consider ourselves as if we had come forth from Egypt" (Exodus 13:8). We have all yearned to travel the path that leads us out of *Mitzraim*.

This recurring theme in the Exodus narrative is one that the early rabbis and sages were almost obsessed with. They were intent on teaching the next generation about our heritage—not just the story itself, but also the ability to integrate it and internalize its messages. Each of us is charged with finding a way to make the Exodus story our own, to locate ourselves in the larger story, and to weave our own narratives into the larger tapestry of our people.

And when we observed Passover at the peak of the pandemic, it wasn't hard to think of ourselves as coming forth from *Mitzraim*. Though we didn't have blood above the doors of our homes, we too stayed behind those doors to prevent the spread of the virus. We knew all too well what it felt like to live narrow and constricted lives. We still do.

As the world turns, situations change. But our values endure. We bring them to bear in every generation, even though our concerns vary from year to year. When my children were young, the plight of Russian Jews occupied a place at our Seder table. Just a few years later, the Ethiopian airlift commanded our attention. When my grandchildren were young, we were horrified by the genocides in Rwanda and then in Darfur. More recently, our hearts broke as we witnessed the breakdown of humanity in the Middle East (and elsewhere) as organizations such as ISIS sank to new depths of depravity. Several years ago, we stared wide-eyed in disbelief as thousands of Syrian refugees risked their lives to escape oppression and death, marching for days or weeks on end with only the clothes on their back, praying to be smuggled aboard battered boats on perilous passages toward freedom. They were the lucky ones. Last year we ached for the endless stream of families walking from Central America, seeking asylum at our country's southern borders. And more recently, our hearts broke as we witnessed the unspeakable atrocities in Ukraine. Our concerns are not limited to the horrors across the globe. They occur on our own streets where some lives, especially Black lives, don't seem to matter. But they do matter; they must. All lives must matter.

Liberation is a never-ending journey of going forth from bondage. It isn't something that happened to other people at another time. It is still happening, in every generation, in every corner of the world, and to you and me. It occurs every time our souls ache with longing to be free of the ways that bind us, hold us back; every time we're still enough to hear the whisper of the small voice inside: "I will be who I will be." Suddenly, we're willing to take a risk and take those first steps into the Sea of Not-Knowing, the same sea our ancestors crossed so many years before.

I like to think, here in our country, that *we* are free. And on one level, we are. Yet Martin Luther King's words echo in my mind: "Whatever affects one directly, affects all indirectly. I can never be what I ought to be until you are what you ought to be." But how many people—who are disadvantaged, disabled, or unjustly discriminated against—never get the chance to be who they ought to be? How many people of color still live such constricted lives because of the structural racism that still exists in our country? I think back to the Civil Rights Movement, the march from Selma to Montgomery, Dr. Martin Luther King Jr., and Rabbi Abraham Joshua Heschel—arms linked in solidarity, testimony of the affinity between the Black and Jewish communities. How the Exodus was the recurring theme of the Movement.

Both King and Heschel believed in an empathic deity responsive to human actions, and that our actions could evoke or suppress what Heschel called "Divine pathos." The work of our generation is to join hands, let our legs march together, and raise our voices in protest, so that our experiences of liberation can bring light to those who are still struggling for theirs.

The work of our generation is to honor all that another of our prophets stood for—the fierce defender of equal justice for women, and role model for generations of women and girls, the Jewish American icon: Justice Ruth Bader Ginsburg. A visionary who cared deeply about all the disenfranchised, who imagined that the world she lived in could be different and *made* it so in her lifetime. Ruth was our Miriam. May we drink from her wells of wisdom, walk the path of the justice she pursued, hold the light she brought to our country, and carry her torch forward.

The Women Who Came Before and Who Come After

As women who follow the more progressive paths of Judaism, we have much for which to be grateful. We stand on the shoulders of generations of women who came before us, women who took great risks to open doors that had been closed to them so they could explore their heritage, deepen their religious experience, make their voices heard, and paint their visions on Judaism's canvas. They have created a space for us to add our visions and voices to theirs. And now it's our turn to nurture the kind of Judaism that we want to leave for the next generation—for tomorrow's women, for our daughters and our sons.

Being recognized in their fullness was not a gift that was bestowed upon these women. They fought for the freedoms they won with grit, determination, patience, community, and a clear sense of what was right. Just as I am grateful and proud to stand on the shoulders of generations of women who preserved the best in our tradition and brought reform to what has been inequitable, I am equally grateful to walk alongside the women I see today—both within Judaism and outside it—who help *educate and empower* those left behind. . .who work to *end violence* against young girls and women and *stop child marriage*, to name just a few vital causes. I'm beyond grateful to see the generation that has come after me expand on these values in ways that I could never have imagined. Sometimes it takes my breath away.

A Balancing Act

When I think about those who came before me and those who will come after, I think about my place in the chain of generations. About the wisdom, strength, and inspiration I drew from my parents and those who came before them. About the legacy I will leave for my children and grandchildren. These concerns were not part of my life years ago when I was busy creating a life for my family and myself. When I felt I was doing a balancing act, trying to make time for all the different pieces of my life—time to work, play, learn, create, love, be with family and friends. When I wound up feeling depleted instead of energized as I tried to live a responsible, fulfilling life that mattered.

That was when I lived in the material realm, thinking that was all that was. Before I realized how much I needed time for solitude and silence, for connecting to spirit and nourishing the soul, for time just to "be," time spent in a way that just might make life matter more. Before I learned that taking time for meditation, prayer, and journaling were among the most important things I could do for myself.

Now when I give myself that time, my whole being softens—my compassion deepens, my circles of concern expand, and boundaries become more permeable, I feel truly connected to all other beings and to my Higher Self. With a clear view of the wide expanse, I get a glimpse of my Promised Land and feel that I am home.

Thank You, Divine Mother for asking us to search our souls
to see how our subjective experiences of enslavement and liberation
can help make redemption a reality for those who still live in the shadows.

Thank You for helping us to see how we can help create a world that reflects
the holiness of every human life, a world that is just, whole, and free.

Thank You for inspiring us to tell our stories to our children and our
children's children, so the message of hope and transformation is renewed
in all the generations to come.

Living the Messages of *Dayenu* and *B'Chol Dor V'Dor*

It is customary at traditional Seders to sings songs of praise to God in gratitude for the countless blessings in our lives. Yet we express gratitude not by song alone. Reflecting on our blessings, sharing the bounty we have enjoyed with others, taking concrete actions to create a smoother path for those who walk alongside us and for the next generation are all expressions of our gratitude to the One. This is the legacy I want to leave for those who come after me.

Food for Thought

Dayenu

- What helps you take those painstakingly small steps to reach a goal?

- How can you prevent disappointment from draining you of the energy you need to move forward?

- Which moments in your life made you feel truly satisfied?

- How does the feeling of being enough impact the way you move through the world?

B'Chol Dor V'Dor

- How has your family's liberation opened a way for you to live a more expansive life?

- How has your personal liberation helped others to become the people they want to be?

- How has working to adopt an attitude of gratitude affected your life?

- What legacy do you hope to leave to the next generation?

CHAPTER THIRTEEN

The Second Cup: The Cup of Healing

Healing may not be so much about getting better, as about letting go of everything that isn't you—all the expectations, all of the beliefs—and becoming who you are.

—Rachel Naomi Remen

HEALING HAS MANY FACES

Healing can be a physical, mental, emotional, psychological, political, and/or spiritual matter. For the ancient Hebrews, healing began with the political—finding the courage to leave the strangling, soul-deadening constraints of slavery.

The work of healing continued as they attended to the myriad ways in which slavery and the escape from it shaped their lives: the challenges of sustaining themselves in the wilderness, of working to overcome a slave mentality, of finding ways to live together as a community, of learning to understand and trust themselves and each other, and of learning to trust in a Higher Power, which they believed could help them to live with a greater sense of freedom.

For those of us fortunate enough to be living in a time and place of relative freedom, matters of healing most often center on physical pain or illness. Only recently have healing circles begun to include emotional/psychological concerns. Because the mind and body are so interconnected, emotional issues often manifest over time into physical issues—reason enough to pay attention. But what of those people who have concerns of grief, loss, depression, anxiety, alienation? A life without authenticity, vitality, meaning, can be a world of suffering unto itself.

The work of psychotherapy and psychoanalysis is to help heal those whose inner lives are tied up in knots of confusion, guilt, feelings of inadequacy, or self-blame; to help those who feel trapped in a *Mitzraim* of brokenness, bitterness, betrayal, despair, hopelessness, or rage. Some people feel empty and alone, emotionally attached to others by a mere string that can be cut at any moment. Others need to let go of toxic relationships, pain, or their one "right" way of seeing things. Many are traumatized, all need healing. They seek therapy with both hope and dread. They desperately want to heal, and at the same time are terrified to explore their feelings and learn of their origins. They want insight and understanding, comfort and support, yet don't believe they will ever find peace or love, or a way to escape from their suffering. *Mitzraim* comes in many shapes and forms.

This is especially the case for those who feel that their worlds have been shattered. How they long for a sense that, beyond the fragmented pieces of their psychological universe, there is a whole. I hold in my mind a vision of the scattered stones of the original Ten Commandments, broken by Moses. How they were gathered up and placed into the Holy Ark, along with the second set. Such are the bits and pieces of our lives—the lost, forgotten, disowned parts of our selves. They too can be gathered up, held in compassion, and integrated back into our lives, creating a different, more complex, and richer whole.

But it's not easy to do this on our own, especially when we're feeling fragile and vulnerable. We need someone to lean on, to hold us. There are many moments when patients experience their psychotherapists as calming, soothing, trusted others with whom they can momentarily merge. But what about when the patients are alone, when the therapist is not available to help soothe overwhelming anxiety?

I have found that those who feel connected to God, the Divine, to Spirit—to whatever it is that they hold sacred—are better able to hold the splintered pieces of their lives in self-reflection and compassion. There is something both subtle and powerful about being able to reach out, cry out, and surrender to something beyond ourselves—beyond words and images—to a force that can somehow lift us beyond the limitations of the small self and provide us with a sense that we are part of a great and enduring whole. Sometimes we need something sacred, like the ark, which is spacious enough to contain all the shards of our lives. For many, *God* is the ark that holds all the bits and pieces of our earthly existence in its Divine embrace.

It may help to think of each fragment of our being as a single stone in a mosaic whose beauty and design is revealed only when seen in its totality—each stone a different dimension of the whole, which is far more rich, varied, and complex than any of its parts.

A Different Dimension of Healing

There are other issues beyond our personal challenges, springing from different sources. While they too may be connected to genetic predispositions, earlier childhood experiences, or family relationships, some are closely linked to the work and social environments in which we find ourselves. Other difficulties are evoked by the state of the world: the brutality, terror, poverty, hunger, and hatred. Some of these concerns may feel at a safe remove from our everyday lives, yet they are close to home—so close that they divide us, polarize us, and keep us separate in noxious ways.

I'm thinking too of our own society, and our own religious tradition. It is sad enough to see the division between religions, but more so to see the division *within* it—where those who practice more orthodox ways look down upon those who are less observant, and those who are more assimilated look down upon those who follow the time-worn path of old. What would it take for the more pious to accept, even embrace, the inclusiveness of those who are more secular, who question their faith, who seek alternative paths? What would it take for the less religious to not disparage the practices of those who may find deeper meanings in ways that they may not comprehend?

And what of the blatant gender discrimination that has long marked our tradition? I applaud the earnest, thoughtful, and significant ways in which it is being addressed in some circles; but it still holds too much sway in others, especially in the more orthodox tradition, where women often live tightly circumscribed lives. Many are "slaves" to large families, sometimes numbering ten or more children, with any desires of their own sublimated to their roles as mothers. Yet it's heartening to hear of the few Orthodox women in Israel and elsewhere who are breaking out of their traditional roles, protesting the attitudes of their sect's "centuries of backwardness" in terms of women's rights and gay rights, and running in local political elections to initiate change, modeling the *chutzpah* of their Israelite foremothers!

And of course, these issues are mirrored in our larger society; its prejudices extended to sexual orientation, to race, class, ethnicity, and disabilities. There is no lack of opportunity to find "otherness"—to keep those who are different at a distance, outside our circles of care and connection.

It is my prayer that we all take seriously the need to heal the divisive "-isms" that perpetuate our separation and isolation and create instead a world where differences are neither denied nor devalued, but acknowledged and embraced, wherever possible. It is not by chance that one of the healing legacies of the Seder is repeated thirty-six times in the Torah: that we are to live with empathy and compassion, to see the world through the eyes of the other (the stranger), "for we were strangers in the land of Egypt."

THE SECOND CUP

I have dedicated this cup to Healing. It honors the freedom to heal from the wounds that bind our souls, and the freedom to become who we are meant to be. Many spiritual traditions correlate feeling liberated and whole with being able to integrate all the fragments of our being. But this can be a formidable task, given how life is so nuanced, complex, filled with paradox and contradictions, and how "truth" is so multilayered. This chapter features many readings that speak to the different dimensions of being, focusing on integrating the fragmented, sometimes divisive, aspects of our psyches and the different paths leading to wholeness. In healing these wounds, we begin to truly know ourselves, learn to accept ourselves in all our multiplicity, and feel free to be who we are.

We lift The Second Cup, which is linked to God's promise to our ancestors and to us: "I will deliver you from servitude." And we bless the fruit of the vine:

B'ruchah at Yah, Eloheinu Ruach ha'olam, boreit p'ri hagafen

Blessed are You, Ruler/Spirit of the world, who creates
the fruit of the vine.

God of our ancestors,
Who brought our people out of the narrow confines of *Mitzraim*,
help us to break free of our own tight spaces,
and stand in the open space of Mystery and Not-Knowing—
the space between our cherished self-images and those we cast aside—
and know that we are more than either.
Help us to be still enough to hear Your still small voice
reminding us that we are still evolving and can create ourselves anew.
Enable us to become spacious enough to know the difference
between how things are and how they ought to be,
between who we are and who we are meant to be.

The Exodus as a Metaphor of Fragmentation and Healing

Although they didn't call it "psychology," Jewish mystics of the past seem to have had a deep understanding of the human soul. Rabbi Isaac Luria, in seeking to make sense of the historical Jewish experience of dislocation in fifteenth- and sixteenth-century Spain, brought forth a spiritual understanding that since has helped many to put the pieces together. It offers a wonderful metaphor for spiritual and psychological fragmentation and healing.

As psychotherapist and spiritual teacher Estelle Frankel suggests, Rabbi Luria proposed a Creation myth conceived within the framework that both the Jewish people and God—the Divine Light of the Infinite—were in exile. For Creation to come into existence, the Infinite pulled in some of its overpowering light in a process of *tzimtzum*, or contraction, thereby creating space for the finite material world.

Tzimtzum can seem like an archaic or abstract concept. And yet the need for it happens in our everyday lives—when parents need to pull in their powerful light of experience and allow their children space to explore life, make mistakes, and learn from their own experiences; when a spouse's expression of concern becomes so overwhelming that it is no longer about care, but about control; when a boss's overbearing need for competency stifles creativity. Even love needs space to breathe.

It was through this process, Rabbi Luria and the mystics believed, that the world, especially humankind, came to be. Each being was thought of as a vessel that would house the Divine Light. But the intensity of the Light was so powerful that the vessels could not contain it—and they shattered, scattering the sparks throughout the material world, where they lived in every being, in every stone, in every grain of sand, trapped in their husks, their shells.

Although the holy sparks lived, they were not fully available—often not even recognizable. So the task of humankind was to repair the fragmented state of the universe by releasing the holy sparks, allowing them to return to their Source. Human consciousness is what would make the holy sparks fly back home: creating sacred moments, higher levels of awareness, acts of loving kindness, and living in harmony with the universe.

As we move toward maturity, many of us become aware that our own divine sparks are trapped in the shells of false selves, in narrow ways of being. We yearn to set them free so that we can live more authentically, liberating ourselves from the enslaving behaviors that keep us feeling tight, closed, and angry. Many of us enter therapy and/or become seekers along spiritual paths to help us emerge from our shells and release the blocked energy that keeps us confined and constrained. We long to fulfill the soul's desire to heal into more authentic, expansive, and vibrant well-being.

Being Good Enough is Enough

"When God completed Creation, God looked and saw it was very good."

—Genesis 1:31

D. W. Winnicott, the much-admired British psychoanalyst and pediatrician, spoke of the "good-enough" mother. At first, she is exquisitely attuned to her baby's every need, both physiologically and psychologically, giving the infant a sense of comfort, control, and connection to her. With time, in keeping with her baby's growing ability to tolerate her failures, the "good-enough" mother intuitively becomes less perfect in adapting to her baby's needs. She is wonderfully *imperfect!* She is not faultless or flawless. She is *real, human, good enough.* Good enough to aid in the healthy development of her baby's internal world. Good enough to facilitate her infant's experience of dependence…loss…reality. Ideally, her *less-than-ideal* mothering contributes to her child's capacity to cope with a less-than-perfect world, softening the inevitable disappointments accompanying the societal strivings for perfection.

What does this mean for us? How many of us live with the sense that our less-than-perfect selves may be good enough? Can we look at ourselves honestly, aware of our strengths as well as our shortcomings?

What is the impact of the "good enough" philosophy? Studies suggest that those who believe they are "enough" live with more ease, confidence, and compassion. They understand that they are where they are supposed to be at this moment in time—perhaps not yet where they *want* to be, but moving toward their ideal; and, for now, that's okay. They are okay. *Imperfect, but good enough.* More importantly, this attitude tends to go beyond the self to treating others with dignity and respect and generosity of spirit. *If God can be satisfied with "very good"—not perfect—why can't we?*

What Is Not Remembered Is Repeated

I hear the "good enough" idea as a subtext for the story of our people. Throughout the Torah, we learn of ancestors who modeled for us what it means to be human. Ancestors both beautiful and blemished, blessed and cursed, who experienced success and suffering, recognition and rejection, who transgressed and who were transformed.

I hear their tales as a plea for us to accept all aspects of our nature—our gifts and our imperfections with nothing excluded. I hear a cry for us to be able to live with seeming contradiction, to become spacious enough to embrace the paradox of our existence so that we may grow and become more whole.

Let us consider the story of Jacob, who—after deceiving his father to obtain his birthright—flees to live with his uncle Laban. Along his journey, he has a divine encounter and dreams of a ladder connecting heaven and earth. Perhaps this is the first realization of his dual nature: the trickster and the one who struggles with God, his Higher Self. Years later, he has another divine encounter in which he wrestles with an angel (which may be his own shadow), and he reunites with his brother Esau (possibly his divided self). God then changes his name to *Israel,* meaning "wrestles with God."

Even as Jacob is spiritually transformed and his higher self, "Israel," prevails, his smaller self, his "Jacob" nature, still lives. And so "Israel" must learn how to manage the "Jacob" within; hearing his cry for recognition, feeling compassion for his pain, and *refusing* to comply with his demands. Israel can *hear* his "inner Jacob," but doesn't have to *listen* to him.

When we are unable to fully recognize ourselves, when we deny or reject parts of ourselves, those parts become our shadows. They lurk in the darkness, out of awareness, only to appear unbidden in moments of conflict or vulnerability, when they betray us with a sudden onslaught of hidden rage, envy, cruelty—and we find ourselves doing to others what was done to us: inflicting on them our long-buried pain. *What is not remembered is repeated.*

Like Abraham binding Isaac, preparing to sacrifice his son to God, doing to his son what had been done to him. *Midrash* (commentary) reminds us that as a child, Abraham was thrown into a furnace as punishment for rejecting the idol-worship of his father. Though he was miraculously saved, he did not emerge unscathed. Repressed trauma became the shadow that enabled him to turn his back on his sons: Ishmael possibly dying in the desert, Isaac on the mountaintop. Only when he heard the true voice of God, the voice of compassion, could he recognize his son's humanity and come to his senses. *What is not remembered is repeated.*

We learn that Moses commanded his army to kill all his Midianite kinsmen—the men, the mature women, and the male infants, even though he lived as and married a Midianite. Moses—who, by the grace of God and the courageous women in his life, was spared from being a victim of a similar decree—did to the Midianite male infants what was almost done to him. Although he lived to become a prophet who was revered for his compassion, his unprocessed trauma also lived—relegated to the domain of the "shadow"—until what had been concealed was later revealed in an act of cruelty.

The Torah often illuminates the battles we wage *outside* ourselves, seldom speaking of the ones that rage *within*. It has been suggested that those are reserved for the white spaces between the black letters, where we're invited to imagine our ancestors' inner turmoil…and explore our own. Torah stories are meant to be just that: invitations to learn about our ancestors' very human victories and vulnerabilities, and in doing so recognize our own. Yes, it helps to read between the lines.

What made our ancestors heroes and allowed their healing to begin were not only their public actions but also their courage to confront their private wars and inner demons. They had to finally face the different aspects of "shadow" breaking through the soil of secrecy.

What about *us*? What will allow *our* healing to begin? Are we even aware that some aspects of our lives *need* healing: that we too have shadows, which may betray us—in our weaker moments of conflict or vulnerability—with an unexpected attack of envy or rage? As with "Jacob," the voices of our smaller selves may never be completely silenced, but neither do they have to overwhelm us. We can hear them, recognize them, and look upon them with compassion, but not do their bidding. We can, instead, hear the wisdom of our "Israel" within.

Beyond the Fragments, There Is a Whole

Teach us, *Sh'khinah*, to create space for,
and embrace, each part of our identity,
both the loved and the unloved parts,
to be grateful for our gifts,
and compassionate toward our limitations.

Teach us, Spirit of the Universe,
to be flexible enough to live with paradox,
spacious enough to contain opposites,
open enough to find the sacred in the ordinary
and meaning in the mundane.

Teach us, Holy One, to be both strong and vulnerable,
to know sometimes we have to "let go"
before we can keep who, and what, we love,
and sometimes we have to lose our way to find ourselves.

Help us, Source of Life, to tend to, and mend, our brokenness.
Like a mother holding her wounded child,
may we hold our imperfections in a cradle of compassion
accepting, understanding, and learning from them.
And may the darker dimensions,
no longer denied, transform our pain into wisdom,
our shame into pride; deepening the soul,
helping us heal, to grow more whole,
more expansive, reflective, creative, and free.

God of Healing, help us to remember
beyond the fragmented pieces of our inner worlds,
that there is a whole.

Me and My Shadow

As with those who came before me,
flashes of my own shadow emerge unbidden
and I try to remember how to get around in the dark.
Try as I may to push the shadow away, it hovers over me,
insisting that I see what I need to see.

It doesn't take too long
before I begin to recognize the fears and insecurities,
the inadequacy and jealousy.
"Hello Darkness, my old friend."
This time, I focus on the feelings in my body,
noticing the tightness in my chest,
the pounding in my head,
and my racing heart.

And though my legs are shaking,
I feel my feet touching the earth,
and I try to ground myself,
letting Mother Earth, the ground beneath my feet,
hold me.

I begin to hold myself more softly,
moving out of my head and into my heart.
I feel stirrings of compassion
for the shamed child,
the broken, confused child.
If only she could have felt held by Mother Earth,
felt safe enough under the wings of *Sh'khinah*,
to hold her shadow up to the light
to be healed.

I relax into my body and feel the space
around my heart begin to expand.
Breath fills my belly.
The knots begin to untangle.
Ego slowly slips away,
and all that is left
are feelings of Safety and Love.

May we find the courage to shine a light on our own shadows,
to accept ourselves for who we are,
and know that change is within our grasp.

Standing in the Spaces

One path toward wholeness is remembering that we don't always stand on solid ground; often, we stand in the gray space of nuance and mystery, of not-knowing. These are the spaces between separateness and Oneness, matter and spirit, love and hate, right and wrong—spaces big enough to contain both the sacred messiness of life, and the light and love of the Infinite.

In spaciousness, we learn to appreciate the complex nature of existence; we can be both gentle and harsh, generous and selfish, passionate and passive. We begin to understand that contradictory needs and feelings don't have to confuse us or diminish our sense of self. They can teach us that we can hold onto the good when things feel bad; we can be angry without withdrawing our love; we can be loving and still set limits, caring for ourselves as well as others.

With spacious hearts, we can hear the whispers of the still small voice inside, urging us to tend with care and compassion to our shadow parts—the wounded, shameful, lost parts—to hold ourselves, in all our complexity, in a full embrace that excludes nothing, allowing all into our conscious image of ourselves; remembering that all dimensions of our being are different parts of the Whole, springing from the same Source. Single stones in a mosaic, each a different dimension of the Whole.

This I Believe

I thank You, God of Healing,
for igniting the spark in me that longs to liberate
my body, my soul.
For the courage to heal from my pain and shame.

Every day, You provide me with opportunities
to grow in understanding.
You live in me as a force of love,
 a source of compassion,
a spirit inspiring me to cope with my challenges
as I move ahead without knowing what lies ahead,
without knowing the right road to take or in whom to put my trust,
to help care for this mind/body that is so in need of healing.
This I believe, even as I cry out to You to feel whole again.

You inspire me to be grateful, to remember that I am not alone.
Even when anxiety and confusion fill me, I know that I am
sustained and supported on this journey.
You remind me that even in suffering (especially in suffering),
blessings are often hidden in pain.

Healing hands, humble hearts, and loving compassion—
taken for granted in good health—
become so valued in vulnerability.
Grace fills me with gratitude.
This I believe, even as I cry out to You to feel whole again.

From You, I have learned to relish the richness of slowing down,
to listen to the deep wisdom of my body/mind,
to know when I need to say "no" and when I need to say "yes,"
to graciously accept the help of others,
to take the hands that reach out to hold mine.

When I am with You, I am open to the beauty that surrounds me:
the endless expanse of sea and sky, the sun that warms my body,
the breeze that caresses me, making me feel alive again,
the mountains, meadows, and marshlands that delight my soul.
Your presence fills me with understanding and trust:
I have all I need, to do what I must.

This I remember, and even as I cry out to You to feel whole again,
my shadow lifts, giving way to clarity and light,
my soul is at peace.
Thank You, God of Healing, thank You.

Food for Thought

- What would help you feel free enough to look at the contradictory aspects of your life?

- What challenges in your life have been repeated because they were not remembered?

- What has helped you find the courage to confront your own shadows?

- How can you embrace each part of your identity without denying the others, accepting both shadow and light?

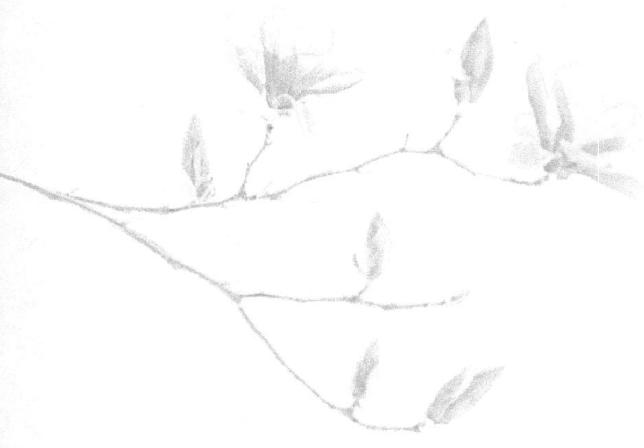

CHAPTER FOURTEEN

Rachtzah: The Second Handwashing and the Seder's Symbolic Foods

Helping hands are better than praying lips.

—Mother Teresa

RACHTZAH

Purification rituals, once the domain of religious observers, are now becoming more mainstream. Guided by celebrities such as Oprah Winfrey, Deepak Chopra, and other spiritually-minded folks, today's people seek cleanses as they prepare for new experiences—be it new relationships, new careers, or new ways of being. They seek to cleanse themselves of negative energy and attachments and create space for change, for new adventures and opportunities to grow mentally, emotionally, and spiritually. As the priests sanctified the Temple by washing and purifying their hands before making an offering at the altar, so we make our homes, our bodies, and our beings holy by cleansing ourselves of imperfections, making ourselves into sanctuaries to receive the blessings of the Universe.

Rachtzah is a second handwashing in the Seder, to cleanse our hands before the next step, the *Motzi/Matzah*. Yet the blessing for *Rachtzah* speaks of "lifting" the hands. What is the connection between purifying and lifting? Just as God's "strong hand and outstretched arm" lifted us out of slavery, so this step implies that we use our hands to do the sacred work of lifting each other up and building a world that is free from suffering. This cleansing is more than a physical purification; it's also a cleansing of the soul-wounds and pain of *Mitzraim*. In our own time, we are still going forth from Egypt, still heeding the call of *Tikkun Olam*, helping to heal the world.

B'ruchah at Yah Eloheinu Ruach ha'olam
asher kidshatnu B'mitzvoteha v'tzivanu al n'tilat yadaim

You are Blessed, Our God, Spirit of the world,
Who makes us holy with *mitzvot* and commands us to wash our hands.

A Blessing for *Rachtzah*

You are Blessed, our God, Who makes us holy
by inspiring us to purify and lift our hands.
May this water, drawn symbolically from Miriam's well,
wash away our transgressions:
the hurt inflicted by our hands and our hardened hearts.
May our hands, like our spirits, be elevated and dedicated
to doing sacred work—
to give and receive, to cleanse, feed, and clothe, to write,
make music and art,
to hug, hold and heal, to reach out and lift each other up.
Purify our hearts, *Sh'khinah*, so we can see the purity
in the hearts of others.

THE SIGNIFICANT SEDER SYMBOLS

Why was Rabbi Gamliel, the great first-century sage who helped create the ancient Passover Seder, insistent upon the elaboration of the *z'roa*, *matzah*, and *maror*? The context of his life explains. Rabbi Gamliel lived after the destruction of the Temple. During the time of the Temple, our ancestors ate the *pesach* (lamb)—a symbol of redemption—to fulfill God's commandment. With the Temple's destruction, the lamb was no longer used as a sacrifice since the ritual could only be conducted by Temple priests. Although the loss of our holy place was shattering, the rabbis would not let it shatter our faith. They were determined to find other ways to bind our ancestors together so that they would survive as a people. They found their answer in the power of the word, through study, memory, and speech. The telling and retelling of our story became a potent and poignant thread that would allow both our narrative and our people to survive. It is as though they knew we would have to hear it repeatedly until it became part of our DNA and we developed a muscle memory for hope, when we would need it most.

Just as we purify more than our hands but also our hearts and souls through the ritual washing, so we do more than taste the Seder's symbolic foods. We discuss them, allowing their essence to rest on our tongues so that we can fully taste the power they represent.

Motzi / Matzah

The *Motzi* (meaning "blessing," usually for bread) and the *Matzah* are often combined into a twofold blessing that is offered to the Creator and Sustainer of Life: first, for the raw materials that sprout from the earth, and second, for the tools—the human hands—that transform them into our daily bread. We offer an additional blessing on Pesach for the commandment to eat *matzah*—the flat bread that had no time to rise, because our ancestors had no time to prepare for their escape. Though not ready, they had to seize the moment that could change the course of their lives.

Matzah—the bread of freedom, the bread of poverty, the bread of our history and hardship—is also the bread of our wandering, a link between our enslavement and our liberation. We recall our ancestors, who were poised to escape slavery on a moment's notice for the possibility of living in freedom, with its accompanying dangers and uncertainties. Yet here we are, centuries later, and experiences of exodus keep occurring. Millions of people fleeing their homelands, taking only what they can carry. Even now, there are many whose "bread" comes in the form of the scraps of food they find, "nourishment" for the most perilous journeys of their lives.

Matzah is a simple bread, stripped of any ingredients to enhance its taste or puff it up. Spiritually, it's the bread of humility, purity, and essence, asking us to strip ourselves of whatever puffs up our egos, and to contemplate our own essence, who we are at our core.

A Blessing for the Matzah

B'rucha at yah Eloheinu Ruach ha'olam hamotzi'a lechem min ha'aretz

You are Blessed, Our God, Spirit of the World,
who brings forth bread from the earth

You are blessed, our God, for making us holy
by commanding us to eat *matzah*.

Just as You widened the narrow straits in which we were enslaved,
may we help widen the narrow places in which others may be caught,
inspiring them to seize the moment of their own redemption.

On Not Being Ready

I was so not ready to take the plunge by leading a Seder. Communicating my ideas, revealing my deepening spirituality, using my voice to express myself in an untraditional *Haggadah* with my larger extended family—all this felt risky. I was afraid that I would be judged and found wanting, and so I was stuck in my own *Mitzraim*, standing on the shores of the sea, afraid to step in, yet unwilling to turn back. The Pharaoh holding me back was my own ego, my clinging to what was familiar: the fear of failing (or maybe succeeding), of being perceived as "holier than thou." To get to the other side, I'd have to *feel* that fear, *let* my voice crack, my heart pound, my knees shake—and not give in to the knot in my stomach. I would have to take the plunge into that sea of self-consciousness and ride the waves before the sea would part.

Initially, the *spiritual energy* of the sea eluded me. Unable to escape the tyranny of my thoughts and projections, I felt as though I were wandering through a dark night of the soul, utterly alone, with no one or nothing to soothe my mounting sense of isolation. I felt myself shutting down—numbed and immobilized.

I don't know when my mind stopped jumping from thought to thought, at last allowing me to arrive at that place of no thought, where there was nothing to do, nowhere to go. When it did, I realized that Spirit had been holding me all along. And now I surrendered to Her soft, strong embrace. I let go, stepping into the unknown, going backward in time.

I thought of our ancestors' story. I imagined those ancient voices reaching down through the generations to shed light on our suffering and healing. I envisioned them sharing with us how they felt as they left the only lives they had ever known—all the doubts and fears that accompanied them on their journey. I imagined them walking toward the Sea of Reeds under the full moon, trembling with dread as they anticipated the formidable task before them. I felt their terror, trepidation, and pain as they immersed themselves in the sea, laboring to birth a new life. In placing my own experience in this larger context, I saw that my dark moments of pain and confusion were also part of a *birthing* process. I came to understand that *all* creation begins in a womb of darkness—even the new day, which, in Jewish tradition, dawns not with the rising sun but with the *setting* of the sun.

If I were to escape my own *Mitzraim*, I too would have to leave behind a part of my identity, let go of my story, my limiting and often imprisoning identification as being "inadequate" and "less than." My consciousness would have to be transformed. I would have to let an aspect of my ego die. I would have to give voice to my own "truth," expose my vulnerability and imperfection, and trust I that would not be destroyed in the process.

Inspired and sustained by *Sh'khinah*, I felt buoyed by a sense of possibility, a willingness to let what needed to change inside me change. I was ready to take the risk, and to share with my extended family not only my *Haggadah* but a deeper part of myself as well. I was prepared for their judgment or discomfort, which might masquerade as laughter and joking, much as my own anxiety had manifested in nervous laughter so many years before. Yet it eventually became clear to me that the only thing that would drown that night was a part of my ego.

In the end, I was not destroyed but transformed, purified. Sparks of divinity were released from my shell. I heard an angel whispering, "Grow, grow, grow!" And I heeded her call.

Z'roa, the Pesach Offering

The shank bone is truly symbolic since the use of the paschal lamb as a sacrifice was discontinued after the destruction of the Temple. Traditionally, it represents God's outstretched arm. Although the destruction of the Temple was devastating for many reasons, a fortuitous unintended consequence is that we no longer sacrifice living creatures. Fortunately, we will never know the taste of the young lamb's bone. That we no longer sacrifice a lamb is progress. That we still sacrifice the lives of animals for human consumption, however, should give us pause, especially when so many of them are treated so inhumanely. We are sacrificing more than God's creatures. We are sacrificing our health and our integrity—our ethical obligation to treat all sentient beings with compassion.

As a young people, unaware of the sanctity of all sentient beings, we sacrificed young animals to express our homage to God. We did not yet know that there were better ways to express our gratitude. As much as we may shrink back from blood and violence, it is part of our story—our past and our present. Too often in the past, blood has been the price of freedom. But must it be part of our future? How can we evolve as a species so that nonviolence, mutual recognition, and understanding—not blood— become the way freedom is won? May the time come when prayer and good deeds, not the sacrifice of life, express our gratitude, our intentions, our atonement.

Maror—Bitter Herbs

Why do we bless the *maror*, the bitter herbs that evoke the harsh reality of slavery that our ancestors endured, and the countless other plagues of the modern world that continue to embitter too many lives? We bless the bitterness because it sensitizes us to pain and helps us to cultivate compassion. It reminds us to be moved by the bitterness in our own lives and in the world, and to try to right the bitter wrongs. But we must also be mindful of not getting stuck in the pain, lest we feel like victims with hardened hearts that cut us off from what is positive in life. Is there a way to experience bitterness but not get trapped by it?

Rabbi Shefa Gold's teachings on such a way draws from the journey of the Israelites after the miracle of the Red Sea, when they walked for three days, finally arriving thirsty at Marah, only to find they could not drink its bitter waters. Frustrated and angry, they railed at Moses, who cried out to God, who instructed him to take a piece of wood (from The Tree of Life) and cast it into the water: as soon as he did, the water was transformed, becoming sweet and drinkable.

I was struck to learn that in the 1700s, the Maggid (teacher) of Mezeritch offered an alternative view of as to why the water was bitter, which is remarkably like Masuro Emoto's theory of the consciousness of water. The Maggid observed when translated literally, the Hebrew words for "because it was bitter," actually mean: "because *they* were bitter." According to this teaching, the reason the water at Marah was undrinkable was because the bitterness of *the Israelites* affected the quality of the water!

Regardless of the reasons for bitterness, Rabbi Shefa Gold reminds us that the Tree of Life is a bridge between Heaven and Earth, between the Infinite Mystery and our finite lives. *Once we reach beyond the boundaries of our own lives and touch the Tree, we connect with all of Creation and no longer feel alone but part of All That Is.* This is the healing that God-consciousness brings.

Whatever the bitter challenges we encounter on life's journey, we too can cast a branch from the Tree into our internal pool—our bitter waters of disappointment, anger, and regret—and sweeten them. We can imagine those small pools as drops in the vast ocean and begin to feel less separate and more a part of a greater Unity, the Wholeness of Life.

Blessing the *Maror*

*B'ruchah at Yah Eloheinu Ruacah ha'olam
asher kidshatnu b'mitzvoteha v'zivatnu al achilat maror*

You are Blessed, Our God, Spirit of the World,
who makes us holy with mitzvot and commands us to eat bitter herbs.

Thank You, Source of Life, for commanding us to eat *maror*.
In Your wisdom You command us to taste the bitterness of slavery,
and internalize its sting, so we can truly feel the joy of freedom.
May the day come when we know bitterness only as a symbol,
and the sweetness of freedom as our reality.

Keeping Bitterness at Bay

I thought that I was far enough away from my daughter Robbi's medical diagnosis to write about it with a sense of calm. Yet even now I am aware of my heart thumping in my chest. I learned from Robbi to pay attention to the sensations coursing through my body without judging them. That's one of the many practices she has committed to since learning that she has chronic blood cancer, which turned her world upside down, mine tumbling along with hers.

From the moment she learned of her diagnosis in 2013, Robbi knew that she would have to deal with her condition as directly as possible. She researched and underwent both traditional and alternative treatment and continues to be diligent about keeping herself healthy and strong in body, mind, and spirit. She has a meditation/mindfulness practice, does bodywork, and practices self-care, compassion, and gratitude—anything that will help her to show up for each challenge.

She's had to learn to take one day, often one hour, at a time. There are good moments and difficult ones, moments of joy and those of grief, when black clouds of loss and defeat temper the optimism. Denying the seriousness of this diagnosis is not an option, but neither is despair. Thoughts of "Why me?" are transformed into "What do I have to do next?" How, I often wonder, is she able to keep from becoming bitter?

Perhaps what helps her do this is her ability to see her individual pool of anger and sadness as a drop in the Greater Ocean of Being. Cancer had stopped her short in her tracks, derailed her, frightened her; but she would not let it define her. Treatment has been a huge part of her life, but it is not her *whole* life. There's so much she wants to learn, experience, and enjoy. Every effort she makes to cast a branch from the Tree of Life into the Ocean sweetens her pool. And there are many branches, mostly those of gratitude: for the care and compassion of the medical community; for her growing ability to keep her personal struggle in perspective; for the blessing of a husband who understands the ways of the Ocean and helps her navigate the rough passages; and for the love and support of her deeply devoted son and her family. It feels like we are all growing taller as we stretch ourselves and reach for branches on the Tree to cast into and help sweeten the water.

Gratefully, her cancer is in remission, but not without consequences from chemotherapy. Her struggle has been transformed from that which was overwhelmingly frightening into a challenge that is manageable. It has allowed her enough moments of calm and resolve to adapt to the changes and limitations in her life. In the process, she's been surprised by the appearance of dormant gifts. Her passion and her pain both are now expressed, not only through her writing but also through her vibrant, joyful, and breathtakingly beautiful art. These are paths of healing, channels through which she shares herself with others. Feeling more connected, she's able to "let in, and trust, the love around me"—the healing that God-consciousness can bring.

Her courage, spirit, and wisdom astonish me. Witnessing how she copes reinforces the work I do to manage my *own* fears and anxiety. Any bitterness that I might feel softens into gratitude. I am profoundly grateful for her healing and for the deep connection and understanding we share. The sweetest fruits from the Tree of Life.

Korech: The Hillel Sandwich

Korech symbolizes the fullness of life, with all its textures and contrasts. To dip the bitter *maror* into the sweet *charoset*—a mixture of apples, nuts, wine, and spices—is to recall the story of this night: bitter and sweet. It is to retell the story of the Exodus, which began with our people's shame and ended with their joy and triumph. More than just the story of this night, it is also the story of our lives.

There is no specific blessing for the *Korech* since each of its elements have already been blessed. Yet we know that often the whole is greater than the sum of its parts; that our separate parts not only complement each other, but also can enhance each other in ways that they could never achieve alone. We may want to add a blessing for the new meaning that emerges when the separate elements, our differing perspectives, are brought together; for how our understanding can be complemented by our differences.

There is so much wisdom embedded in the *Korech*. Which may be one of the keys to our survival as a people, our ability to understand a deep truth of life—that no life is exempt from pain and suffering, and even our greatest moments of happiness may contain seeds of sadness and loss. Yet our tradition reminds us, again and again, not to let bitterness become so overwhelming that we lose our capacity to savor all that is beautiful, sweet, and good in life; that even in sorrow, there are seeds of healing, even in pain there are blessings to be found.

After the destruction of the Temple, use of the paschal lamb as a sacrifice was discontinued. Some sources state that the lamb was substituted with *charoset*, which symbolizes the clay and straw from which our ancestors toiled to make bricks to build Pharaoh's cities. The apple further represents the courage of the women of Israel who bore their babies in secret under the apple trees of *Mitzraim*, without security or safety. Its sweetness tempers the bitterness of bondage, just as the women's fierce devotion may have sweetened the misery of enslavement. The *Korech*—the combining of bitter and sweet—becomes our "Hillel sandwich," embodying what the revered sage Hillel saw as one of life's greatest challenges: *to taste freedom amidst oppression and remember the suffering of others even as we enjoy our freedom.* Just as the broken pieces of *matzah* are held together by *maror* and *charoset*, may our compassion be the ingredient of life that holds all our broken pieces together.

This truth was written in bold relief when we observed Passover during the pandemic. Our *maror* took the form of disease and the pain, sorrow, and grief left in its wake. Yet it was sweetened by a *charoset* made of courage, kindness, and generosity of spirit of those who put their lives on the line to soften the pain and bitterness of those who were suffering. May we carry this blessing of true *Korech* as we go forth in healing and, I pray, well-being.

The Sweetness that Softens

We all thought she would live forever. My mother began her ninety-sixth year with her typical *joie de vivre*, but within months, signs of decline began to peek through her vibrant persona, culminating in a downward spiral just before her next milestone. Still, my sister and I were able to mark her ninety-seventh birthday with such joy that when the inevitable end came just a few weeks later, the bittersweet memory of that day held us, in our grief, like a strong and loving maternal embrace.

May 6, 2014 was a warm and beautiful day, sunshine and tender green leaves on the trees surrounded the patio of the Rehab Center. Like a plant seeking light, Mom's face kept turning toward the sun, and we kept turning our chairs to face her so she could see and hear us full on. As usual, her daily report about the bad food and slow aides quickly turned to the more gratifying conversation about her family, especially her fifteen great-grand-children, her *raison d'etre*. But on this day, Mom was holding court. She had an agenda; she had important things to discuss. She spoke of a recurring thought that was close to her heart: "I want to know, when my time comes, how we can tell 'the audience' how I felt about my family." As if it were possible to not know!

Then she segued into her absolute, most favorite topic: her two daughters, whom she believed were the best. As she extolled our virtues and sang our praises with typical exaggeration, it was hard to keep our eyes from rolling. We knew she was serious, but we were embarrassed and uncomfortable and didn't know how to react except to become our silly, laughing, childlike selves. So we began to spontaneously create new verses to an old Irving Berlin song, "You're Just in Love," that lovingly poked fun of her over-the-top expressive-ness. Before we knew it, she joined in the fun, adding her own words. Here's what we came up with:

> *My two daughters are the—very best.*
> *Telling you has been my—last request*

It's what I want—before I'm laid to rest.
But please don't run, I'm not quite done.

For the rest of the day, all conversation was interspersed with new verses and the reminder:

"Girls, I want you to sing this song at my funeral. I'm serious."

"Right, Mom," we countered, "we'll sing it. We'll even have the words written on a screen with a bouncing ball so everyone can sing along!"

As the sun faded, we hoped that her inspiration would, too. We thought the beautiful dinner we planned for her would change the channel. It didn't. She just wanted more singing. We obliged. Old favorites—and the new one— were met with applause by her roommate and the staff members. Mom was in all her glory, having "the best birthday ever." Until she suffered the first of two heart attacks.

Levity gave way to gravity. Her time had come, and she welcomed it. She'd had a long and loving life. But living had become too difficult. She could barely see, hear, or walk. Even family visits weren't enough to sustain her will to go on. She just wanted "to go to sleep."

As we discussed the funeral service with our families, to our surprise they asked, "You're going to sing the song, right?"

"Wrong!" This was not what we had planned. Yet there was something that kept me thinking. *What if I changed some of the sillier verses and wrote a lighthearted song that honored her expression of gratitude for the family she was blessed with?* Unable to sleep, I wrote, with sweet memories softening the pain. My sister reluctantly agreed to sing it with me if we could pull it together. So we refined my nighttime musings via cell phone the following day, as we each drove to the funeral home. And we rehearsed it as we drove back to our homes, grateful for the traffic that gave us more time, and the laughter that lightened the grief.

Yes, we sang her "Swan Song," and once again it was met with applause. The audience loved our tribute to her, the tender words, and the celebratory vibe. What we loved was the sweet memory of our extraordinary day with Mom, creating a space for her to share what was in her heart. It felt as though we were helping to birth her into the next world, just as she had birthed us into this one. "To everything there is a season: a time to live and a time to die. A time to mourn and a time to dance"—or to sing.

As she prepared to leave us, Mom knew that our song was not intended for her "audience" alone, but for her family as well. She knew, in the way that mothers do, that the memories and laughter would comfort us, like the beautiful blankets she once had made for each of us. Sweetness and sorrow stitched together, covering us all in her warmth.

Food for Thought

Rachtzah

- How does it feel to pour water over your hands with the intention of blessing and elevating them?

- In what ways have you used your hands to comfort or create?

- Whose hands have soothed you, lifted you up, harvested your food, sewn your clothing, built your home, or touched you with love?

- How can you use your hands, your life, to build a better world?

The Symbolic Foods
Z'roa

- Can you allow yourself to acknowledge those things you've come to regret?

- Are there ways in which you have committed violence that you didn't then recognize as such at the time?

- What aspects of your life have you sacrificed to feel accepted or get what you wanted?

- What aspects of your life have you sacrificed to help bring about a greater good?

Matzah

- What change do you need to make, even though you don't feel ready?

- Which internal doubts, fears, and desire for security are you fearful of letting go?

- How might holding on to them be at the expense of your personal growth?

- What would it feel like to seize the day, follow your dream, and trust that the seas will part?

Maror

- Have your disappointments, regrets, or rage become stagnant pools of bitterness?

- Or have you been able to work with them and move beyond them?

- Which branches from the Tree of Life can sweeten those pools when challenges arise?

- How do you feel when you cast those branches into the Ocean of Being?

Korech

- Can you truly taste the *Korech* and digest its message?

- How can you experience your challenges as part of the fullness of life with all its contrasts and textures?

- How has the sweetness in your life softened your struggles?

- What can you do to soften some of the bitterness in the world?

CHAPTER FIFTEEN

Shulchan Orech and *Tzafun*: What Is on the Table and What Is Hidden

*Better is a dry morsel and quietness therewith,
than a house full of feasting in strife.*

—Proverbs 17:1

SHULCHAN ORECH—THE FESTIVE MEAL

As with many of our celebrations, dinner is often the high point of the event. The Seder's Festive Meal is no exception. Still, while it is usually so much more than a dry morsel, there's also a sense of inner quietness within the joyful celebration. As a formal Seder step, it's meant to be more than having family and friends get together for dinner; it's the part of the ritual that ties the different parts of the Seder together—the first part that tells of our past and the second part that speaks to our future. The meal is about our present: what

225

is happening right now, this evening, at this table. It creates a space between the parts of the Seder, offering a sense of balance and integration. *The Festive Meal stimulates our minds, touches our souls, nurtures our bodies, and delights our senses.*

The meal itself often begins before we taste the first foods—be it an egg, gefilte fish, chopped liver, or chicken soup, traditional Ashkenazi dishes. For many, it starts as we inhale the aromas redolent of Seders past. It's as though our mothers, aunts, and grandmothers are still in the kitchen, getting ready to delight us with their time-honored recipes. But just as Seders themselves evolve, so do many festive meals. In addition to the familiar, favorite foods, you're likely to enjoy the culinary creativity of those who try to appeal to more contemporary palates, including vegetarian and vegan dishes and decadent deserts.

Now it's time to enjoy the abundance of the festive meal, and share the thoughts, feelings, and questions evoked by the Seder. It's also a time to connect to family and old friends, get to know new guests, share old memories, and create new ones. A time for singing and offering blessings that spring from the heart. It's all very much a part of the greater whole of the evening.

Though it's a formal *step*, it's not a formal, serious *meal*. Instead, it's one with a good blend of solemnity and levity, a meal that can be eaten quickly, sometimes ravenously, or lingered over for hours. More traditional Seders follow the meal with the blessing for the third cup of wine and proceed to the next, shorter part of the Seder. At more contemporary Seders, the complete ritual—meaning as much or as little as is considered enough—may be performed and concluded before the meal is served. Whatever its variations, the festive meal is meant to be savored.

That the traditional *Haggadah* doesn't acknowledge those who create the festive meal should not surprise us, given how women's stories and contributions have been *passed over*! Yet we all know who plans, prepares, shops, cooks for this evening, who sets the beautiful table, and gathers us together. As more women become involved in the Seder, they are choosing the prayers, blessings, and songs that will be used as well as the themes that will stimulate meaningful conversation and taking responsibility for all the remaining details to make the Seder flow with ease. Not to speak of serving the food and cleaning up the wine-stained linens and trails of *matzah* crumbs afterward. Without the women, there would not be a truly Festive Meal. Not to say that this is a one-woman show; it isn't always, nor should it be. Today, Seders are often joint efforts, with guests—including the men—being responsible for different parts of the meal. In our family, my son often provides us with super-delicious dishes. But traditionally, this has been women's work, and our contributions should be acknowledged, even when it's not experienced as a chore but as a meaningful, creative endeavor—which it can be for more of us.

With a shift of focus, even the shopping can be a blessing instead of a burden. Just think of how fortunate you are to have the means to create a sumptuous meal. When you are cooking, you can take time to appreciate the miracle of the food's journey from the depths of the earth to your kitchen; enjoy the colors, textures, and aromas of the ingredients. And when all is done, look at the beauty of your holiday table and imagine your guests sitting around it, enjoying your Seder and each other. You are not merely making a holiday dinner; you are passing on our ancient tradition to the next generation. You are touching people in ways you may not know. You are creating memories, a gift for all.

The Egg and the Salt Water

The meal often begins with a hard-boiled egg dipped in salt water, a symbolic food that celebrates change, new beginnings, and birth. And Passover is very much a holiday about birth: the rebirth of the earth, the birthing season of the lambs, the birth of the Israelite nation, and our personal rebirth as we heal and become more whole. Indeed, there is much to celebrate.

Yet when dipping the egg in salt water, we also remember those for whom there is little to celebrate, those who are still stuck in the many forms of *Mitrzaim* that continue to plague them. May they soon experience the birth or rebirth of justice, freedom, and peace.

Although the egg holds the potential for new life before that can happen its protective shell must be broken. Before our ancestors could begin new lives as free people, they had to break the yoke ("yolk") of slavery and give up any illusion that Pharaoh would protect them. The only protector whom they could trust was their God. The Holy One would help them transform from fragile souls into a solid people, as a raw egg is transformed when cooked in boiling water. Similarly, to become our authentic selves, we must give up any illusion that we will be genuinely protected by the false self we have adopted: its values, coping mechanisms, unappeasably self-critical dictates, and views of life.

At the end of the day, when you're alone with yourself, you may want to think about any *illusions* you may have. Have you been hiding your vulnerability so that you appear strong and independent? Or have you been showing up in the world as if you're totally confident and successful, so that you'll get the admiration and respect you seek?

As with the *matzah* that represents both the bread of freedom and the bread of affliction, the egg too is a paradoxical symbol, both of new life and of mourning. It is the first food to be eaten upon returning from the cemetery and entering a house of *Shiva*, a mourning ritual. Because the egg is a food that hardens the longer it is cooked, it is as though our tradition is reminding us that we must learn to steel ourselves when death occurs, so that we can continue to go on being. So too just as we mourn the illusion of the false self, we strengthen ourselves with the knowledge that growing in our womb-space are the seeds of an authentic life, waiting to be born.

The Orange

Now that Susannah Heschel, the feminist writer, and scholar, has introduced and popularized the idea of including an orange on the Seder plate, more Seders—particularly Women's Seders— begin the festive meal with the orange. While it may not be apparent, the orange can be a strong female symbol, its seeds symbolizing the future in the same way as the egg. The mature fruit carries within it the seeds of the future.

This new tradition began when Susannah Heschel was visiting Oberlin College and came across a feminist *Haggadah* containing a ritual in which a crust of bread was placed on the Seder plate. It was meant as a symbol of solidarity with Jewish lesbians and a statement of defiance against a rabbi's wife who stated, "There's as much room for lesbians in Judaism as there is for a crust of bread on a Seder plate."

Heschel, too, felt the need to acknowledge those who had been excluded from Judaism, but she thought that bread was a poor symbol because it suggested that lesbians were truly out of place in their tradition. And so, at her own Seder the following year, she used an orange as a symbol of inclusion, signifying the fruitfulness for all Jews who have been left out—women, in general; lesbians; and gay men—who now have a place and are active, participating members of the Jewish community.

Heschel then tells how her intention to affirm lesbians and gay men was distorted by a widely circulated rumor about a man coming up to her after a lecture, angrily stating that a woman belongs on the *bimah* (platform for reading Torah) as much as an orange belongs on a Seder plate. We can feel her ire as she relates how *her* idea of using an orange was attributed to a man—all too typical of what has happened to women in Judaism.

Because the orange seeds symbolize the future, they represent the potential of new fruit. It's all too fitting that the need to spit out some of its seeds has become a metaphor for the need to spit out Judaism's chauvinism. Imagine Susannah Heschel relishing the juiciness of this gesture!

Food for Thought

The Egg

- When alone with your own thoughts, do you wonder who you really are?

- Is your authenticity still sealed inside the shell of the false self you present to the world?

- What would help you break the shell?

- Are you willing to let that die so that more of your true self, who you are inside, can be birthed?

The Orange

- In what ways have you felt marginalized—in your religion, your family, a social group?

- What do you attribute this to? Your gender, sexual orientation, race, ethnicity, disability?

- What would it take for societal attitudes to change, to be more inclusive, to finally spit out the seeds of any kind of chauvinism?

- What is it that you, with support from others, can do to help create this change?

TZAFUN—FINDING WHAT IS HIDDEN

Things are not as they seem. Much in life is hidden: God, the less loved parts of us, and the parts yet to be discovered. While hiding the truth suggests something sinister; it can also be a propitious way to protect what is precious. Let us honor the courageous but often secret acts, especially those of the women in our history—and the women among us today—who knew when to conceal and when to reveal.

In our own history:

- The midwives hid the truth from Pharaoh.

- *Yocheved*, a young mother, hid her baby, sparing him from Pharaoh's decree.

- Her daughter Miriam hid herself in the reeds by the Nile, watching over the baby.

- Pharaoh's daughter drew the basket from the water, hid the identity of the infant from her father, and raised him as her own.

- Miriam hid the identity of *Yocheved*, who would help Pharaoh's daughter nurse the baby—her own mother and the mother of Moses.

- Moses wasn't the only male newborn to be hidden. The Hebrew women hid among the apple orchards to birth their babies undetected.

- In another time and place, Queen Esther hid her Jewish heritage from her husband, Ahasuerus.

- And later, in fifteenth-century Spain and Portugal, our people hid their identities as Jews, fleeing or converting to escape death.

- Not so long ago, in Germany and elsewhere, we hid our identities and our physical bodies: in the attics and haylofts of compassionate Christians, in tunnels and sewers under Polish streets, and in forests.

- And here in our own country, how long was it before we felt safe enough as a people to come out of hiding, to find and reconnect with our roots, to openly reclaim a relationship to our heritage?

We cannot fall into complacency. We know that there are far too many who are still hiding behind doors of discrimination and oppression. How many women have felt the need to hide their talents so that men would not feel threatened? How many women, everywhere, have had to conceal their intelligence, their desire to learn and study, sometimes hiding their female identity to gain access to knowledge because their traditions did not allow this for women? How many women—and men—still feel the need to conceal their sexual orientations because revealing it is simply not safe? And how many refugees and illegal and undocumented immigrants are still in hiding? As long as there are those who are not free, *we* are not really free.

Hiding is so much more than a children's game.

Yet all of us may still be hiding some aspect of who we are. Sometimes this is the prudent, wise thing to do to keep ourselves safe. But very often it comes at a cost, and the price we pay may be higher than we realize. Truth cannot be long hidden.

 ## Julia's Story:

When my patient Julia was five years old, her father left the family, taking her with him. Wanting all traces of who she had been to be gone, he called her by a new name, one that she can barely utter now. She reported living alone with him until his "wife" moved in, and that she was abused both physically and sexually and terrorized, left alone, hidden, and locked in their apartment all day. She lived in mostly dissociated states, traumatized by painful feelings with no context to make sense of her experience and little ability to regulate her emotions. Like a feral child, bereft of human care.

Julia recalled a pivotal moment when she was about ten years old. A woman knocked at her door, slid a religious book underneath it, and said, "I know what's going on." Nothing more. That someone on the outside knew of her existence was a lifeline that she held onto. Because she didn't go to school after the abduction, she wasn't able to read the book, but she found solace in the illustrations and identified with the woman's compassion. It somehow made her feel that she wasn't the crazy, bad child she was constantly told she was, if "God" had sent someone to care about her. She never saw or heard from the woman again; nor did she find out if what the woman knew contributed to her being found and returned to her family about a year or two later. Julia's memory, like her soul, was filled with holes.

She was slowly reintegrated into "what was never a fully functional family" (her then-"sober" alcoholic mother and brother) and called once again by her birth name. She returned to school and was placed in special needs classes, supported by extensive individualized attention and tutoring. There were a few unsuccessful attempts at therapy, but because she was not ready to come out of hiding, not enough real work could be done. Still, she made remarkable strides, given her horrendous history.

Julia and I started our work together years later, when she was married and had a daughter of her own. We worked intensely for several years and were able to put many of the pieces of the puzzle of her life together. She finally found enough of her true self to know that she wanted to end the marriage to her successful husband, because "it was all a show, a sham. I was his trophy wife because on the outside I had pulled myself together enough to be what people called 'very attractive.' As much as my father kept me hidden, my husband loved to show me off—business dinners, golf outings—but he didn't know me at all. How could he? I wouldn't let him in and, besides, I didn't know myself! I was a sham too. I lived my life pretending I was smart, pretending to be 'normal.' I sometimes amaze myself about how well I covered up and passed for normal. But I was far from it. I'm still not, although I feel closer to it now than ever before."

Julia's painful awareness of this "sham" was the first step out of her *Mitzraim*, the marriage that she described as a "prison, like being in solitary confinement" because for too long she couldn't risk communicating to her husband her feelings or fears, her traumas and triumphs, her needs, desires, and dreams. Until, along with the dawning light of a new day, she found the courage to do so.

I would like to say that Julia came fully out of hiding, found herself again, and lived happily ever after. Although I pray she will, I don't know how her story will end. Our work ended when she accepted the "golden" opportunity for a job and different lifestyle in a different state and moved there with her daughter to start their lives anew. She didn't experience this as running away or hiding again in a new place, but as a new beginning. She was just trying to let go of her shamed childhood and begin again. I was not so sure. But we both felt that she would benefit from a long-distance (telephone) relationship until she transitioned into her new life.

Almost every call contained an expression of gratitude for my helping her to come out of hiding. She made my heart happy when she told me, in one of her warm Christmas greetings, that she had begun therapy again to continue her journey. She wrote, "I'm so tired of trying to find the lost parts of my life, but I can't stop. I have to do whatever I can so I can be the mother I want to be for my daughter. I may have lost my childhood, but I'm not going to lose the rest of my life, and I want her to have a real mother, who can fully be there for her…The more I understand about myself, the freer I feel to be the real 'me,' not hiding or pretending, but open and present. It's so liberating…."

Julia's story is extreme yet common. Every day, we hear stories of personal suffering and loss greater than our own, making it easy to minimize our own pain. How can we dare to compare *our* issues—that we aren't living fully or truthfully—with those who are living without food, money, homes, or health, with those who are profoundly traumatized? Please do not compare. Life is not a contest to see who has suffered more; everyone knows the experience of pain. What is important is to let the pain that we concealed be revealed by bringing it into the light, where it can be seen, tended to, and hopefully mended. And to be aware of and sensitive to others' pain—sometimes seen, and sometimes still hidden, waiting to feel safe enough to come out of hiding.

Today, finding the *afikomen* is the highlight of the Seder for young people, a children's game in which the finder gets a reward. I don't know which is the most fun for them: the search, the finding, or the monetary reward. This game may be for kids but searching is a lifelong pursuit for all of us. The process may evoke a familiar sense of excitement as we try to find the missing pieces of our lives that we believe will make us feel more complete. Or we may feel a sense of restlessness, unsure of what we're looking for, yet feel compelled to search. Often the search itself is the reward.

In traditional Seders, the hidden piece of *matzah* must be found and brought back into the ritual so that each guest can have a piece of it, and the

Seder can be brought to its conclusion. Originally, the *pesach* lamb was eaten at the end of the meal when guests were sated, the taste of *sacrifice* lingering in the mouth. But the sages reversed this, counseling that the *afikomen*, the symbolic taste of *freedom*, should be the taste to linger in our bodies and memories.

The Healing Message of *Tzafun*

We break the matzah at the start of the Seder
--as our spirits were once broken.
Having journeyed through the Seder
we find the missing piece and join the two in wholeness.
Let us honor all that remains hidden
and strive to restore all that is broken.
Let us shine a compassionate light
on our own shadows and on those of others
bringing us to all toward greater healing and wholeness.

Food for Thought

While it is sometimes necessary to keep things hidden, there are times when truth can be liberating, even when we feel helpless. May we have the wisdom and the courage to know when to conceal and when to reveal.

- Which parts of your life are you still hiding?

- Why have you chosen to keep them hidden, and at what cost?

- How might unveiling your secrets help you feel more complete?

- What secret have you brought out of hiding, and how has it changed your life?

CHAPTER SIXTEEN

Barech: Blessing

Just to be is a blessing. Just to live is holy.

—Rabbi Abraham Joseph Heschel

Blessings connect us to the abundance in our lives, to forgotten parts of ourselves, to what we may need to learn. Blessings are everywhere. We can find them in the most ordinary experiences, in the humblest places. They are not magical, but they do have the power to affect us in ways beyond our understanding. Have you ever felt so touched by something that time stopped you in your tracks? That your heart leaped out of your chest to merge with something beyond? That you found yourself saying, "Oh my God," or heard yourself murmuring, "Thank you, thank you"? Then you know how it feels when an ordinary moment is transformed into a blessing. Sometimes all we need to do is pay attention to the sensations flowing through us.

Barech refers to the *Birkat hamazon*, the blessing recited after a meal, thanking God for the land given to our ancestors and the food grown on it. The essence of our blessing is a heartfelt expression of gratitude for Earth's bounty, for our nourishment and sustenance. Yet the full blessing is not limited to the foods that nourish us but also includes varied forms of nourishment, including prayers for the rebuilding of Jerusalem and God's continued abundance, mercy, and grace. We see that a blessing can express gratitude or longing; it can be a prayer for protection or favor; it can be a plea or a call to action, or a quality or experience that we wish for ourselves and/or someone else. Taking the time to offer a blessing can be a blessing itself. *When we bless the Source of Life, we too are blessed, infused with a sense of strength and hope that may have felt lost to us before—a reminder of the abundance in our lives that we often take for granted.* This is the healing message of *Barech*.

THE BLESSING OF HEALING FROM PERSONAL *MITZRAIM*

I have often felt blessed by the wisdom of our tradition and the sages' understanding that struggle is part of life, and that we all need to have an undergirding sense of hope that we can survive our difficulties. This includes not only the injustices and indignities that we face in the external world, but also when we feel enslaved by our own inner pharaohs: when we're overcome with self-doubt; when we forget (or never experienced) a sense of self-worth; when the life we're living feels small and dull—when we know that there is much more of life to be experienced, but we don't feel free to explore the possibilities or the passions that may be stirring beneath the surface.

Just as our ancestors went from being slaves to becoming a free people—physically, psychologically, and spiritually, with the help of a power within and beyond themselves—so can we. Sometimes miracles appear just by our seeing the same situation from an unfamiliar perspective, as if with new eyes. And *that* is a blessing. As Gandhi stated, "The moment the slave resolves that he will no longer be a slave, his fetters fall. Freedom and slavery are mental states."

Am I Free?

The struggle for freedom echoes through the generations.
Since ours is a different kind of bondage than that of our ancestors,
we don't always recognize it for what it is.
Living a lifeless life long enough entraps you in a
deadening routine that slowly morphs into a new reality.

That's the thing about enslavement:
it has an insidious way of becoming the norm.
It happens to us one infringement at a time,
so we don't quite notice
until a nagging ache dares us to ask:

Am I enjoying the blessings in my life?
Does my life feel expansive and creative,
or circumscribed, narrow, and tight?
Is there too much clutter in my mind?
Are there too many self-doubting voices, judgmental voices,
obsessive and depressive thoughts?
Am I free to love, create, make mistakes, fall on my face,
get up and begin again, so I can find out
who I'm meant to be, and become who I want to be?
Or am I barely aware of the freedom that is mine to claim?

Barely Aware

Oh, the pull of old habits!
The tug that draws me back to a place I know too well,
so subtle that I'm barely aware of feeling like a child again.
"A, my name is Alice"— remember Alice in Wonderland?
Barely aware of feeling smaller,
I have just fallen into a rabbit hole.
I'm under the spell of the Trickster
who has me believing again:

I'm not who I like to think I am.
Others' needs are more important than my own.
Their opinions are more valid than mine.
I need to prove my worth.

Barely aware, but awake enough to know
it's not the Red Queen and the White Rabbit
(absurd characters of a child's story)
who are filling me with questions and doubts.

It's *me*, falling back into a familiar pattern,
forgetting my essential nature, losing touch with
Who I Am.

I sit in solitude, confused and alone.
There are no magic mushrooms to make me feel taller again.
Yet in the deep silence, I hear a soul-whispering…
the voice I most need to hear.
Barely aware of Your presence, I breathe in Your spirit.
It rises inside me, filling me with lightness.
You bless me by asking me to
connect to my true self, to remember
Who I Am.

Your simple question, and my humble answer,
infuse me with a sense of freedom, of choice.
I can choose to fall prey to the Trickster,
or to be lifted by You.

More than barely aware, I am now more than a bit in awe:
You have transformed a dark rabbit hole into a portal of light.

Knowing our essence—beings made in the image of God—is integral to transformation. It serves to ground us in our internal reality, holding us in the sometimes agonizing process of change. As much as change may be desired, it can be frightening. So remembering who we are, remembering our intrinsic worth, is a profound blessing. Discovering how we mirror nature in our struggle to grow—the metamorphosis from caterpillar to butterfly is particularly poignant—and relevant!

TRANSFORMATION

There is a story about a well-intentioned man who patiently observed a butterfly as it struggled to emerge through a small opening in its cocoon. But then (unfortunately for the chrysalis on its way to a butterfly), he tried to help by enlarging the cocoon's opening. While this helped the butterfly to emerge, there was an unintended consequence—it was unable to fly!

Struggle is often a necessary precursor to growth. Even the seed of a plant must break through the soil's hardened crust to reach the sunlight and fulfill its potential. What the "helpful" man in the story didn't know was that the struggle required for the butterfly to pass through the narrow opening was Nature's way of forcing fluid from the body into the wings. This process prepares the butterfly for flight once it has achieved its freedom from the restricting cocoon.

How different are we in our desire to avoid pain and struggle? Who among us doesn't want to break through our constricting cocoons and soar beyond our familiar existence with a minimum of discomfort? How often do we sidestep change because we know that moving from one stage to another entails struggle? Yet who *doesn't* feel that push to be all we can be? Enter (again) the caterpillar. In the caterpillar's growing body are small clusters of cells called *imaginal buds*. They embody the blueprint of the butterfly-to-be. As the buds grow and link together, the caterpillar's immune system experiences them as foreign, and a struggle ensues. The immune system tries to destroy the cells until they break down and disintegrate. And only then can the butterfly, encased in its protective shell, emerge.

Within our own body/minds there is also a blueprint embodying our *true self*—the self we dare to imagine, the self we were meant to be. Buried deep, it remains hidden until the day—maybe after *hundreds* of days of feeling that we are not living the lives we were meant to live—when we find ourselves feeling confined and restless, longing to break through the false self: the shell we have built to protect ourselves from early trauma so that we could keep the bonds with those we love intact. We begin to remember who we really are, our essential nature.

Like the caterpillar, we may experience this budding self as foreign. We dare not trust it, lest we fall prey to disappointment and hurt once again. But it is far from foreign. It's as natural and essential to us as our own breath. So with hope and dread, we dare to change.

But we don't go softly into the night. We *struggle* as we question: "How do I let go of the only life I've known, but in many ways outgrown? How do I remain grateful for its having served me to this point, as I now surrender to a process in which part of the *self* must die?"

Our ancestors' experience serves us well once again. Before being transformed from slaves to free people, they had to let some aspect of their reality die. When they jumped into the Sea of Reeds to flee the Pharaoh's army, all they had to cling to was their faith—a basic sense of trust in the essential goodness of a power beyond them, one that would help them release their doubt and fear long enough to take a leap of faith and step into the unknown.

They trusted with all their hearts and might that the Divine Presence would hold, guide, and grace them with what they needed. And instead of them drowning, all that drowned in that transcendent moment was an aspect of ego: the small part of themselves that once had served them well, the part of themselves they once mistook to be the whole of who they were. From this story, and our own inner counterparts, we learn that consciousness cannot be truly transformed until we are willing to let the ego temporarily dissolve into "No-thing." *Just when the caterpillar thought the world was over, it became a butterfly!*

Just when we think we are nothing, a new world may be waiting in the wings. *Nothingness* is also one of the Hebrew names of God (*Ayn Sof*—literally, without end), corresponding to the highest level of spiritual and psychological development. This nothingness is a fertile spaciousness, close to what other traditions call "emptiness"—a state of receptivity, of being open and able to hear what springs up from within, no longer bound to constraining habit and memory. A state in which new ways of being are waiting to be. And it is our *struggle* that strengthens our wings, prepares us for flight as we emerge from our own restricting cocoons, transforming us from who we thought we were to who we really are, by connecting to our true selves. *Just to be is a blessing.*

We are blessed when we are to be able to connect to our essence. We are blessed when our heritage holds us on our journeys of transformation, and the field of science supports us as we travel. We are blessed when we are connected to others.

Although *Barech* does not speak specifically of connection, it is implied, for Judaism is a religion of community, of connection. Even as we engage in private prayer, our public prayer services require us to have a *minyan*, a quorum of ten adults. Because the blessing of connection—in its infinite variety—is so vital to our well-being, women, have been making group gatherings part of their lives in ways they hadn't before: book groups, support groups, advocacy groups, and spirituality groups, to name a few. As one woman said of our Women's Seder, "I love being part of such a warm, caring community of interesting women. Today, with so much social media and screen time, it's such a treat to take a few hours to be with a group of women and to connect around the annual ritual of the Seder." Another woman echoed these feelings, adding, "I feel so blessed. It's something I wish for all the women in my life." Spiritual gatherings such as Women's Seders can nourish our sense of connection to the generations of women who came before us, to those with whom we share our journeys, and to different parts of ourselves. Below is an adaptation of a ritual that can easily be incorporated into a Women's Seder. The women stand in a circle and welcome the spirits of our female ancestors, whose wisdom has been a source of guidance in our lives. In blessing them we connect to our own wisdom, compassion, strength:

We bless **Sarah**, for teaching us that having children is not the only way we can be mothers. Even before she was a mother — Sarah was "ninety" when Isaac was born— she was the Mother of our People. Her insight, courage, and patience helped birth a new world.

We bless **Rebecca**, who reminds us to pursue our dreams even if the odds are against us. Rebecca persevered to have her favored son Jacob receive the blessing meant for his brother Esau.

We bless **Rachel**, compassionate mother, always with us in our grief. Rachel, Jacob's true love, died giving birth to their son Benjamin. Known as the Mother of Our Sorrows, she extends her compassion to all who suffer, who grieve.

We bless **Leah**, womb of our people, in whom we were nurtured and sustained. Leah, who competed with her sister Rachel for Jacob's love, was the mother of ten of the twelve tribes of Israel.

We bless **Dinah**, beloved sister, who reminds us to care for women who survive abuse. Dina's "rape" was violently avenged by her brothers, but in many *midrashim*, the focus is shifted to the care and healing of the women who were abused.

We bless **Miriam**, desert prophetess, who modeled for us how women lead and inspire. Miriam appears in the bible in the shadow of her brother Moses. Now she is an icon of women's leadership and inspiration for her role in the Exodus.

We bless **Ruth**, who chose Judaism and the bonds of love and friendship between women. After Ruth's husband died, rather than return to her people she remained with her mother-in-law, Naomi, avowing "your people will be my people."

We bless **Esther**, who risked her life by revealing her Jewish identity to save our people. By disclosing her Jewish identity to her husband, King Ahasuerus, Esther saved the people of Persia from a plot to annihilate all the Jews in the kingdom.

We bless **Deborah**, judge, and prophetess, for her wisdom, compassion, and strength. Deborah inspired the Israelites to a victory over their Canaanite oppressors, modeling how to be a strong, wise leader.

This is followed by an opportunity to express gratitude for a woman in the participants' lives who has been a source of blessing, and/or to offer a prayer to a woman—or the many women in the world—who are so in need of blessings.

Expressions of Gratitude

Barech is said over the third cup of wine after the traditional blessing. The numerous parts of the traditional blessing stand in contrast to the few offered at more contemporary ones, where you may hear simple alternative expressions of gratitude like this one:

We thank you, Mother Earth,
for providing the healing nourishment and sustenance
that allows us to survive and thrive,

and we thank all those whose strong backs prepare the earth,
whose knowing hands turn the soil, nurturing it,
tending the crops, harvesting the plants,
those whose hands prepare Your bounty
and set this feast before us.

We thank you, Spirit of the Universe,
for blessing us with sacred moments,
celebrated with family and friends,
for the Torah's teachings, the soul-food
that heals and inspires us
to nurture and sustain one another
and the Universe of which we are a part.

A Blessed Encounter

In preparing for a holiday meal, I would often find myself overwhelmed with the planning, preparing, shopping, and cooking. Although I made lists, I'd invariably forget something and would have to return to the market again and again. Like a lot of women, I suffered from "what-if-I-don't-have-enough-itis," and I'd prepare way more than what was needed. Before long, I'd be flooded with misgivings. I'd think to myself, "Why am I doing all this? It's too much food and too much work." I didn't know back then that sometimes less is more. And I'd continue with the preparations, joyless.

I remember once shopping for a holiday dinner, my cart filled to the brim. All the checkout lines were busy, and the one I chose turned out to be particularly slow; shoppers, myself included, were growing impatient, mumbling, and grumbling. Slowly, and with considerable effort, the frail, elderly woman standing in front of me, with just a few items in her cart, turned around, looked at me, and said, "*Mamale*" (a Yiddish term of endearment for young girl, or "little mother"), "just thank God that you can fill up your wagon." She turned again and carefully drew the food stamps from her purse to pay the cashier.

Rather than a reprimand, it felt more like she was reminding me of how blessed I was. I knew what she meant; I remembered the elderly neighborhood women of my youth who scrimped and saved to feed themselves, and

I thought of all who do the same today. Still, I felt a burning sensation of shame. Her words went to my core. I'd been complaining about having too much food on my holiday table and having to wait too long in line. Had I once stopped to acknowledge the blessing of being able to create an evening that was plentiful, delicious, and beautiful? Not until then.

That was about forty years ago, and the woman's words have stayed with me, transforming something inside me, getting me out of my own small world. They connected me to a part of myself that easily gets lost when I'm involved in creating something of "importance" and losing sight of what's *really* important—how blessed I am for being able to create something meaningful and inspiring. Gratitude for this blessing was barely even a background presence because what was in the forefront of my mind was a running list of all the things I had to do and the anxiety that it generated.

Now, when I feel myself becoming overwhelmed, I reframe my thinking: I remind myself that I'm setting an abundant table as an offering for all that I am blessed with in my life. It's a way of giving back, a way of saying, "Thank You." This attitude of gratitude even affects the way I cook. I try to slow down instead of rushing to get things done. I often look at the ingredients and remember where they came from—not the market, but from the earth—their miraculous journey from seed to my table. I sometimes marvel at the intense colors of the tomatoes: red, yellow, orange, purple, and green; at the heady fragrance of spices; the texture of the grains. It's a reminder of my intention to prepare the dishes with gratitude, attention, and love—that I'm making this dinner with my heart as well as my hands. This mindset infuses the holiday dinner with a different energy: the food seems to taste better, the mood feels warmer and more relaxed, and my anxiety slowly melts away. All this because a wise old woman once blessed me with her simple truth and words of wisdom.

And I've blessed her ever since, thanking her, wishing her well in my thoughts, even though she is gone from this Earth by now. I can't see her face, but I still hear her words that touched my heart. Wherever she is, I hope she can somehow sense that. The moment was fleeting but her blessing lingers.

Food for Thought

A blessing is a way of paying attention to things so that we notice them more fully, seeing things as if with new eyes, being infused with strength, hope, and abundance.

- What blessings in your life have gone unnoticed?

- What does it feel like to realize that freedom is a mental state as well as a physical one?

- Think of when an ordinary moment felt transformed into something extraordinary. What was the experience like?

- How has your awareness of the power of blessings inspired you to live your life differently?

CHAPTER SEVENTEEN

The Third Cup: The Cup of Connection

Human connections are deeply nurtured in the field of shared stories.

—Jean Houston

EXPLORING OUR CONNECTION AND DISCONNECTION

Rabbi Harold Schulweis has written that God is known not in isolation but in relationship—through kinship, friendship, healing, binding, raising each other up. God is known in connection, in community; the betweenness that binds and holds together.

With a similar sensibility, Persian mystic and poet Rumi wrote: "Out beyond ideas of right-doing and wrong-doing there is a field. I'll meet you there." We connect to each other when we let go of our ideas of right and wrong and listen. Both teachings transcend boundaries within religions and dissolve divisions between people.

The Third Cup seeks to do the same. It honors the freedom to soften our internal walls of separation that isolate, disconnect, and cut us off from each other. The reflections in this chapter explore our sense of separateness from and connection to each other. They are meant to help us embrace both our uniqueness and the common humanity that we all share, and to heal our sense of isolation and alienation. They are meant to give breadth and depth to the concept of connection and to serve as a springboard to facilitate connection among Seder guests.

Blessing for the Third Cup

B'ruchah at Yah Eloheinu Ruach ha'olam boreit p'ri hagafen.

You are Blessed, Our God, Spirit of the World,
who creates the fruit of the vine.

Thank You, God, for Your promise to redeem us,
for Your outstretched arms reaching out to us, delivering us.
Made in Your image, may our arms reach out to others,
connecting us all in an endless circle of care and compassion.
And may our hearts, too often hardened, preoccupied with protection,
soften and open with the loving-kindness You have implanted in us.
We thank You, God, for the gifts of connection, relationship, and love
that gladden the heart.

TOWARD MUTUAL RECOGNITION:
THE PSYCHOLOGY OF CONNECTION

As with most spiritual traditions, one of the goals of psychology is to help us live with a greater awareness of the world around us and a greater capacity for empathy and mutual recognition. *Empathy*, as defined by esteemed psychoanalyst Heinz Kohut, is the capacity to think and feel oneself into the inner life of another person. Kohut felt that the capacity to understand others' experiences is as basic to our lives as our five senses—so vital to our existence that we can no more survive psychologically without empathy than we can survive physically in an atmosphere without oxygen.

Yet empathy is not a given. For some people, this critical faculty has not been sufficiently developed or has somehow gotten derailed; they do not understand that in the fundamental yearnings of the heart, we are all very much the same. If only we could take as a mantra for humankind the essence of Martin Buber's "I-Thou relationship": that when we relate to another, we relate to them as a "Thou" rather than as an "it." A "Thou" stance is respectful of their personhood, their uniqueness; whereas an "it" stance sees the other as one who merely provides a function: pumping our gas or filling our order at the deli. From Buber's perspective, when we meet the other as a "Thou," we may also find *ourselves* being met and known. When we touch the other's essence, we may discover our own, and get a momentary glimpse of the "eternal You" that lies at the heart of this way of relating. "When two people relate to each other authentically and humanly," as Buber puts it, "God is the electricity that surges between them."

Buber further reminds us that every person born into this world represents something new, original, and unique—something that never existed before. There is great truth to this. Yet as members of the human family, we are also more alike than different, as many philosophers and poets have observed. In a spacious mind that can hold all possibilities, both are true.

Breathing in the same air, warmed by the same sun, guided by the same stars and moon, we are bound together by our shared humanity. Do we not share the desire to live in peace and health, to pursue our dreams and contribute meaningfully to a purpose beyond ourselves? I believe most of us do, even as we recognize that how we work toward our dreams and desires may differ greatly.

In opening to the process of *mutual recognition*, we are not asked to agree with or excuse the other or to lose our own perspective. Mutual recognition is about opening our minds and our hearts a little wider, so that *all* feelings are recognized—not your truth or my truth, but one that honors both. This extended space of mutual recognition is the ground that nourishes our sense of safety and trust, the rich soil in which relationships grow and blossom. And when they do, they often become moments of healing and transformation: small, personal encounters in which two people come to know each other more intimately, each feeling less alienated and more connected.

To me, this process is the cornerstone of healthy, respectful relationships, be they intimate, professional, familial, social, or global. Now more than ever, it is imperative that we learn to truly recognize the other, create dialogue, and build relationships to foster understanding and healing. The sanity of the world depends upon it—on *us*. And because our personal healing reverberates in the larger world, in bringing about mutual recognition we are contributing to global healing, *tikkun olam*, one relationship at a time.

I often wonder, "What can we do to nourish connectedness, to see others as singular pieces of the human puzzle, held together by the same cosmic glue?"

Sometimes, all it takes is a genuine curiosity, an open stance, a desire to learn from those who see things—and live—differently from us. Finding commonalities as seemingly inconsequential as sports teams, music, or food can begin to break down walls of separation. Try a variation of "Jewish geography": when you meet someone for the first time, ask where they come from, or if they've been to a place that you're familiar with; see if there are people or experiences you have in common. Or tap into a feeling that you recognize. You can casually say, "You look excited; your smile is contagious," "You look like you need a hand; is there something I can do?" "You look lost; can I help you?" You might be amazed at the "friends" you just haven't met yet!

 ## Bob's Story:

We met Bob when we ducked into a covered patio to avoid the downpour. This week of rain was unusual for Mexico, but there it was, forcing my husband and me to share some protected space with a stranger. We chatted for a while, exchanging pleasantries that began with "So where are you from?" It continued with our sharing common interests in books and baseball and ended with "Really good talking with you" when the rain subsided, each of us going our separate ways.

Until we met again, when Bob and his family were leaving the restaurant where we had just ordered dinner. He stopped to chat when my husband asked if he'd like to sit down for a few minutes. He did. In the ten or fifteen minutes of conversation we had that included something again about baseball, Bob—who was from the Midwest—shared that he and his son had gone to Yankee Stadium, compliments of the Make-A-Wish Foundation, an organization that tries to make wishes come true for children fighting life-threatening diseases. A year later, Bob related, his son lost his fight to cancer. I guess the expression on my face and my tear-filled eyes conveyed more than the polite condolence I offered.

The conversation resumed, with not much more being said about his loss. But when he got up to leave and we said our good-byes and shook hands, Bob squeezed my hand and held it for a long moment. More than a good-bye, it felt like we were both acknowledging that when he spoke of his son's death, there was a meeting of two souls—as if he were saying, without words, "Thank you for sharing my pain."

TIKKUN OLAM: HEALING THE WORLD

The world is a sacred place. Helping to heal human suffering, to liberate people from all forms of bondage, is sacred work. This work is at the heart of the Passover narrative; for me, it is my temple.

I tend to see the world through global glasses. I am painfully aware of those caught in the crossfires of actual physical wars and ideological conflicts: victims of oppression, persecution, discrimination, and unspeakable violence; victims of poverty, famine, and disasters.

I am no less aware of those in our own families and communities who may or may not have suffered from the same events, but who experience the same feelings. With today's technology collapsing distances between us, bringing the pain, and suffering of both neighbors and strangers into our immediate experience, I cannot close my eyes to what has become "up close and personal." Too many of the sounds I hear sound like plaintive cries instead of a "joyful noise."

But a soothing song comes through the music of the Torah—"Love your neighbor as yourself" (Leviticus 19:18), and "Love the stranger, for you were strangers in the land of Egypt" (Deuteronomy 10:10)—repeating the refrain no less than thirty-six times. Like mantras deeply embedded in our beings, they ask us to live with a deep sense of empathy and compassion, to try to see the world through the eyes of the "other." They are enduring legacies of the Exodus.

Because the experience of enslavement is engraved in our collective conscious, it is presumed that we understand the heart of the stranger, even if the trials they face are alien to our own; that we can empathize with their feelings, if not their specific struggles. In caring about and for strangers—both those among us and those living on foreign soil—by embracing the essence of *Tikkun Olam*, we become humanity's healers-without-borders.

And yet I would be remiss if did not acknowledge the sorrowful situation in Israel with their Palestinian neighbors. The inability of the powers that be on both sides to be able to see beyond their own concerns and feel their way into the inner experiences of the other is tragic. Perhaps it will be the work of the women again—the Israeli and Palestinian mothers who have lost children in the ongoing, senseless wars—who will bring healing to both peoples. I pray that the intimate sharing of their pain and their dreams will crack the hearts of their leaders open and let the light of understanding and peace prevail. I pray that the Israeli and Palestinian children who take part in programs like Seeds of Peace will inspire their leaders to transform their communities, to find those seeds of healing that live within all their sorrows, that—like *karpas* on our Seder table—they will push through the depths and wind up in a holy place, a place of peace.

But healing the divide between people doesn't have to be born from tragedy. It can be born from *desire*. Consider the individuals or groups who create innovative programs like The Silk Road Project, an exchange program that brings together performers and composers from around the world. Founded by cellist Yo-Yo Ma, its intention is to forge connections across generations and cultures. When I first heard them perform, a deep chord was struck in me—not only by their haunting, exotic, gorgeous music, but also by their commitment to bring people together through music.

It was their expressed hope that as members of the human family, we could better address our differences by appreciating our commonalities. This hope so resonated with my own. The Project embodies the magic that is possible when strangers meet, crossing boundaries of time and space. As Hans Christian Andersen wrote, "When words fail, music speaks," and as several of the musicians described it—listening to each other's music, meeting each other's friends and families, tasting each other's foods, and learning bits of each other's languages—all helped to create a feeling of "being changed, not only musically, but inside."

Estelle Frankel, psychotherapist and teacher of Jewish mysticism, speaks of how in Hebrew, many words combine opposite meanings or qualities, connecting them to a Unified source. For example, she explains that the word "stranger"—*nochri* in Hebrew—comes from the same root as the word for "recognition," *hakara*. In other words, we are strangers to those who don't recognize us. But once we feel recognized, then we cease to be strangers.

What might it be like for you to know the soul of the stranger, to step inside his or her skin? I often wonder why mutual recognition so often eludes us, keeping us strangers in each other's eyes; what keeps us from empathically entering the experience of the other. If we could achieve a stance of mutual recognition, might we find that we are more alike than different, that we might, under similar circumstances to theirs, behave in the same ways for which we demonize others? Are we afraid of our own "shadows," the unacknowledged fears that we project onto the other? What it might be like if we grew up in another time and place? How might we have acted if we were ordinary citizens in Germany, for example, during the Holocaust? Would we have hidden Jews in our attics—or obeyed orders and been complicit in their annihilation, as we tried to keep our own families safe? If we were male and conscripted into military service in the Middle East today, would we commit unspeakable acts of atrocity—or have the courage to stand up against oppression and injustice (assuming that the culture in which we were raised enabled us to cultivate these values in the first place)? How have we responded to the injustices in *our* midst? Have we acted on our ideals as nobly as we hoped we would?

Though we can't be certain of how we may act in moments of crises, we can cultivate an ethos that inspires principled behavior. We can try to live by the philosophies of religious and spiritual traditions that transcend the boundaries of ideology—by the teachings of the Torah or those of the Dalai Lama, which implore us to work not only for our individual selves, family, or nation, but also for the benefit of all humankind. While the realities of limited resources and necessity make our priorities center around those closest to us, we must expand the notion of care from self to neighbor to stranger and widen our circles to include those outside our groups to the causes and concerns in the world beyond us. Distance does not protect us from suffering. As we have learned from chaos theory, a butterfly flapping its wings in New Mexico can contribute to a hurricane in China. It may take a long time, but the connection is real. The wars, poverty, diseases, and hunger happening across the ocean will be felt in some way on our own shores. We are all affected, if not individually, then collectively; if not now, then at another time in another way. Because at the deepest levels of being, we are all connected. Distinctions between "us" and "them" fall away, and all that remains is the essence of who we are.

Walking Through the Gate

We are in Phnom Penh, Cambodia, at the Ridgewood Village School. Before we walk through the gate and down the aisle between two lines of sweet, smiling students, we hear the soft voices of the middle schoolers singing a song of welcome. Their unrestrained joy brings tears to our eyes.

My daughter Karen is leading Ridgewood, New Jersey's Cambodia Club, on their annual trip to the school to bring educational material, sundries, and mostly our presence to let these children know that they are not forgotten.

The Club has built the school, and continues to sponsor it, so that some of this generation's children will have the benefit of education. The plight of the Cambodians who survived their own Holocaust and who live under the inhospitable rule of a less-than-benevolent government is—in a word—heartbreaking.

Yet what we bring them pales in comparison to what we are given. Being with these sweet and gentle youngsters and their young teachers—feeling their warmth, appreciation, gratitude, their eagerness to learn, and their happiness—fills us with a quiet joy of our own. They inspire us with a profound sense of gratitude and hope, and a desire to ensure that the radiant light of these children will shine.

My daughter-in-law Stephanie walks with a different group through a different gate, in a different place, Greece, with different children—Syrian, this time—and the same need to offer a sense of solidarity, to listen to the stories of these beyond brave souls who fled their homelands in fear of their lives, *to let them know that they are not forgotten.*

After a few days, the group makes their way to a camp in Germany, where the horror of the Holocaust is only a heartbeat away from the genocide these refugees miraculously escaped. Here they are offered shelter, a place to rebuild their lives in what we pray will be freedom and peace.

Again, those who went to offer solidarity and support returned with so much more than they gave: the feeling that they helped those whom they met to feel human again. Their sense of what it means to be part of the family of humankind deepened, transforming them in ways that perhaps only face-to-face, heart-to-heart encounters can.

They are carrying concrete to create a courtyard for a school in Ghana, painting classrooms in Peru, teaching English to children in Tanzania, and working with disabled children in Viet Nam. This is the work that our children, my grandchildren, and yours, are doing in countries across the world, seeing firsthand the communities they have been trying to help with their fund-raising, consciousness-raising, and letter writing: *letting their "brothers and sisters" on the other side of the world know that they are not forgotten.*

Yet neither have our children forgotten their "brothers and sisters" who live in our *own* communities, whose families are struggling with poverty, illness, and more.

My family is just one of many families whose open hearts have inspired the compassionate actions at the heart of *Tikkun Olam*, bringing blessings to those both close to and far from home. I am in awe of the compassion of so many of our young people, who I imagine absorbed from their families the spiritual wisdom that guides us all—if only we listen to their music.

Blessings for a Wounded Healer

When I empathically enter the world of another, as I am privileged to do as a psychotherapist, things often look different than I initially imagined. This is especially true when my intention has more to do with healing and serving than about helping and fixing (a state in which we tend to focus on the brokenness and lose sight of the wholeness—both in our clients and in ourselves).

Serving reminds us that our *wholeness* is what helps us heal. Wholeness includes not only our strengths, but also our pain, wounds, and struggles—the sources of our compassion and empathy. When I come to my therapeutic work with the intention of serving as well as helping, I experience more mystery than mastery. It is this sense of not knowing, this awe, this possibility, and this connection that makes the work sacred.

We are *all* wounded healers!

So I try to be truly present with my whole self: my beliefs, unconscious prejudices, and limitations, as well as my "expertise." I try to be engaged in a process of mutual recognition where *it's not only my clients* who need enlightenment, but also me. To be with my clients in this way, I try to see more than what's on the surface. I try to hear not only what *is* said, but also what is *not* said; to understand what their experience of the world feels like; to walk in their shoes; to live in their skin. When I look at things from the client's vantage point, from the "inside out," things often make perfect sense. What may be problematic for them is the narrow window through which they view their experience. When I help them to feel understood, then together we open the window a bit wider, allowing them to glimpse other perspectives that can go a long way toward untangling the knots of frustration, misunderstanding, and anger.

 **Ellen's Story:**

Ellen was angry, disappointed, and cut off from her Judaism. Her feelings about her faith mirrored her feelings toward her parents. She felt that the God of her tradition was an empty concept characterized by distance and judgment, much the way she viewed her mother. She could not imagine a compassionate and loving God. Yet over the course of our years of work together, she was able to understand and work through the rage she felt toward her parents, and to open and soften her feelings toward them— and not surprisingly, toward God as well.

Amid this process, Ellen connected to a progressive church like the one she had been involved with years before. She enjoyed the music, the presence of like-minded others, and a deep sense of caring among the congregants. She didn't speak to me about belief or doctrine, just about how this warm, welcoming place made her feel like she had "come home," like she was "a child of God." And when she shared with me the teachings of some of the homilies she enjoyed, I was struck by their similarity to those of Judaism—a perfect opening for me to speak more intimately about religion.

So I let her know that while my experience of Judaism was very different from hers, I could understand why she felt as she did. I shared with her that for a long time, I couldn't connect to Judaism as deeply as I would have liked; that I struggled with what didn't resonate with me yet was able to embrace much that did. The issue of religion shifted between being the background and the foreground of our work, until she told me that she was going to be baptized in her new church!

I was stunned, as if I had taken a hard punch to my gut! In my mind, I could see the writing on my tombstone: "She Lost One of the Fold!" It took me a while to process my disappointment and ground myself; to remember that the possibility of her reconnecting to Judaism was *my* hope, *not hers*. But this was not about me.

It was time for *tzimtzum*—time for me to contract, to pull back, and let go of my theories and expectations. I had to create a larger space for Ellen to share her story of what her church meant to her. Listening to her, less encumbered now by my own hopes, I understood how earlier childhood experiences had contributed to her rejection of Judaism and why she felt she had found a spiritual home in her church. The encounters between us became more intimate and alive, giving her "permission" to ask how I *really* felt about all this.

I was able to tell her that, even as I could understand her choice, I felt sad that all that was good and beautiful in our shared heritage would be lost to her. In turn, she explained that although *I* felt that she was rejecting Judaism, *she* did not feel she was giving up her heritage, but rather was deepening her spirituality. In fact, she felt that our work together had been successful in making her feel more expansive; that she was not limiting herself to *one* path but finding a way to have the best of both worlds. Her journey was less about finding religion and more about finding a path leading her "home" to God, to her higher self—to all that she held sacred.

My capacity to understand her at such a deep level expanded my *own* sense of self. The spaciousness that accompanied this understanding allowed me to contain her experience without compromising my own. Paradoxically, learning about and accepting her diminished Jewish identity helped me to deepen my own.

Moments of mutual recognition—I-Thou connections—are the place where compassion is born, both for those with whom we are in relationship, and in our relationship to ourselves. For both Ellen and me, our connection felt so open, honest, and safe that we both experienced it as something sacred.

Yes, God is known through our relationships that transcend boundaries of religion and dissolve divisions between people.

Food for Thought

- How can you experience yourself as being a separate entity *and* part of a larger whole?

- When words fail you, how do you communicate caring and concern?

- If you've felt like a "stranger," how has this influenced the way you relate to others?

- How does it feel for you to recognize the subjectivity of someone whose experiences and feelings are very different from your own?

CHAPTER EIGHTEEN

Elijah, the Prophet

The ego seeks to divide and separate. Spirit seeks to unify and heal.

—Pema Chodron

A FLAWED PROPHET

Like so many of those held in high esteem—celebrities, world leaders, and others who, because of their inflated egos, have fallen off their pedestals—the prophet Elijah fell from his. Yet like some who have redeemed themselves, Elijah did as well.

Elijah became such a beloved mystical figure and prophet that—in addition to being associated with several other rituals, blessings, and holidays in our tradition—he merited *two* rituals in his honor performed at the Seder: Opening the Door for Elijah and Filling the Cup of Elijah. He is remembered as the prophet who would appear to the Jewish people in times of trouble to help those in need, to fight for justice. Because the belief was that he never died but ascended to heaven on a chariot, he could be sent back to earth with a message of hope, inspiring the people to return to God and avoid utter destruction. Elijah would announce the coming of the Messiah, signaling the world's redemption, and he would turn the heart of the parents (God?) toward the children (the people of Israel?), and the hearts of the children toward the parents. Jewish folklore envisioned him as a savior who interceded on behalf of the powerless, bringing them comfort through centuries of persecution and wandering. Out of nowhere and often disguised, Elijah, like a holy Superman, would appear to foil the plot.

Elijah's legacy is one of compassion and kindness, as a doer of good deeds. But this was not always so. When the lesser-known, darker side of Elijah was revealed—a side that accompanied his prophecies and the miracles God worked through him—it cast him in a very different light. It turned out that Elijah was a furious, fire-and-brimstone prophet, at a far remove from the people he hoped to influence and from his legacy as a legal authority. In his zeal for God, he overstepped the boundaries differentiating *prophet* from *God,* separating himself from the people and assuming a stance of God the Father. His ego-driven beliefs were so strong that he could not hear the larger truth until it was too late: that the Divine Spirit would not be found in thunder or in the grand miraculous acts attributed to him.

So filled with righteousness and his professed love of truth, Elijah could not tolerate those who did not see the truth as he did. It took too long for the doors of his heart to open wide enough to hear that still, small voice beneath the thunder. Too long for him to understand that his concern for God's people was too extreme, that his efforts (which may have sprung from a source of innate goodness and belief in the goodness of God) were misguided. Ultimately, he had to hand his mantle on to a disciple. Religious leadership called for guidance and compassion, virtues different from those Elijah possessed.

Yet this overzealous defender of justice became a true messenger of God, beloved throughout our history. How do we understand this? Judaism repeatedly reminds that we are made in the image of God; and Elijah created himself in the image of a wrathful, all-powerful God, imposing his fixed beliefs on the people he tried to protect. Only after he fell from his pedestal, which brought him into the realm of humanity, did he strive to re-create himself in the image of the loving, benevolent, compassionate God he could not see while enamored with his own passions. With the doors of his heart now open, Elijah's better angels prevailed. No longer separating himself from the people he tried to influence, he was at one with them—hearing them, tending them, healing them.

Again, Biblical wisdom reminds us of the complex nature of our humanity. Like Elijah and our forefathers, we may be compassionate, but only to those who think like us. We may be righteous but be too quick to condemn those whose ways we don't understand. And yet we can still be redeemed. Our blemishes are not erased and though they shaped our lives, they don't have to mark us for life. They don't have to determine the people we are to become. Like Elijah and the patriarchs, we earn a place in history because the better angels of our nature transcend our shadows.

God's Unconditional Love

Don't hide them from Me:
the buried, broken,
conflicted, contradictory,
discarded, disowned,
hated, hidden,
shameful, shadowed,
tainted, tarnished
parts of your Self.
You are vast, you are multitudes,
infinitely more than the sum of these parts.
And I love you for all you are.

WAITING FOR ELIJAH

Opening the door for Elijah is a time-honored Seder ritual, a metaphor for the announcement of a redeemed world. It reminds us that "Blood above the door" was the mark of protection to keep our ancestors safe on the night of the tenth plague, which ravaged Egypt. Thousands of years later, we still keep our doors closed for protection from the elements, danger, and intrusion. Yet doors open two ways: as Access or Barrier, Invitation or Rejection.

For the Jewish community, doors have too long represented the latter; the closed doors of ghettos separating us from the rest of the world, doors torn open to drag us from our homes into the night. The scenario repeats itself for different people in different eras. There are still so many closed doors, so much darkness covering Earth. In every corner of the world, from the far reaches of Africa and the Middle East to the hurt and hungry in our own communities, there are those who suffer from countless forms of hatred and ignorance, from unspeakable acts of violence, cruelty, and brutality inflicted by human hearts and hands.

Yet we also remember doors that have been opened by others, Christians who hid us in attics and barns, providing us with food, shelter, and hope. Polish survivors of Auschwitz who returned to their homes after liberation and opened their doors to their fellow Jewish survivors, feeding and clothing them, sheltering them, and binding their wounds. And so, we invoke this openhearted energy each year at this part of the Seder by opening the doors of our homes to invite the spirit of Prophet Elijah's kinder nature in.

We open the door for Elijah with the hope that he will herald the arrival of the Messiah and usher in an era of peace and justice not only for us, but for all humankind. Every year we enact this ritual, and we wait… But how long must we wait before all people can live in freedom, with dignity and equality, before we take the necessary actions to save the planet that nourishes and sustains us? It has been said that Elijah, who brings hope to those in despair, visits the Earth from time to time when the doors of the heart are open and the need for peace is great. That time is now.

And yet according to rabbinic legend, Elijah is already here, although his identity is not revealed to us. There is a story set in Biblical times about Elijah disguised as a leper, sitting at the gates of Jerusalem binding his wounds (today he might appear as one of the homeless people among us). He sat unnoticed as the passersby tended to their own needs. Not a single heart was open to him; his disguise remained intact. He is more than ready to reveal himself, but only when people treat each other, especially a stranger or an unwelcome other, with kindness. The world will not be healed by the Messiah but by our own efforts. Mystical thought tells us that our own ethical behavior has the power to unite *Sh'khinah* with her Divine lover. We are the conduits through which the virtues of Heaven flow to Earth. Hopefully, opening the door for Elijah will open the doors of our hearts, inspiring us to act in ways that will usher in an era of peace and justice for us all.

Another ritual enacted at some Seders is to have guests share their visions of what a redeemed world might look like by pouring a drop of wine out of their cups into Elijah's. It symbolizes our willingness to give up something to achieve our collective dream, because it is only through our shared acts and sacrifices that the world will be redeemed. This is an opportune moment to ask ourselves, "What am I willing to sacrifice for the greater good? For whom can I open a door?"

Opening the Heart

Miracle-maker, peacemaker, prophet of consolation,
it is said that you will return to Earth to usher in
a new age of peace and prosperity—
one that is dependent on our actions,
on the way we treat
each other, all living creatures, and the Earth—
a new age that will be realized only when
we truly practice loving-kindness in all aspects of our lives.

Elijah,
tonight, we do not just sit and wait for you.
We actively feel your presence.
We open our hearts so your spirit can fill our Seder.
Inspired by you, we teach our children
to act with compassion, courage, intellect, and grace,
to hear the Seder ritual as a cry against indifference,
a call for hope, and a commitment to heal and transform the world.

Elijah and Our Sisters

Elijah, compassionate healer, binder of wounds,
we're still waiting for you to grace our planet with your presence.
But the world isn't ready for you.
There are still too many who don't understand
that your arrival is dependent on the ways we treat one another.
But don't despair.
We know your heart breaks as ours do,
so we'll continue to do what we learned from you—
we'll keep reaching out to those who hide in shadows of shame:
our sisters, who mistakenly accept the blame
for being abused, misused, unloved, unlettered,

still fettered—by hatred and ignorance.
With deep humility and respect for all they endured, we'll ask:
"How can we help you make your gifts and beauty shine?
Will you allow us to mentor you, empower you,
even as we learn from you
just how connected we all are?
Because in the end,
there is no 'you' or 'me.'
There is only 'we'
and the space between us where Spirit dwells."

POUR OUT YOUR WRATH

As a response to the periodic massacres of the Middle Ages, the passage *Shefoch Chamatcha* was added to the *Haggadah* in the Elijah section. It is a plea to God to pour out fury and destruction upon all those who have oppressed, and tried to destroy, the Jewish people. Some communities opened their doors and cried out to God, "Pour out your wrath on those who do not know You...," implying that we must be able to express our rage at the violence done to us before the world can be redeemed.

Though crying out for revenge may be natural, we are taught that this passage is a *fantasy to be recited*, not something to be acted out—a cathartic, therapeutic release for those who have known violence and oppression. There are many ways to respond to those who oppress. I like to invoke the insightful interpretation of Beruriah, the revered female second-century scholar of Jewish law, often quoted by the sages. It's refreshing and instructive to hear this woman's wisdom float above the sea of male voices whose authority has been the basis of our laws. With typical feminine sensibility, Beruriah advised that we pray not for the death of the sinners, but for *the death of their sins*. We hear about her wisdom, but not much about the pain that may have inspired it. Not surprising—but more about that shortly.

Important as it is to give voice to traumatic experiences, pain, rage, and trauma, these raw emotions are difficult to express, especially at communal gatherings. Because the *Shefoch Chamatchma* is disturbing and unnerving, many communities have omitted it completely, choosing to sing the plaintive

Elijah chant instead to invoke the spirit of the prophet and healer. And yet some of the rules changed after the Holocaust. For many, the rage could not, should not, be contained; and this section became a deeply resonant passage and a place in the Seder for remembering the many who resisted, the millions who perished, and the few who survived.

How Have We Allowed This to Happen?

Just as we are required to remember the Exodus, the total enslavement of a people, we are inspired to remember the Holocaust, the systematic annihilation of a people. Perhaps when we speak of the ordeal of the victims and survivors on this sacred night, it will ignite a flame, a burning desire to do more than we have done to put an end to the unimaginable depths of depravity to which some humans can sink.

How did this happen, the seeming ease with which one human can turn another into an object, a thing, an "other," an enemy believed to be a threat to what we hold dear, reviled creatures to be exterminated like rodents? As though they were no longer human, no longer professors, farmers, doctors, or poets. As though they were not fathers who read bedtime stories to their children, who taught them to ride their bicycles; or mothers who fed, bathed, loved, and kept their children safe from the monsters under the bed—or from the monsters now at their door....

Let Us Remember

Let us remember all those who were rounded up—
the hardy and the frail,
the grandmothers and toddlers,
the disabled who could no longer walk
and the infants who had not yet learned to walk,
the adolescents discovering the sweet, wild taste of young love,
and those who've grown old together
knowing the sweetness of real love.
All those who were ripped from their homes,
beaten in the streets, crammed into transports to "labor" camps:
Auschwitz,
Bergen-Belsen,

Buchenwald,
Dachau,
Theresienstadt,
Treblinka....

Let us remember those who suffered degradation and humiliation,
those who could not stand up to their captors and those who did,
those who fought and resisted oppression,
those who breathe no more,
and those whose breath miraculously did *not* stop.

We pour out our wrath and plead with You to pour out Yours.
Yet it is not so much Your wrath we seek,
but Your help in ending the senseless slaughter in our midst.
Beneath our rage is profound sadness and helplessness.
After learning of the atrocities
committed behind barbed-wire fences,
we vowed never to forget, never to allow this to happen again.
Yet what we vowed would never happen again, happened again.
Bosnia,
Cambodia,
Rwanda,
Darfur,
Myanmar,
Yemen,
Ukraine.
When will it stop?
When will we no longer have to bear witness to the rising number
of fundamentalists, extremists, and radicals
who are beating, killing, and blowing up "others"
in the name of self-defense, nationalism, patriotism?
How can we make the words "Never Again" *mean* Never Again?

By ensuring that no child
is ever so humiliated, shamed, or demeaned

that he turns his rage on another,
doing to the "other" what was done to him.

By ensuring that every child feels loved, valued, and cherished
so they see the value and the divinity in everyone,
and no one is made to feel the sting of being labeled as "other."
By modeling compassion, teaching tolerance, and remembering
that as different as we may be,
we are all members of the same family,
the family of humankind.

May the lives of all who perished not have been in vain.

Remembering Beruriah's Wisdom and Courage

Because we don't hear much about the women who contributed to our history, they are often portrayed as one-dimensional figures. We hear of Beruriah's wisdom, but not of her courage. Did she acquire her wisdom because she was the daughter of an esteemed rabbi as well as the wife of one? Was she gifted with a particularly intuitive nature at birth, one that inspired even the sages of her time to seek her advice? Or did it arise from the courage and wisdom with which she faced the overwhelming tragedies in her life: it is said that her father was martyred by the Romans, her mother and brothers died violently, her sister was exiled, and she lost her two sons in a single day? Whatever the truth, she is legendary because of her wisdom, courage, and fortitude.

Rather than being remembered because she was able to gently persuade her husband to see the merit of her words without diminishing his ego, she should be acknowledged for challenging the misogynistic attitudes of the men who surrounded her. It pains me even now to write of a story that was superimposed on her character in the Middle Ages by the widely respected teacher Rashi. He wrote that her husband arranged for her seduction by one of his pupils to prove the validity of the Talmudic claim that women are weak-minded and vulnerable to seduction, and that after many refusals, Beruriah finally yielded to the student's sexual advances. I rage at her husband, while my heart aches in learning of her response to his betrayal—she hung herself.

Why was this story written? To prove that if women like Beruriah existed in the second century it was an exception, or perhaps a legend? Even if she were fictional or a composite of more than one woman, why did Rashi need to denigrate the reputation of a learned and righteous woman who could have served as an exemplary heroine for Jewish women? Was he worried that her sarcastic, biting, and arrogant side—as described by the *men* who wrote about her—would incite the women to abandon their nurturing, soothing, and peacemaker sides? I can't help thinking how many men, then—like their contemporary counterparts—wanted to keep the status quo, wanted to keep women well-schooled in suppressing expressions of anger.

Nor can I help but think of the women who have been coming forth in the #Me Too movement. Women who are speaking their truth to power, even though the direct expression of anger, especially at men, makes us "unlady-like," "unfeminine," "un–maternal," "sexually unattractive," or more recently, "strident" or "nasty women," even though they may be ridiculed, disbelieved, accused of seeking attention, or worse. And I think too of those women, like Beruriah, who succumbed to the shame. Let us remember and admire not only Beruriah's wisdom but also her "arrogance" (aka courage), which inspired her to challenge the beliefs of the sages. She could not remain silent. And neither can we.

We—both women *and* men—need to express our rage. We need to speak up, because we are painfully aware that shame breeds more shame, helplessness creates more helplessness, and hatred gives rise to more hatred and violence. Women are speaking out because their anger is energizing them with holy *chutzpah* (nerve/daring), fueling their strength and dedication to work for real change. They're working to change the status quo and to hold accountable those who believe that "male prerogative" includes violating the humanity of women. Like Beruriah, they're using their voices to create awareness of how pervasive this is in our culture, working to bring it to an end. May their courage empower them to stand strong against discrimination and shame. May their voices deepen our capacity for love and compassion and inspire us to connect to each other in more significant, more respectful ways. Expanding on Elijah's mission, maybe such use of our voices will not only turn the hearts of parents toward children and the hearts of children toward their parents but will do the same in the hearts and souls of women and men.

Food for Thought

Elijah

- Who has opened a door for you, and at what personal cost to them?

- Is there someone for whom you can open a door?

- How do you keep your passions from becoming overzealous?

- Have you had to reconcile the admired aspects of your nature with those that evoke shame? How have you done so?

Beruriah

We all experience pain, sometimes injustice, if not trauma.

- How have you dealt with the rage you have experienced?

- Have you sought revenge? Have you sought justice?

- Have you spoken out? Or have you remained silent because speaking out felt dangerous, shameful, or isolating?

- How can you express your rage or anguish in an optimally effective way?

CHAPTER NINETEEN

The Fourth Cup: The Cup of Wholeness

She made broken look beautiful and strong look invincible. She walked with the Universe on her shoulders and made it look like a pair of wings.

—Ariana Dancu

INTEGRATING ALL DIMENSIONS OF OUR BEING

To see ourselves as Whole, we must see ourselves in our fullness, to accept the complexity of our humanity—both the loved and less-loved aspects of our nature—as more than just the fragmented parts of our being. And so, this cup speaks to our ability to integrate the different dimensions of our beings: our materiality and our spirituality, our uniqueness and our common humanity, our weaknesses and our strengths. Like our biblical ancestors who were troubled as well as triumphant, for us our potential for growth and transformation lies in the wholeness of our being, not in our parts.

As we move closer to the end of our Seder, a sense of gratitude rises in us as we recount our escape from *Mitzraim*: from Egypt, and from the *Mitzraim* of the mind. We review the progression of The Four Cups and their three-tiered concerns: the enslavement of our ancestors, our own constrained lives, and the constraints on women in our tradition.

The First Cup was dedicated to *Awareness*: our ancestors' growing awareness of the pain of physical, political, and spiritual enslavement; our emerging awareness of the psychological imprisonment in our personal lives; and women's evolving awareness of their patriarchal enslavement in our own tradition and beyond.

The Second Cup was dedicated to *Healing*: our ancestors' journey to heal from a slave mentality and learn to think for themselves; our personal journeys of healing from the behaviors and habits that no longer serve us; and women's healing from the yoke of patriarchy—giving up some measure of "security" in the service of autonomy.

The Third Cup was dedicated to *Connection*: our ancestors' connection to their God and their community, to achieve what couldn't be achieved alone; our own growth from seeing ourselves as separate beings to embracing a consciousness of connection; and women's expanding connection to other women, to create a feminist movement.

And now the Fourth Cup, dedicated to *Wholeness*, reminds us of the different facets of our being—how they contribute to the fullness of who we are, and how each of us is part of something larger than our singular selves. Just as our individual lives are part of the greater whole of humanity, so is Judaism a thread in the tapestry of the rich and varied religious and spiritual paths of the world. I am heartened to know that while all branches of Judaism work steadfastly to maintain our identity, there is also an openness to learning from the diverse traditions of the larger world and sharing their spiritual wisdom. While we may never have one universal religion, I would love to see the establishment of an interreligious organization—a United Nations of Religions. Such a body would promote respect and collaboration among different faiths and facilitate the goal of all religions: to create an enduring connection to a Higher Power, find meaning in our lives, live according to our values, and pave a path toward personal and world peace.

Blessing the Fourth Cup

B'ruchah at Yah, Eloheinu Ruach ha olam, boreit p'ri hagafen

Blessed are You, Spirit of the Universe, who creates the fruit of the vine.

We thank You, for making us aware
of the narrow places in our lives that yearn to be free.
May that longing be fulfilled.
We thank You, Source of All Life, for healing
the narrowness in our still-too-broken world.
May it soon become a more welcoming, spacious, and safe place for all.
Thank You, Holy One of Being, for helping us weave connections
between our internal divisions and those between ourselves and others.
May we continue to strengthen the ties that bind us to each other and You.
Thank You, *Sh'khinah*, Divine Mother, for loving us in our wholeness,
for helping us to learn to love ourselves, to be at peace with ourselves,
for all we are.

Being Peace

Bringing unity to humanity is a noble goal, perhaps even an impossible dream. But what if each of us were to work toward creating a freer, more peaceful world starting with ourselves—with the freedom and peace that we feel inside? In the spirit of *Dayenu*, maybe that would be enough. As esteemed Buddhist monk, spiritual leader, and peace activist Thich Nhat Hanh taught, we must *be peace* to make peace. As he put it, the depth of our consciousness is like a garden that holds many varieties of seeds. If we water the seeds of love, understanding, and acceptance, every day we will cultivate our capacity for compassion and peace.

But our gardens also contain seeds of ignorance, fear, and hatred. We all have the capacity to seek suffering for those whom we believe caused us to suffer. Watering those seeds will make them stronger, too. But what if we could *pause* when we feel hurt, and remember that others' actions may have come from their own hurt or limitations and have little to do with us? If we don't take their actions personally, we may find that we don't need to strike back or seek revenge. And by taking a deep breath, we may find ourselves with space to make better choices.

What if we let the light of compassion shine on our fears—if instead of reacting to them, we could see them as states of mind that let us know that something in our lives may need attention? If we can stay with them long enough, we may come to understand their origins and how they served us at one time, maybe even protected us, but no longer do. We may begin to seek healthier ways to feel safe and whole, accepted and loved. Seeing ourselves in our totality, aware of both our lightness of being and the darker, less-loved parts of ourselves allows us to embrace the fullness of our existence. The kind of garden we choose to grow is up to us. The choice is ours—but only if we accept the wholeness of our being and nurture the attributes we wish to see prevail. To help create peace in the world, we must cultivate it in ourselves, nourishing it in our hearts.

Perhaps one way to do this is to work towards a state of equanimity—to try to go with the flow of life, to know that we are part of a cosmic cycle of darkness and light, growth and decay, sweetness and sorrow, trials and triumphs. To remember the words of the nineteenth-century poet Rainer Maria Rilke:

> Let everything happen to you.
> Beauty and Terror.
> Just keep going.
> No feeling is final.

No feeling is final. Not the beauty of cherished moments, nor the terror we feel when we are overwhelmed by the dark moments in our lives, the experiences that shatter us and convince us that we can never be put back together again. It is true that we may be forever changed—we will never be again as we once were; the broken pieces will live on in us like the shards of the broken tablets living alongside the Ten Commandments. But with time to grieve and space to grow, they can become sources of insight and compassion, helping our hardened hearts begin to open again to love; reminding us of the intimacy, tenderness, memories, and wisdom that survive our losses.

But how do we move from brokenness toward wholeness, from narrowness to expansiveness?

The Exodus as a Journey Toward Wholeness

The Exodus, our ancestral journey that began close to four thousand years ago, continues to unfold. Just as our forebears moved from the narrowness of their *Mitzraim* to the Promised Land, each of us can move from the narrow places in our own lives toward becoming more expansive. But these journeys often take us through uncharted waters, through the depths of the misty, shadowy underworld of our psyches. And the only way to get from here to there is by allowing ourselves to feel the ache in our souls that lets us know that something is desperately in need of our attention, and by realizing that denying or disregarding the source of our pain—our vulnerabilities and limitations—will only prolong the journey, preventing us from attaining the more spacious, peaceful ways of being we long for.

How to navigate this journey was a central question for Rebbe Nachman of Breslov, the eighteenth-century Hasidic spiritual master, guide, and "mystic for modern times" whose teachings are particularly relevant to the all-too-familiar angst of the twenty-first century. His prescription for healing and wholeness was both spiritual and practical: if we are to transcend the inner emptiness, he said, we must integrate the diverse physical and spiritual elements of our beings.

Having experienced depression for much of his short life, he understood negative emotions to be an inescapable aspect of our humanity, but he knew all too well that disowning them was not the path that would help us feel more whole. Quite the opposite: only by accepting them—by shining the light of inquiry into our internal struggles, confronting the dark holes of our alienated, fragmented selves, and being willing to take responsibility for our own humanity could we begin to heal them—can we become whole.

His teachings focused on hope and joy. He urged his followers to believe that even in the darkness of despair, divine sparks of light are waiting to be released; that truth is the light by which we find our way out of the darkness, and that it is *our* responsibility to turn the light on! He viewed as an important truth the ability to see ourselves in our fullness, to acknowledge and take responsibility for our negative tendencies, and to work to heal/transcend them so that they become *part* of who we are, not *who* we are. And to hold us as we navigate these stormy seas, he stressed the importance of connecting the mind and the heart, empowering the self with faith, simplicity, truth, and finding the good in others and in oneself: "Let the good in me connect with the good in others, until all the world is transformed through the compelling power of love." For Rabbi Nachman, focusing on the good through meditation and prayer could help turn depression into joy. Regardless of what happens to us on our journeys, we can still be grateful for the meaning and love in our lives, and for our ability to live according to our values, knowing that kindness, integrity, and generosity of spirit matter.

"Focus on the good, not on fear" must have been his personal mantra. He tried to live by the words "All the world is a narrow bridge, and the most important thing is not to be afraid." He understood what it felt like to be afraid; but he also knew that—as with all our emotions—fear has a purpose: it cautions us to be aware of danger. Our world, too, is fraught with danger, filled with narrow bridges—just listen to the news, read the papers or the posts on social media. No one is immune to fear. It is real. Yet "not to be afraid" doesn't mean not feeling fear; it means not being rendered powerless by it. A more accurate translation of Rabbi Nachman's counsel is "the most important thing is not to be *immobilized* by fear."

Reb Nachman's teachings focused on working with and managing our fears so that they don't stop us from living, from moving forward. In this way, we move ahead despite them; we learn to cope with them, to take the next right action. To keep us moving forward, this biblical guru asked: "If you are not a better person tomorrow than you are today, what need have you for a tomorrow?" His teachings built on the lessons from the Exodus regarding our psychological freedom: our ability to grow, to change, and to transform our lives from narrow ways of being to more expansive ones; from being immobilized by our fears and insecurities to transcending them so that we can become the people we want to be.

In my own process of "transformation," I've often experienced a strong need to do more to help heal the world, to be a "better person tomorrow" than I am today. But attached to this desire was a fear of being judged as pretentious, as standing out, apart from others, which caused me to limit myself and keep myself "small"—in my dreams, my aspirations, and my impact on others. But why the fear? I've worked mightily to shed my constricted way of being. I've come a long way; I'm more expansive and comfortable owning my needs and desires. And then I understood: I was carrying the remnants of my childhood trauma. The body-memory of *using* my voice was still unconsciously linked to *losing* my voice. If I screamed as I had as a child, about the suffering in the world and thought that somehow, *I* could help heal it, I would stand apart from others. People would see me as being self-important. They would shun me. Silence me.

I needed to reframe my thinking. I had to name my emotions, feeling them once again in my body, and noting what I've done to create a new narrative. Another help was noting my work with clients: how my focus has always been on the "leading edge"—on their gifts, not on their deficits, conveying my belief that by shining our inner light, we help illuminate the world, lighting the way for others.

Didn't this apply to me as well?

If I have been given the ability to help heal, how does minimizing or withholding that gift serve anyone? I shifted my perspective: helping others to speak their truth, to feel more whole—as I have been helped by my mentors and teachers to become more whole—was what I was meant to do. Especially because my belief that *becoming more whole inspires others to do the same* is embedded in my work.

I thought about the words of one of my clients: "After we focused on my need to stand up for myself, I finally asked my supervisor for what I needed. I was shaking like a leaf, and I almost persuaded myself to just let things be as they were. But my heart ached for my daughter, who I could see was beginning to follow in my footsteps. That's what gave me the courage to speak up. If I were to teach her how to take care of herself, my words alone wouldn't be enough. I had to model a better way of taking care of myself. I had to use the voice and the strength I had within me to give her permission to use hers."

Another client's journey came to mind, and with it the Talmudic teaching, "To save one life is to save the world" (Sanhedrin: 37). I remember her words clearly: "I feel like I'm watching myself in labor giving birth to a new life, a new *me*—and I like the '*me*' I'm becoming. Sometimes the pain is excruciating, but it's also liberating. The freedom to be who I was meant to be, to do what I was meant to do is such a gift. I don't know what I'll do to make this world a better place, but somehow, I know I will. Even if I bring light to just one person's life, I'll feel I'm fulfilling my life's purpose. That's the biggest blessing."

Witnessing my clients' resilience—their willingness to endure the painstaking process of change; their efforts to release the past so they can move into the now and the new; how they are turning brokenness into beauty—fills me with a sense of awe and gratitude for how much I learn from them. Like my client wanting to be a liberating model for her daughter, I too needed to model for my clients that I can use my voice and my strength to be with them as they deal with their difficulties, allowing my inner light to kindle theirs. When I do this, I feel I am helping to heal the world—one person at a time! This is not pretentious. It is a gift for which I say, "thank You." I still want to be better tomorrow than I am today, but I now know *it's not about doing more*; it's about *doing what feels right*, aligning my values with my actions, and not focusing on the judgments of others. Everything I do to help heal myself will help heal others. Which brings up another nugget of wisdom from Reb Nachman: "Work at not needing approval from anyone else and you will be free to be who you really are."

On Brokenness and Wholeness

Imagine if we expanded our understanding of life to know that we are *all* "shattered vessels"; if we knew from the start that brokenness, like darkness, is not "bad"; that often, it's the place where Light can enter. What if we really understood Rabbi Nachman's teaching that "a broken heart is simply a sign of our humanity…a gateway to healing," as well as the Kabbalist teaching that pain and suffering are inevitable—that *all* of life is in need of healing—which is possible even when (*especially* when) our lives feel most hopeless? Though we may not think of it in this way, healing—becoming more whole—is a holy process. It's no coincidence that the words "heal," "holy," and "whole" all share the same root.

How much more resilient might we be if we could believe in our hearts that even what we lose doesn't have to be lost forever? If we had a deep knowing that we can *remember*—put back together—the bits and pieces of what has shattered in our lives, and reweave the fragments into a new whole? This may feel like an impossible task when our lives have been altered so dramatically that some aspects of them are rendered unrecognizable. Still, we are reminded by the eighteenth-century Hasidic master Reb Dov Baer of Mezritch,

"Sometimes we have to sift through the ashes to find a single spark." Though it may feel beyond our grasp, there is always something that survives in us after a loss, something indestructible and eternal that will allow us to begin again. Though we may feel reduced to ashes, our *essence* does not die in the flames; that single spark has not been extinguished.

And from that spark, we can begin to remember all that is precious in life and live from the values at our core with grace and dignity. Our capacity to give and receive love—to live with courage, strength, and compassion—is eternal. We can find a way to remain open to life after sustaining a tragic loss. We can become more compassionate to ourselves and to others. In time, we can live with renewed purpose; we can become part of some meaningful change in the world and do what we can so that our suffering will not have been in vain. We can find beauty and meaning in unexpected places, hope and love in the smallest gestures; we can rebuild our lives and rise from the ashes. We can transform the weight of the world on our shoulders into wings that lift us to a higher place.

Perhaps that spark is what we call God, Soul, or Spirit—the force that pushes us to go on being, to choose life despite the dark, uncertain times ahead. Perhaps it is the feeling that we are part of something far greater than our individual lives, part of the Universe's enduring patterns—birth and death, creation and destruction, ebbing and flowing—which allow us to feel held in our suffering, to know that although we are in the dark, we are not alone. That, in the somber stillness, a life force quietly pulses within us, pushing us to reach for the light that we don't believe will come.

Expanding Our Understanding of Darkness

It helps to expand our understanding of this realm by remembering that *all* creation begins in chaos—in the dark, silent womb of the Divine, where seeds are held in Eternal connection, awaiting birth and growth: a baby in its mother's womb; tender shoots in the dark earth; creativity and visions in our dreams. Within darkness are seeds of Light.

And it helps to remember the wisdom of our tradition: that the days of our lives begin in darkness and move toward light. It's comforting to know that each new day begins with the *setting* of the sun the evening before, rather than when it rises—as it is written in Genesis, "There was evening and there was morning." But this view is also at the core of Jewish philosophy, which holds that we are on upward journeys from darkness to light, that our challenges can be pathways to illumination.

In the Jewish tradition, we face the darkness—the night—with the *Sh'ma,* the quintessential Jewish expression of faith; the prayer that teaches us to see all of life, the dark and the light, as part of a Whole. Accepting the darker dimensions as an aspect of the Divine is a testament to our faith in God's Oneness.

This hidden, mysterious realm flows softly beneath the surface, animating our lives, inviting us into the silent space of self-reflection, where we can come to know ourselves at the deepest levels of being and hear the soul-whisperings of the Divine: "Come, sit close to me. Be still. 'Just be.' Stay here until your pain turns into compassion, your suffering into strength, your mourning into dancing. Stay until you return, once more, to your Self. Your beautiful broken, mended, whole Self. You are not alone. I am with you."

Sh'khinah's Blessing

In the quiet of your mind,
in the stillness of your heart,
in the depth of your soul,
I am with you.
Living within you, moving through you,
I dwell in you
as Peace and Wholeness,
as Softness and Strength,
as Compassion and Love
as Understanding and Acceptance
as Openness and Receptivity
as Beauty and as Grace.
Seek me—I will not hide my face from you.
Reach for me—I am as near to you as your own breath.
Return to me—I will lead you home to the Jerusalem of your soul.
I am with you. I am you.
We are One.
Listen. Listen.

Bringing *Sh'khinahh* Home

As we focus on Wholeness and a sense of Oneness, it's important to apply this to Spirit's immanent dimension of *Sh'khinah*, the feminine face of the God accompanying the Jewish people on their journeys and in their exile throughout history. As our Divine Mother, She accompanies all of us in our spiritual exile, when we are suffering, broken, lost or afraid. When we long for a mother's touch She is right there, holding us in a maternal embrace—especially when we are wandering or stuck in the darker dimensions of being. Since the Kabbalistic period, She has been depicted as being in exile along with Her people, going into the places of our pain and suffering in order to enliven us again, making Her pulsing energy felt in our daily lives.

With the current resurgence of spirituality and the growing interest in alternative healing practices, which values the nurturing qualities associated with the Goddess and the Divine Mother, as well as the mystical notion that Her presence exists within all things (stones, plants, animals, and humans), Her energy is flourishing. Though we still have far to go toward creating the kind of world She would want for all of us, Her consciousness—with its goddess-like attributes of love, empathy, connectedness, healing, and nurturance—is on the rise. Acts of kindness and compassion are activating Her presence, which is palpable.

I'd like to reframe our thinking about *Sh'khinahh* energy and focus less on exile and more on Presence—how this energy dwells within us wherever we are. How women are embodying Her attributes of intuition and compassion—opening to and owning the wisdom of who we truly are. How the feminine traits of intuition, collaboration, and cooperation are coming to redefine the meaning of strength—taking its place alongside the prevailing masculine energy, joining it in sacred union, becoming a powerful source of creation and empowerment. Our Divine Mother knows that balancing and integrating the two energies is the way for us all to grow more whole; the way to create the change we desperately need; and the way we write a new chapter in the evolution of humanity in which all men, women, and children may blossom.

The Fourth Cup brings together the fragmented parts of our lives into a cohesive whole, helping us to expand our understanding of ourselves—physically, emotionally, psychologically, and spiritually—in a holistic way. It helps us see ourselves as sparks of the Divine, as *single drops in the Ocean of God*. Taken together, the four cups are progressive steps along a path that brings us all to a higher level of personal freedom, functioning, and well-being—always in service of creating a more peaceful, just, and free world.

Food for Thought

- How can you "be peace to create peace"?

- How has truth been the light that helped you out of the darkness?

- How have you been able to reweave the fragments of what felt shattered into a new whole?

- How has *Sh'khinah* consciousness impacted the way you move in the world?

CHAPTER TWENTY

Hallel: Praise

*Our goal should be to live life in radical amazement, to get up in the morning
and look at the world in a way that takes nothing for granted . . . .
To be spiritual is to be amazed.*

—Rabbi Abraham Joshua Heschel

THE SACRED UNDERPINNINGS OF PRAISE

What is it about praise that makes the heart expand? It's about being touched by wonder, beauty, small acts of kindness that make our hearts sing—"Thank You, thank You, thank You." Gratitude grows into praise for the privilege of being alive!

Hallel asks us to put aside our intellect and experience the emotional joy of freedom—to allow ourselves to feel transported from anguish to elation, from mourning to celebration, from slavery to freedom. It is said that songs, psalms, and poetry are expressions of a joyful soul, a way to break out of oneself and reach for freedom.

At traditional Seders, the *Hallel* section praises God for the countless blessings bestowed on us. Yet the sheer volume of psalms—those that thank God for liberating us from Egypt and those that express hopes for future redemption—often don't speak to the more secular among us, who experience the repetitive praises to God as "over the top," making them question why we worship a God who is so in need of adoration and praise.

But that misses the point of praise. The Holy One does not need our praise, does not need to be adored. The point of praise is that it awakens *our* capacity to be amazed by the everyday miracles in our own lives—the occurrences that go beyond our expectations or comprehension, the ones we experience when we're truly alive and awake. The word Jew (*Yehuda*) comes from the Hebrew word *hoda'ah*: to give thanks. The root of all our blessings is the awareness of these miracles.

So while this step of praising is often omitted or abbreviated at many contemporary Seders, at others it has become a space where the traditional liturgy is distilled down to its essence. This gives participants an opportunity to express gratitude to the invisible, ineffable Power/Spirit in the Universe, Who evokes the feeling that *it's a blessing just to be alive*. To be part of an ongoing story of creation. To experience beauty. To ease suffering. To move through the world with compassion and courage. To know joy and love. To know that the power of this love can heal the brokenness of the world. Because even amidst darkness, there is light; amidst death, there is life; amidst hate, there is love. Remembering this, we can share the philosophy that Leonard Cohen expresses in his evocative song, "Hallelujah": that even when things go wrong, we can stand before the Lord of Song, with just one word on our tongues—Hallelujah!

I've enjoyed hearing voices sing praises to the One for opening them to awe and wonder—for blessing them with something that has touched them deeply—for inspiring them to work for the change they want to see in the world. The *Hallel* is a perfect place in the Seder to offer a spontaneous blessing, sing a joyful song, or just pause to take in the magic of the moment. Or—in the spirit of the words of Oscar Wilde that "imitation is the sincerest form of praise"—to emulate the Holy One by conferring kindness and compassion on others, making each day a song of praise to God.

What moves *you* to express gratitude? A child's first words, a walk on the beach, a song you love, a return to health? What if *Hallel* is more than a step in the Seder? What if we infused our lives with the awareness of the blessings that so often go unnoticed? If we took nothing for granted? If we made the "attitude of gratitude" a practice, might we experience what research reveals: that such a practice becomes reflected in our bodies, with increased levels of hormones that create a sense of well-being; that it improves mental and physical health, leads to greater empathy and less aggression, and fosters resilience? Might our gratitude organically grow into praise?

A Moving Experience

My husband and I were more than eager to sell the house that we had made our home for forty-six years; we were ready to begin the next chapter of our lives. And finally, we had buyers. Except that on their end, they had just four to six weeks to move in!

This felt like an impossible task. We hadn't yet begun the painstaking process of discarding the accumulated keepsakes of a lifetime—books, photos, records, report cards, camp letters, drawings.... We weren't even clear on where we wanted to relocate. And the one area where we had hoped to rent held very little promise.

Overwhelmed both emotionally and physically, we kept telling ourselves that we would find a way to make it work—and then we'd be inundated with doubt, apprehension, and fear. Sometimes we were both on the same page; other times, one of us had to hold the other up. And all this was happening while I had to prepare to lead another Women's Seder! I couldn't renege on my commitment, but I didn't know how I could do it all. My head hurt from thinking about the task in front of me.

Yet at some point, I remembered one of the truly valuable lessons of the Exodus: often the seas don't part until you take the plunge! So, like my ancestors, I got into action mode, put one foot in front of the other, and kept doing what I had to do. Day after day, with some help, I went through closets, cabinets, and crawlspaces. I pondered, cried, discarded, and packed. I prayed that Spirit would guide me to do what I had to do, both in the move and in leading the Women's Seder. I wanted to be able to lead it with a sense of calm and confidence, but my frazzled and fatigued state was taking its toll on me physically and mentally.

I forced myself to take some time to sit in stillness, to hear the voice of Spirit. In the quiet of my mind, I heard Her pointing me to the Passover miracles of old—that a path through the sea of apprehension would open.

I took the story to heart. I kept it in my mind when I was in Seder mode, when I was packing, when I was working. It became no longer a story for me, but a lifeline to hold onto when I felt like I was drowning. The Exodus narrative became alive for me in a way I had never experienced before. The ancient Israelites were more than my ancestors, my people; they were my relatives. I took comfort especially from the women: my foremothers, my mothers, my sisters, and my aunts. I identified with their strength and their resolve.

I thought about the courage it took to leave the only life they had known for a future that was completely unknown, except for knowing that they would no longer be under the yoke of a tyrant. I envisioned them leaving in the dark of night, carrying with them only what was essential, leaving all else behind: the grains stored to feed their families, the herbs and plants to soothe their aches and pains, the tent where they gathered when they bled and birthed. I imagined their fears as well as their faith in the ineffable power guiding them on this journey to a place and a life they did not know. Their story put things in perspective, evoking the gratitude that had been eluding me.

They left with the absolute essentials; I could choose what to leave behind.

They didn't know where they were being led; I could choose where to settle.

They were escaping from slavery along a path to freedom fraught with danger;

I had the luxury of leaving my home for something that better suited my needs.

It took them "forty" years to have a homeland; I'd have a new home within one.

The circumstances couldn't have been more different, but I too was on a journey of liberation—not from the land of Egypt, but from my psychological *Mitzraim.* Although the course ahead of me was strewn with obstacles and challenges, there were shafts of light that illuminated the path. As in meditation, when my mind was filled with doubts and fear gripped my heart, I tried to return to my breath, breathing out the anxiety, breathing in a sense of trust. Again and again, I made attempts to name what I was feeling and to locate the sensations in my body until they slowly subsided. Less overwhelmed now, I was better able to reframe my experience, to see this challenge as an opportunity for growth. Neither the constant self-talk nor self-soothing came easily but come they did. They centered me when I was verging on panic, and I began to find more calm spaces where the uncertainty was tolerable. At times it felt like I was in the presence of Mystery—something that was exciting and held a sense of promise—and I made a concerted effort to be present, open, and receptive to the moment. I learned that I had more strength than I realized; the constriction was giving way to a feeling of expansion. I was so grateful for being part of a tradition whose narrative guided me through a challenging time, connecting me to long-gone ancestors who suffered, endured, and prevailed; ancestors whose stories still serve as role models for us all, thousands of years later.

Because I was now personally immersed in the experience, the Women's Seder felt particularly meaningful to me. As did the family Seder I hosted in our home about two weeks afterward and just a few weeks before our actual move. This "Last Supper" was a bittersweet evening, with the emphasis on sweet. We all felt some sense of loss, knowing that this was the last time we would be sitting around our dining room table together in this home, celebrating Passover. We reminisced about Seders past, still connected to those who were no longer with us but whose presence was still felt, and we looked forward to whatever form our future Seders might take. There was a palpable sense of excitement for our new adventure. Mostly, the immediacy of our situation made the messages of the Exodus more meaningful, helping us all to feel "as though we were personally leaving *Mitzraim*," our own narrow places.

Then, just when my husband and I had almost despaired of finding a place we could call home, we did! We closed the door on the home and the life we had known, with a deep sense of gratitude for having been able to live for so long in a home that was good for and to our family. We were ready for a new family to love and care for it as we once had, and we offered them our blessings. In return, the new occupants blessed us for helping make their dream happen. And for offering them many of the books we had collected over the years. The man of the family, a proud father of two young daughters, told us: "I didn't have books in my house, growing up, but it's something I've always wanted for my girls. So, thank you, bless you." It was one of those beautiful moments of connection.

And when we finally opened the door to our new home and the next chapter in our lives, it was with a song in our hearts and praise to the Mystery and Spirit that had brought us here.

A JOYFUL EXPERIENCE OF PRAISE

Praise and Song inspire fulfilling the injunction to "make a joyful noise unto God." We are told that in ancient times, men were the musicians and singers of our Temple rituals, and women were the teachers, the song-leaders, the weavers of melody and drummers of spirit. We still are. Our voices have become even more clear, confident, beautiful, and resonant. We make joyful noises with song, dance, in our poetry, prose, and in our art. Sometimes it's a loud expression that bursts from our spirits in wild abandon, like the singing and dancing at many Women's Seders.

I remember the first *Ma'ayan* Women's Seder I attended. Thanks to Debbie Friedman and her drummers of Spirit, there was much joyful singing and clapping at each table. But when they played her version of *Hallelu*, Spirit inspired me to get up from the table, take the hands of the two women on either side of me, and dance around the table. Within moments, each woman took the hand of another, who took the hand of yet another, and another, until there was an unbroken, undulating line of women weaving in and out around the tables. It was pure joy!

But joy isn't always expressed with wild abandon. Sometimes, it's a quiet expression of praise and gratitude for all that is good and beautiful in the world. Sometimes silence is praise.

Thank You, *Sh'khinah*

Thank You, *Sh'khinah*, Mother of Compassion,
Healer of heavy hearts,
for Your ongoing, in-dwelling presence.
You carry us on eagle's wings
and help us transcend the woes of our world
by illuminating all that is beautiful and good,
by returning us to Gratitude, Mystery, and Presence.

Walking in the woods, along a leaf-strewn path,
I look down and feel the colors inside me,
crimson and gold, brilliant and muted,
bright yellow, coppery orange, green leaves
whose youth have faded.
Their energy warms me, fills me, and flows through me,
like the birds and geese that fly overhead
and the silent sound of ducks paddling home.
My heart leaps with unrestrained joy to be so close to You.

Being here, with senses heightened,
I remember that I, too, am part of Your glorious Creation.
I, too, shed my leaves and let them fall,
and return to the earth so that new buds may blossom.
One by one, I work at shedding my narrow ways…
of needing to know what lies around the next corner,
of doubting myself, instead learning to trust myself and You,
to be open and receptive to possibilities and surprises that delight.

Made in Your image, the One whose breath
created the trees, the birds, and fish…
a world where all is subject to ebb and flow,
I, too, am a work-in-progress,
continually creating and re-creating my life.
My branches grow higher as I move
toward becoming my Highest Self
reaching for You.

And all You ask of me is to aspire toward the
highest, deepest, and widest
love and freedom
of which I am capable,
to live with generosity of heart and spirit,
to listen to my silent yearnings,
to give voice to the songs in my heart.

And so, I offer songs of Praise to You,
Halleluyah!

 ### *Elsa's Story:*

Elsa was going through an early midlife crisis. Her marriage to a "really good man who truly loves me" felt stale, just as her career did, despite creative attempts to revitalize both. She craved a sense of passion, wanting to connect to the sense of aliveness she had felt earlier in life "when everything felt new and exciting. I was totally energized by my profession; I still felt the high of the 'honeymoon' phase, by our discovering each other and places in the world we never thought we'd see...."

Elsa just wanted to feel happy again. But she was driven, always on her way "somewhere" to find that "something" that would make her feel fulfilled. Her efforts were linked to circumstances, to externals—a new career, a new home, new discoveries, a better body. If one thing didn't work, she'd find something else. Everything was filled with possibility. Until it wasn't!

Her story reminds me of a teaching story/joke, one I've heard in various iterations, about a man going through a midlife crisis and a divorce. Wanting a different kind of life, job, and wife because the old ones were simply not enough, he went through a total makeover. He lost weight, toned his muscles, dressed in designer clothes, got a new car and a new hairstyle. On his way out of the salon, a bus hit him. And he screamed, "God, all I wanted was to be happy, how could you do this to me?" To which God replied, "To tell you the truth, I didn't recognize you!"

Elsa came to see me at the point in her life when she felt a bus had hit her emotionally. She was devastated by a series of setbacks: feeling harassed and undermined at work, the sudden loss of her father, and a pervasive sense of emptiness—all of which left her feeling ashamed, unlovable, and alone. Her pain drove her to "work the program" in therapy and outside of it. With the same urgency that characterized her way of being in the world, she found books and podcasts that elaborated on the themes that resonated with our therapeutic work. She took a course in meditation and downloaded more self-help apps to her digital devices than I knew existed.

And they were helpful. They laid the groundwork for cultivating the presence to be with her emotions. Mostly, she was willing to be still enough in our sessions to feel whatever was happening in the moment: the emptiness, the sadness, the fullness…. It was not easy, but it was good for her to be able to be with herself, to stay with herself. As an "attitude of gratitude" became her focus of attention and intention, she became more present to her own bodily sensations. She experienced the process of creating new body memories—the way her body softened, and her heart opened when she tasted the sweetness of gratitude. Elsa began to understand that what she was looking for was within her.

Which reminds me of another story: Here, God is pondering the issue of how humanity could find the key to happiness and wondering where to place this elusive quality. The answer is revealed when a rabbi suggests placing it right in the human body, in the heart—the last place people look!

Elsa worked on training her body-mind with the same dedication she brought to strengthening her body, as though she were enrolled in a "gratitude gym." She did the exercises offered in the workbooks and talks. She made it a point to reach out to people with both random and intentional acts of kindness, offering smiles, compliments, and heartfelt compassion, and she savored the reciprocated kindness, especially when students and colleagues noticed how radiant she looked.

I could feel myself smiling at Elsa's astonishment when she realized that her previous "small, empty life" had somehow expanded dramatically. And yet the only thing that had changed was the way she looked at it, including her new-found awareness of the everyday miracles that were already part of her life: the pleasure she got from gardening, from the sense of mastery she felt as a potter, and from the scent of the woods when she hiked or ran.

She continues to pursue many of the same activities, but now with less of the craving and grasping that ultimately blocked the happiness she was seeking. A bright and determined student, Elsa has resolved to let go of her "have-to-have it" attitude. She has resolved to accept that life will not always cooperate with her wishes—that it will hurt and disappoint—and to accept "what is," trusting that the Universe will provide what she needs, and often, what she wants. Both in our sessions and on her own, she works to track when she gets *off*-track, practicing U-turns (or what we've come to call "*you*-turns")—the pause that helps her to come back to herself, to be present to "what is," to the open heart-space of acceptance.

Elsa is beyond grateful to God for helping her see life with new eyes, for helping her stay more in her heart than in her head as she walks through life; as she ponders what really matters; as she asks herself what stands between her and happiness; and as she hears the answers that spring from her heart. Elsa is passionate in her quest for the kind of happiness that is less dependent on circumstance and more on being present to whatever is and being with her own heart—what Buddhist teacher Tara Brach calls "happiness for no reason."

I never take patients' progress for granted, and Elsa's flowering has made my heart swell. I sing praises for the blessing of participating in a process that has transformed an empty, driven life into one that now feels rooted in acceptance, trust, and gratitude.

Food for Thought

Gratitude is an expression of praise to God for all the blessings in our lives, a feeling that can make our hearts sing or take our breath away. *To praise Spirit is to be reminded of the strength we have that sometimes eludes us, and that beneath our pain there is hope, love, and kindness.* This is how *Hallel* heals.

- What are the blessings in your life that you have taken for granted?

- How can you awaken your gratitude, cultivate a spirit of "radical amazement"?

- What do praise and song feel like in your body? Do they feed your soul?

- In what ways are your joy and gratitude reflected in your relationships, in the ways you move through the world?

Gratitude Suggestions

A few ways of cultivating gratitude include:

- Keeping a gratitude journal.

- Keeping a daily list of three things for which you feel grateful.

- Writing a note to someone for whom you feel grateful.

- Bestowing a random act of kindness on someone.

- Savoring the grace of that which evokes gratitude.

- Looking at all the things you have instead of what you don't.

- Focusing more on what you need rather than what you want.

- When you find yourself wanting, seek from a place of fullness instead of from a place of lack. This fullness draws positive energy into our lives, often attracting more abundance.

CHAPTER TWENTY-ONE

Nirtzah: Conclusion

The ache for home lives in all of us.
The safe place where we can go as we are. . . .

—Maya Angelou

"NEXT YEAR IN JERUSALEM"

Most traditional Seders conclude with the iconic words, "Next year in Jerusalem"—an expression of longing to return "home" to Jerusalem, whose name means "City of Peace." How we wish that this city, home to the three Abrahamic faiths—Judaism, Christianity, and Islam—could be a true reflection of its name; a city where Israelis and Palestinians, Jews, Christians, and Muslims can live in peaceful coexistence instead of anxiety and animosity. More than simply the absence of conflict, the name expresses the yearning for it to be a place of abundance, wholeness, and peace; a place where we can share our bounty and the gifts of life; a place that is safe for each of us to be who we are—a metaphor for a perfected world, the Jerusalem of the Heart.

Jerusalem of the Heart

A world where both women and men are strong and empowered,
kind and compassionate, courageous, and vulnerable,
intuitive and wise in the ways of the world,
where welcoming strangers is the most natural thing to do,
and embracing diversity enriches our lives.

A world that teaches compassion instead of fear,
that cultivates the soil so that each of us can blossom
like flowers in a wild and gorgeous country garden —
rich, colorful, and varied.

A world that nurtures its young, cares for its old,
lifts the weak and fallen, humbles the mighty and arrogant,
where no one is subjected to another's will and
no one has power over another or is put down by another.

A world where the competition is less between "us" and "them"
and more between the different aspects of ourselves,
where we transform our more complacent tendencies
into motivation that inspires us to be the best we can be.

A world where Mother Earth is respected and cared for
instead of being heavily trod upon,
where She and all Her creatures are nurtured and sustained,
treated as our partners in this reciprocal dance of life.

Returning Home

Living in the world as we know it, this vision of Jerusalem sounds like an impossible dream. But if we think about the Jewish mystics' concept of humanity, maybe it's not. They imagined us as shimmering threads in the web of Being; complete expressions of the Holy One, the Whole-y One, with each of our lives containing the seeds of all we need to become our highest selves. But they were also cognizant that these seeds are buried beneath our awareness, hidden between layers of consciousness, compelling us to go on endless journeys of exploring, discovering, and remembering before—as the poet T. S. Eliot wrote—we can arrive at where we started and know the place for the first time.

Just as we as Jewish people have a spiritual longing to return to the land of our beginnings, so most of us share a universal, personal longing to arrive "home" at the place where we started; a longing to return to that place where we can be as we are, to be who we were before we learned to conform to societal expectations and the stresses accompanying them; a place where we can remember our essential natures, our innate nobility. The place where we remember who we are.

What lies at the heart of this journey? Could it be that to arrive where we started—to return home—is to know the true nature of our being before we were born, before we lost touch with our basic goodness? To know the natural nobility of the heart—the openness, warmth, and love that abides at our core, unconstrained by fear. To experience the flowing and giving heart is to know and trust ourselves as if for the first time.

This may feel beyond our reach; but might a Jerusalem of the Heart be within our grasp? Some say it's as close to us as our next breath, that heaven and earth are one-tenth of an inch apart, and all that separates them are our own perceptions, the ways we see reality.

The moment we remember that the world of spirit is just as real as the world of materiality, a pathway out of the many *Mitzraims* that keep us locked into narrow spaces appears. The seas part, and suddenly we can see and touch a piece of sky, the Jerusalem of the Heart—a place of wholeness and peace, potential and possibility, Light and Love.

In Jerusalem's golden light, we return to our Selves, and remember the wisdom that was ours before we were born. We can return home—to our essential nature, to our innate nobility— not next year, but now.

Our Essential Nature

Buddhist monk Jack Kornfield tells a story about the ancient clay Buddha that stood in a large temple, north of Thailand's ancient capital Sukotai. It had been tended for five hundred years and revered for its sheer longevity. Storms, governments, and armies had come and gone, but the Buddha endured.

At some point, the monks noticed cracks in the statue, in need of repair. After a stretch of particularly hot, dry weather, one of the cracks became so wide that a curious monk was able to take a flashlight and peer inside. What shone back at him was a brilliant flash of gold! Inside this plain statue, it was discovered, was one of the largest and most luminous images of the Buddha—crafted of pure gold—ever to be created in Southeast Asia. The monks believed that the shining work of art had been covered in plaster to protect it during times of conflict.

In much the same way, we too have encountered threatening situations that led us to cover our innate nobility. Created in the image of God, each of us has a unique purpose that cannot be fulfilled by any other being. We are small but significant parts of an unfolding plan. But just as the people of Sukotai had forgotten about the golden Buddha, so we have forgotten our essential natures. Yet only by accepting and honoring our divinity can we know what we are called to do in this world and when. If we are seeking meaning in our lives, we have to remember who we really are under the exterior coverings.

Remembering Who We Really Are: A Parable

Jewish legend tells us that from the time before time,
when we were safely ensconced in the comfort of the womb,
the Holy One of Being sent a personal angel to sit beside each of us
and teach us all the wisdom we would ever need to know.
And then, just before we were born, the angel "tapped" us
between the nose and upper lip, creating the indention
shared by all humankind,
and all we had learned was forgotten,
including the noble truth of our beings—
Who We Really Are.

In God's wisdom, and as the Buddha also discovered,
the wisdom of the Universe is best retained through self-exploration.
And so we had to forget what we originally knew,
and discover for ourselves what each of our life-journeys is meant to teach—
Who We Really Are.
Beings created in the image of God:

Compassionate, Courageous, and Creative,
Kind, Patient, and Wise, Beings of Goodness,
Wholeness, Peace, and Love.

Because this also happened to our parents,
and they forgot who *they* really were,
they couldn't always express the deep love they felt for us,
and we couldn't see the longed-for gleam in their eyes,
the wordless warmth that would have reminded us of Who We Really Are.
And we took this to mean that we were unloved.
Because we were too young to realize that they were only human,
with burdens and wounds of their own,
we built walls around our hearts to soften the pain of not feeling loved.
And the walls grew thicker with every relationship that evoked that memory,
until we lost touch with our own luminosity, our basic goodness.
And we became creatures of all the thought patterns
of our parents, grandparents, all our ancestors,
and all the conditioning that has ever been.
We learned to behave according to the laws of the land,
the customs of our "tribe,"
the traditions of our families—
absorbing their values, attitudes, dreams, and fears.
We learned to obey rules, to be polite.
And we developed ultrasensitive antennae to detect
when our parents were angry, unhappy, or disappointed with us.
Again, without our realizing it,
what appeared to be the Truth of our Being
was most often a "false self," which longed to feel safe and loved,
until we no longer felt the truths of our own hearts.
The thoughts, dreams, and fears of those we loved
too often became our own.
Unaware of this, our lives began to feel dull, dry, deadened—
and we felt unbearably limited and enslaved.

Until one day, we imagined ourselves
breaking out of our conditioned cocoons.

Like the caterpillar who must become less and less a caterpillar
before it can become a butterfly,
we need to become less limited by that "false self"
before we can once again become Who We Really Are.
It was as though we were wearing masks.
And once we realized this, we asked ourselves:
"Is this fearful person really me?
Am I unlovable, unworthy?"
Once we understood that we were
so much more than our limited perceptions—
that we are not our thoughts—
we felt free not to believe them.
Like Moses—who first assumed
that his stammering disqualified him from being a leader,
but then came to believe in that possibility—
we began to let go of one conditioned thought at a time,
one limiting belief that drained us of energy,
one limiting belief that created fear and doubt,
one limiting belief that made us feel defeated.
And we continued to challenge those limiting beliefs
until we felt lighter and more open,
until a sense of freedom came over us,
as though we just had parted the sea.

Then we felt a different kind of Light
surrounding us and holding us in its glow:
a Light that was warm, open, and kind.
It was the Light of *Sh'khinah*,
the feminine face of God,
the Divine Mother of all creation,
of every soul.
Sh'khinah, who cries with us, comforts us, and inspires us.
Sh'khinah, who sings with us, prays with us, and rejoices with us.
Sh'khinah, the Divine Mother, in whose arms we soften and settle.
Like children coming to rest in a sustained maternal embrace,

with space just to be, we felt held, supported, and loved,
part of an ancient timelessness.
Warmed by the glow of our True Self,
with its openness, vitality, and radiant spirit,
we began to remember everything we needed to know.
We began to remember Who We Really Are:
Compassionate, Courageous, and Creative,
Kind, Patient, and Wise.

Toward the Jerusalem of the Heart

I like to think of the Exodus as the beginning of an ongoing process of our evolution that brings us closer to the Jerusalem of the Heart. Though it began with the Israelites' struggle to be free of physical enslavement, the process continued with the struggle to be liberated from the confines of their slave mentality—a significant legacy. They bequeathed to us the belief that "with God, anything is possible." As we continued to grow, collectively and individually, we discovered that just as our God evolved, we could too. We didn't have to be stuck with a limited and limiting one-dimensional view of ourselves; we contain multitudes, free to become our best selves by becoming our authentic, imperfect, loveable, worthy, and whole selves. Many of us learned to become more whole by gathering the split-off, fragmented, less-loved parts of our lives and accepting ourselves in all our complexity—our empathy and our indifference, our compassion and our cruelty. We grew in awareness and acceptance of our own vulnerabilities and limitations, and became more spacious, more present, more compassionate to our own darkness (the seeds from which compassion toward others is born).

And then, slowly, something extraordinary began to happen. Because of our shared humanity, our personal growth toward wholeness inspired a similar growth in those to whom we were connected, helping them feel a greater sense of wholeness and holiness in their individual worlds.

If only it inspired such growth in the whole world, *Dayenu*! It would be enough. But there is still much work to be done. Every generation must live the lessons of the Exodus, remembering that freedom from physical enslavement is just the first, imperative step on an ongoing journey. Then we must free ourselves from our own personal *Mitzraims*, the narrow, constricted consciousness where our inner Pharaohs enslave us. *If returning to who we really are—Beings of Love, Wholeness, Goodness, and Peace—is our destination, then we must honor the gift of our freedom to grow. This journey is not out of reach; it isn't in the heavens, and it isn't across the sea. It is as near to us as our breath, it is in the words we speak, it dwells in our open hearts. This is the healing message of Nirtzah.* And while absolute freedom, peace, and wholeness may be unattainable, they are goals toward which we must strive with our whole being, focusing on them much as desert travelers train their eyes on the one guiding star that will lead them home.

Our Guiding Star

May the star that leads us home be our commitment
to honor our roots and tend to the soil of our ancestors' teachings.
May their wisdom bring us closer to the Jerusalem of the Heart.
May every generation be inspired to plant seeds of its own,
so that our tradition will always be a Tree of Life
that keeps growing, living, and giving.
May its roots grow deep and wide, with branches reaching toward heaven,
bearing fruit for body and soul.
May our Tree keep blossoming beyond the desert—
scattering its seeds in every soul and in the soul of the world—
with all we need to grow in Love, Wholeness, Goodness, and Peace—
bringing us home…where we can be who we are.

A PERSONAL LOOK BACKWARD AND FORWARD

The Exodus was a journey that began with our ancestors' *Mitzraim*—their enslavement in Egypt—and ended with their liberation. As slaves, they were voiceless; but with freedom, their voices keep echoing through the generations. My personal journey mirrors that of my ancestors in that I, too, had been voiceless, constricted in my own *Mitzraim*, and had to wander through the wilderness before I felt free to use my own voice.

As I embarked on my quest for a more authentic, expansive spiritual life, I braced myself for the trek, knowing that there would be no clear paths in the wilderness. And I learned that if I were willing to look under its countless stones, I could find my way. Leaving few of those stones unturned, I eventually found a connection to the profound wisdom of my tradition and to *Sh'khinah*. This bond transformed the Seders of my childhood, marked by anxiety, into a joyful and meaningful ritual that fills me with a sense of pride and gratitude. This bond transformed and healed me.

The ritual also eased my fear that the Judaism I have come to love would be lost to my grandchildren and was my inspiration to create the kind of Seders that would nurture an appreciation of our heritage. I look at all my children and grandchildren with such pride; they are each, in their own way, embodiments of the best of our tradition, compassionate carriers of *Tikkun Olam*. To think that our family Seders helped them to appreciate previously unrecognized aspects of our tradition and has contributed to the development of their values makes me eternally grateful. While for the most part my children and grandchildren are not involved with organized religion, they personify the spiritual qualities religion seeks to nurture and cultivate—compassion, kindness, courage, wisdom, a strong sense of justice, and generosity of spirit. This is what I pray will be preserved for future generations, along with the source from which these values came.

On a broader note, when I think about the Passover Seder, I'm still struck by the irony that the women—those on whom so much of the Exodus depended—have been mere footnotes in our people's Story. Would our ancestors have been redeemed without the courage and creativity of the midwives Shifra, Puah, Miriam, Yocheved, and Batya? How different would the world be if they hadn't challenged the prevailing patriarchy of our tradition, and if so many courageous women throughout history hadn't done similarly? I like to think that they were role models for what it means for contemporary women to have the courage of their convictions, to be the inspiration for women today to become engaged in activism and seek the political power that has long been denied them. I can't help but think that some of the unspeakable events that have happened in our broken world might have been far less likely to occur had we been guided by the energy of the Divine Mother. We have made much progress, but we have not fully left *Mitzraim* when there are still so many who are enslaved, politically or psychologically; who are designated as "other," the stranger among us, who are discriminated against. This is not the Promised Land.

And so we must continue to build on the forward movement that we have made. What gives me hope that we will do so is witnessing the arc of history bending back to its beginnings: honoring once again this feminine energy, whose roots are so intertwined with the early Goddess culture. With all the *Sh'khinah* energy that today's women are bringing into their lives and into their rituals—making Seders more creative, innovative, and meaningful—comes the hope and the confidence that our Story, which is all our stories, will continue to be told. Like ripples in a pond, its messages will reverberate in ever-widening circles, touching others; and our healing, our becoming more whole will contribute to the healing of the world.

BRINGING THE SEDER TO A CLOSE

The Seder is ending. We look back on the evening—the warmth of family and community, breaking "bread," drinking wine, eating, laughing, praying, and talking with one another. We look back at the moments that opened our hearts, filling our eyes with tears of sadness and of joy.

And we look forward. How will we carry the hope and inspiration, the sense of community, wonder, and gratitude of this evening into the year ahead? Are there commitments that we have made this night, to realize our dreams of a future world built on love, peace, justice, and wholeness? How will we implement them?

Let these questions serve as an intention for each of us to take one action toward fulfilling our vision of building a true Jerusalem.

Food for Thought

I hope that the Seder's healing legacy and the ancient wisdom offered on these pages speak to your lives today—especially to the women who, for far too long, have lived in a psychological *Mitzraim* imposed by patriarchy. I hope that you will look back at your own beginnings and feel that you too, have made quite a journey, individually and collectively. Mostly, I trust that you will look forward—beyond your accomplishments or disappointments, beneath whatever covers your essential nature—and remember who you are. I trust that you will allow your essence to shine and will find ways of carrying your personal hopes and dreams— and those of our tradition's "season of liberation"—into the year ahead. May the fullness and freedom that you feel touch others, spreading outward in an ever-expanding web of connection.

This is how we ensure the Seder's legacy as a gift for all humanity—one that will continue to blossom beyond the desert.

For Further Reading

Chapter 1

Arnow, David. *Creating Lively Passover Seders*. Woodstock, VT: Jewish Lights, 2001.

Chapter 2

Cooper, Rabbi David. *God is a Verb*. New York: Riverhead Books, 1997.

Kamenetz, Roger. *The Jew in the Lotus*. New York: HarperCollins, 1994.

Kushner, Rabbi Lawrence. *Invisible Lines of Connections*. Woodstock, VT: Jewish Lights Publishing, 1998.

Chapter 3

Gottlieb, Rabbi Lynn. *She Who Dwells Within*. San Francisco: Harper One, 1995.

Hammer, Rabbi Jill. *The Hebrew Priestess*. Teaneck, NJ: Ben Yehuda Press, 2015.

Heschel, Rabbi Abraham Joshua. *The Sabbath: Its Meaning for Modern Man*. New York: Farrar, Straus and Giroux, 1996.

Novick, Rabbi Leah. *On The Wings of Shekhinah*. Wheaton IL: Quest Books, 2008.

Chapter 6

Brandchaft, Bernard. *Toward An Emancipatory Psychoanalysis*. New York: Routledge, 2010.

Greenberg, Rabbi Irving. *The Jewish Way*. New York: Touchstone, Simon and Schuster, 1988.

Lerner, Rabbi Michael. *Jewish Renewal*. New York: G.P. Putnam's Sons, 1994.

Schneider, Pat. *How the Light Gets In*. New York: Oxford University Press, 2013.

Chapter 7

Emoto, Masuru. *The Hidden Messages in Water*. New York: Atria Books, 2004.

Chapter 9

Aachan Cha in Epstein, Mark. *Psychotherapy Without a Self*. New Haven, CT: Yale University Press, 2008.

Chapter 11

Frankel, Estelle. *Sacred Therapy*. Boston, MA: Shambala Publications, 2003.

Gold, Rabbi Shefa. *Torah Journeys*. Teaneck, NJ: Ben Yehuda Press, 2006.

Chapter 13

Remen, Rachel Naomi. *Helping, Fixing, or Serving*. CA: Shambala Sun, 1999.

Winnicott, Dr. D. W. *Playing and Reality*. London: Tavistock, 1971.

Chapter 16

Thompson, K. *IONS Review #52.* "What the Butterfly Knows." Sausalito, CA: Institute of Noetic Sciences, 2000.

Chapter 17

Buber, Martin. *I and Thou.* (W. Kauffman, Trans.) New York: Scribners, 1970.

Kohut, Heinz. Eds. Goldberg, Arnold, and Stepansky, Paul E. *How Does Analysis Cure?* Chicago: University of Chicago Press, 1984.

Shulweis, Rabbi Harold. *Passages in Poetry.* Encino, CA: Valley Beth Shalom, 1990.

Chapter 18

Thich Nhat Hanh. *Being Peace.* Berkeley, CA: Parallax Press, 2005.

Chapter 19

Mykoff, Moshe. *The Empty Chair: Finding Hope and Joy—Timeless Wisdom from a Hasidic Master, Rebbe Nachman of Breslov.* Woodstock, CT: Jewish Lights Publishing, 1996.

Reb Dov Baer of Mezrich, in Lesser, Elizabeth. *Broken Open.* New York: Villard Books, 2005.

Chapter 21

Kornfield, Jack. *The Wise Heart.* New York: Bantam Dell, 2008.

Acknowledgments

I could not have begun to write this book without the help of all those who inspired, guided, and supported me in this endeavor:

All the generations who have kept this ritual alive for more than three thousand years. I'm grateful to the sages who taught that the Seder, while providing order and continuity, was like a recurring dream that could be infused with new meaning every time we open ourselves up to the experience. It seems they knew that by telling and retelling the Passover story with old and young reliving the experience together, our families would become the transmitters of memory; that by asking each of us in every generation to imagine ourselves as being personally redeemed, the past could become present, and the meaning of the Exodus could come alive.

My family. Although Judaism has always been part of the fabric of my life, it is only in recent years that I've become more fully awakened to its beauty and spirituality. For that, I thank my husband Stan for encouraging me to learn more, trusting that I'd discover what I needed to find. Thanks to my children Robbi, Karen, and Michael, whose thoughtful questions, doubts, and feelings prompted my explorations; and I want to thank my sons and daughter (in-law, in-love), Steve, Bart, and Stephanie, for their responsiveness to my creative efforts. You have all made me feel that I have something worth sharing. Mostly, I am grateful for the sparks of curiosity and joy in my grandchildren's eyes as they learned about our traditions. Jeremy, Emily, Ben, Becca, Hannah, and Ava—this book is for you.

And I want to thank my parents, Ronnie and Murray Stein, for their incredible warmth, love, and acceptance. For ninety-six years, we were blessed by my mother's presence in our lives. She taught us by the example of her life how to age with grace and dignity, wisdom, and compassion, how to live and grow and change. Barely a month after turning ninety-seven, the arc of her life on earth completed its journey. Even her dying was a teaching moment, an example of dying the way she lived, with grace and dignity.

My father, with his reverence for our religious heritage and his deep well of gratitude. Gone for thirty-two years, he has always felt so much a part of our celebrations, a shining tribute to how God works in the world. I like to think that part of the warmth and light that illuminates all our holiday celebrations is the spark that both my parents kindled in my sister and in me, in our children, and in our children's children.

And my sister Sandi Swerdloff, whose love and friendship I treasure. I don't know how I would have survived this process intact if not for her endless patience, technical expertise, and generosity of spirit.

I extend deep gratitude to *my spiritual teachers and companions*: Dina Kushnir and my Path of the Priestess sisters; authors Rabbi Shefa Gold and Estelle Frankel; fellow seekers, friends, colleagues; and my clients—I have learned so much from all of you. And my gratitude goes out to the Women's Spirituality group at the Reform Temple of Rockland in Nyack, NY (formerly Temple Beth Torah), and especially Cantor Sally Neff, for making Judaism joyful, spiritual, and beautiful, and for her generosity of spirit. Her support and encouragement to lead our Women's Seders helped me find my voice.

Special thanks to two *editors*: Naomi Rose, whose patient and gentle spirit helped me nurture the seeds of this book. Her soulful, supportive, and wise guidance gave me the confidence to trust my heart to speak its truth. And Elizabeth Kracht, who motivated and inspired me to explore my roots further, to dig deeper into the soil of my own experiences. Their expertise helped the wisdom of this ritual blossom.

And to *Sh'khinah*, the Divine Mother, whose presence sustains my spirit and feeds my soul.

About the Author

Shelle Goldstein, LCSW, is a seasoned psychotherapist whose strong interest in spirituality informs her work. She received her MSW from New York University, and certification in Psychoanalysis from the Institute for the Psychoanalytic Study of Subjectivity in NYC. She is the author of *Psychoanalysis and Spirituality: Convergence, Divergence and Transformation*, and has authored numerous family and children's *Haggadot*. She has led community workshops on psychology and spirituality; created and led Women's Seders for fifteen years at her Temple; facilitated and led *"It's A Girl Thing": Building Self-Esteem for Adolescent Girls*, as well as a monthly Spirituality program for women. Well-versed in spiritual matters, particularly as they pertain to women, Shelle has considerable access to women and what they claim to be important in their lives and what they experience as healing.

Shelle feels blessed to live with her husband in Piermont, New York, near the mountains, meadows, and marshlands that nourish her spirit. *Blossoming Beyond the Desert* is her first book.

www.ingramcontent.com/pod-product-compliance
Lightning Source LLC
Chambersburg PA
CBHW031526150726
47990CB00001B/74